**sociology
and
modern systems theory**

PRENTICE-HALL SOCIOLOGY SERIES
Herbert Blumer, Editor

PRENTICE-HALL, INC., *Englewood Cliffs, New Jersey*

WALTER BUCKLEY

sociology
and
modern systems theory

Printed in the United States of America
Library of Congress Catalog Card No.: 66–30824

37022

PRENTICE-HALL INTERNATIONAL, INC., *London*
PRENTICE-HALL OF AUSTRALIA, PTY. LTD., *Sydney*
PRENTICE-HALL OF CANADA, LTD., *Toronto*
PRENTICE-HALL OF INDIA (PRIVATE) LTD., *New Delhi*
PRENTICE-HALL OF JAPAN, INC., *Tokyo*

To my mother and the memory
of my father

preface

This book is intended as an exploratory sketch of a revolutionary scientific perspective and conceptual framework as it might be applied to the sociocultural system. This point of view and still developing framework, as interpreted here, stems from the General Systems Research movement and the now closely allied fields of cybernetics and information or communication theory. The principal goal of the book is to bring to the attention of a larger number of social scientists, particularly sociologists, the wealth of principles, ideas, and insights that have already brought a higher degree of scientific order and understanding to many areas of biology, psychology, and some physical sciences, to say nothing of the applied areas of technology to which they are essential.

The modern systems view, which flowered during World War II (though building on principles in the wind much earlier), has already borne its first fruits and is in danger of a superficial acceptance into the corpus of sociology by way of the incorporation of some of its now common vocabulary. Hardly any of the intellectual ferment it has occasioned has penetrated sociology, though there are recent signs of such stirrings. It is hoped that the ensuing discussion will stimulate a desire to delve deeply underneath such terms as "input," "output," "feedback," "boundary," and "system." In particular, I have been concerned about the possibility that the now standard use of the notion of "social system"—derived principally from equilibrium and organismic models—is deluding us into believing that we have been using modern systems theory for some time. This book, in fact, grew out of a feeling of the inadequacies of the mechanical equilibrium and organismic models, as well as a belief that modern systems research can provide the basis of a framework more capable of doing justice to the complexities and dynamic properties of the sociocultural system.

This brings up the question of the role of theoretical frameworks or perspectives in structuring scientific investigation—in selecting our assumptions, metaphors, analogies, and models, and hence pre-forming our observations and how we conceptualize them. I believe that we show little faith in the principles suggested by our own sociology of knowledge, and de-emphasize the role of general theoretical frameworks or models. Just as some believe in an immaculate perception of events and objects "out there," others believe it possible to build a logically systematic, deductive theory free of any explicit or implicit guiding perspective, model, or philosophy. Scientific work, analytically speaking, goes on at three, not two, distinguishable levels: besides empirical research and logico-deductive theory we have the equally important, though all too implicit, frameworks, models, or philosophies that inform our approach to both of the former. I believe the subject matter of this book is especially sensitive to such considerations, and the reader should be prepared to meet the issue at several points along the way. I cannot promise him any definitive arguments, but I attempt to convey my conviction that the modern systems approach has a significant contribution to make to sociocultural system theory and research even though it is not itself a deductive theory and has no large body of supporting research as yet. This is to warn the reader, then, that he will not find here a new sociological theory in the stricter sense of that term. He will, however, find that a number of current middle-level theories, which are outlined in the last three chapters of this book, suggest strongly that modern systems theory is not radically different from, or foreign to, much of the pioneering work currently produced and can make more explicit and systematic many of the assumptions and principles that appear to underlie this contemporary research. In other words, I am concerned to dispel the feeling that modern systems theory, including cybernetics and information theory, is so "far out" that its articulation with social science lies in the distant future and that no immediate gains can be expected by attempting to apply it to current investigation. By "applying," I mean to study the literature seriously enough to absorb its ideas, principles, and models into one's cognitive map so as to be able to perceive and structure one's subject matter in its terms. This is not an easy matter, given our predilections and prior intellectual investments, but the payoff may be well worth the gamble of time and energy.

This book was written first and foremost as a contribution to the science of society, but some consideration was also given to its use by the advanced student. Thus, summaries of important ideas and principles are repeated more than might otherwise be necessary, and some background or introductory materials are provided for the central areas of General Systems Research, Cybernetics, and Information Theory that will be unnecessary and perhaps oversimplified to the more widely-read scholar. However, the book cannot be taken as an adequate introduction to the wide-ranging and voluminous literature in the fields of what we are calling modern systems theory.

It is always difficult to do justice to the numerous sources of inspiration, intellectual support, and concrete aid that contribute to a book that is three or so years in the making. Particularly important in the formative stage were discussions and informal seminars with Tamotsu Shibutani and Thomas J. Scheff, who also gave of their time to read a draft of the manuscript and contribute important comments. I am likewise greatly indebted to Aaron Cicourel for his constructive critical review of the manuscript, and for pages of helpful comment that went well beyond any call of duty. Valuable suggestions have come from a number of undergraduates and graduate students who have responded to some of the material presented in my sociology classes and in informal discussions; in particular I wish to thank graduate students John Walton and John Shiflett for subjecting themselves patiently to the complete manuscript and for providing several hours of fruitful discussion of its contents. I am grateful for the professional way in which Miss Gloria Nakagawa aided my library research, deciphered my scrawl, and typed and retyped the bulk of the manuscript, and to the ladies of the sociology department office of the University of California, Santa Barbara, who came through in the pinch of time to help complete the final draft. Finally, I wish to acknowledge the support provided by the Research Committee of that University.

W.B.

contents

It may be noted, to paraphrase Whitehead, that sociological theory has been living for some time off the intellectual capital of previous centuries. This helps to account for the fact that the great bulk of empirical research in sociology conducted in the last decades is little informed by and even less cumulative for the dominant theoretical perspective currently in vogue, namely, that referred to variously as equilibrium, consensus, or functional theory. It also underlies the sizable chorus of critics and skeptics of the last few years toward such theory. It is the central theme of this book that the difficulty, at base, lies in the fact that current dominant theory is built on mechanical and organic (more exactly, organismic) system models laid down during previous centuries which are quite inappropriate in dealing with the type of system represented by the sociocultural[1] realm. Although it is all too obvious, once said, that sociocultural systems show fundamental features that are unique vis à vis physical systems and biological organisms, we are still left with the question why our theories of the former still appeal to sterile analogies with the latter. The unfortunate answers undoubtedly involve the great success and prestige of the physical sciences and the seductive and often shallow similarities and affinities between the biological and social spheres developed by great, but often grossly inaccurate, intellects of other eras.

Since World War II there has been great intellectual ferment in the other sciences, which is bringing to a head a number of general shifts in perspective developing at least since the turn of the century. We refer to the closely related developments going under the names of cybernetics, information and communication theory, general systems research, and the like. Their growth marks the transition from a concern for eternal substance and the dynamics of energy transformation to a focus on *organization* and its dynamics based on

---

1 We shall use the term "sociocultural" throughout the book to make explicit the difference between the human level of organization and the lower, merely "social," level of certain animal or insect species.

introduction 1

the "triggering" effects of information transmission. Here is to be found the secret distinguishing living from nonliving matter, adaptive, morphogenic processes from equilibrating, entropic processes. Both sociology and modern systems theory study many scientific problems in common: wholes and how to deal with them as such; the general analysis of organization—the complex and dynamic relations of parts, especially when the parts are themselves complex and changing and the relationships are nonrigid, symbolically mediated, often circular, and with many degrees of freedom; problems of intimate interchange with an environment, of goal-seeking, of continual elaboration and creation of structure, or more or less adaptive evolution; the mechanics of "control," of self-regulation or self-direction.

The interdisciplinary generalizing and integrating potential of this newer systems theory has been widely accepted and utilized in all the major scientific fields, but sociology has remained virtually untouched by it. On the other hand, though it has led to some significant payoffs in a few specific areas of science, it is probably fair to say that the full extent of its promise is still an open question. It is the intent of the present volume to investigate the principles and methods of modern systems research as the basis for a more adequate model or theoretical framework for analysis of the sociocultural system. It is our working bias that such a new and more viable model will eventually develop out of the modern systems approach, and our present endeavor can only be seen as tentative and probing, in the hope that a larger number of sociologists will recognize the potential, profit by our errors, and carry the task further.

It should be said at the outset that ours is not an attempt at a definitive review of current systems theory in all its sprawling ramifications, but rather a selective emphasis on contributions of potential significance to the sociological perspective. Further, our emphasis is on drawing out principles and their implications, with a consequent lack of concern for more specialized techniques and tools, such as the mathematical techniques of "information" (i.e., signal) theory or "game" (i.e., payoff) theory. On the other hand, we cannot overlook the significance of such procedures as stochastic process analysis or the non-numerical, set theoretic techniques of the "new mathematics," for the analysis of certain kinds of sociological phenomena.

Finally, it might be well to try to head off at this early point a likely criticism of many sociologists and others to the effect that, whereas we have rightly eschewed the older physical analogies we are now about to plunge into an orgy of just such analogizing via cybernetics, signal transmission theory, and other such "hard science" disciplines. We believe there is gross misunderstanding here of the very fundamental significance of these recent developments, which can only be unfolded with extensive and sympathetic consideration. We can simply state our case briefly here.

Aside from the fact that cautious analogizing has always been basic to scientific advance, there is a difference between analogizing and discerning fundamental similarities of structure (unless we define analogy so broadly as to make it synonymous with scientific theory, as some have done). As Abraham Kaplan has argued:

> Working with these concepts of communication and control, cybernetics becomes relevant to the study of man because human behavior is paralleled in many respects by the communication machines. This parallel is no mere metaphor, but consists in a similarity of structure between the machine processes and those of human behavior. The Darwinian continuity between man and the rest of nature has now been carried to completion . . . With communication and control as the key, a similarity of structure can also be traced between an individual . . . and a society . . . The metaphor of Plato and Hobbes can now be given a literalist interpretation.[2]

To pursue the point further, the critic is unwittingly arguing for the eternal substantive differences between types of systems, thus missing the main point mentioned earlier, that the newer systems view is building on the insight that the key to substantive differences in systems lies in the way they are *organized,* in the particular mechanisms and dynamics of the interrelations among the parts and with the environment. Thus, we now understand, in principle, the particular kinds of mechanisms or internal linkages of parts that must underlie any goal-seeking, or purposive, behavior, whether of machine, man, or group (though the writer would argue that it does not at all follow that cybernetic machines therefore have their own purposes, or that computers really think in any fully psychological sense). Thus, a major goal of the General Systems Research movement is to trace out just such structural similarities, *and structural differences,* between "substantively" differing types of systems.

It should not be forgotten that borrowing and analogizing between the behavioral and physical sciences has never been a one-way street, and that cybernetics, and information theory in particular have been inspired by major clues specifically borrowed from behavioral principles, which they have then systematized in terms of the structural mechanisms involved. Furthermore, it is not without significance that the late Norbert Wiener, major pioneer in these areas, chose the analysis of society as the vehicle for presenting his cybernetic conception to the general public.[3] And we must not be misled by the frequent use in the literature of mechanistic terms—the "Turing machine,"[4] John von Neumann's theory

---

2 Abraham Kaplan, "Sociology Learns the Language of Mathematics," *Commentary,* 14 (1952), 274–84.

3 Norbert Wiener, *The Human Use of Human Beings* (Garden City, N.Y.: Doubleday & Company, Inc., 1954).

4 A. M. Turing, "On Computable Numbers, with an Application to the Entscheidungsproblem," *Proceedings of the London Mathematical Society* (Series 2), 42 (1937), 230–65.

of "automata,"[5] or Ashby's general theory of the "Machine"[6]—since the major concern is with models of organization sufficiently general and complex, though built from simple units, to embrace behavior systems of any type—physical, biological, psychological, or sociocultural. Once again, to base our skepticism on some inherent "substantive" difference among such systems is to retreat to an older philosophical position and miss the whole point of the current scientific trend.

Plan of the Chapters

The next chapter sets the stage with a brief discussion of the use of mechanical and organic models, as well as the opposing "process" perspective, in sociology. The current dominance of the mechanical and organic models is then outlined by way of a critical comparison of the theoretical frameworks of two leading theorists, George C. Homans and Talcott Parsons. The weaknesses of these views is examined in terms of the breakdown of the underlying models in the face of persistent problem foci of social science: structurally induced and maintained conflict and dissensus; the structure-elaborating and changing feature of all societies; the theoretical status of less-structured "collective" behavior as a neglected but important aspect of the social system; the systemic status of "deviance" and "social control"; and others. The chapter concludes with a brief overview of the newer systems approach as a potential basis of a more viable sociocultural system model.

In the third chapter we examine the concept of "system" with brief excursions into the problem areas of "wholeness," degrees of systemness or "entitivity," and the ontological-problem. Our main concern, however, is not with the more abstract and often otiose discussion of features common to any system, but rather with a comparative characterization of the principal features distinguishing mechanical, organic, and sociocultural systems in an attempt to make more precise the manner in which mechanical and organic models are inappropriate to the analysis of sociocultural systems, and to provide more particular points of attack on the development of a newer model. For example, we are concerned with the fact that an isolated physical system typically proceeds to its most probable state of minimal organization (equilibrium), and that organic systems (more exactly, organismic systems) characteristically work to maintain a specific, genetically given structure within fairly definite limits (homeostasis), whereas systems on the phylogenetic, higher psychological, and sociocultural levels, are characterized primarily by their morphogenic properties.

---

[5] John von Neumann, "The General and Logical Theory of Automata," in *Cerebral Mechanisms in Behavior: The Hixon Symposium,* ed. Lloyd A. Jeffress, (New York: John Wiley & Sons, Inc., 1959) pp. 1–31.

[6] W. Ross Ashby, *An Introduction to Cybernetics* (New York: John Wiley & Sons, Inc., 1956).

That is, these latter are distinguished precisely by the fact that, rather than minimize organization, or preserve a given fixed structure, they typically create, elaborate, or change structure as a prerequisite to remaining viable, as ongoing systems. It is our concern to understand what it is about complex adaptive systems—as we shall often refer to them—that gives them this capability. Our investigation leads us to an examination of the cybernetic principles of control, positive and negative feedbacks, communication and information processing, goal-seeking, self-awareness and self-direction, and the like. In addition, we devote some space to the methodological issues raised, in particular, a discussion of causal, teleological or functional, and cybernetic methods of approach to complex adaptive system analysis.

Further methodological issues are raised here (and later) in pointing out the many different types of relations between parts found in complex adaptive systems. Over and above the more simple cause and effect relations, or correlations, found between elements or events in a sociocultural system (and our research tools are currently confined to a very great extent to such relations), we must at least begin to worry about the problem of handling such types of relations as step-functions, "precipitants," "buffer mechanisms," complex positive and negative feedback interrelations, and the like. The relevance for sociology of some of the analytical techniques of systems theory are suggested, such as the mathematical logic of relations as a tool for analyzing structure *per se,* and the stochastic analysis of certain complex system processes. A main concern here is simply to promote awareness of the possibility that advanced calculus and factor analysis are not the only or even the best bets as tools for future sociology, and mathematics is not at all synonymous with the manipulation of numbers and numerical measurement.

One of the central insights deriving from discussions in the third chapter is that a *system,* as a continuous, boundary-maintaining, variously related assembly of parts, is not to be confused with *the structure or organization its components may take on at any particular time.* In Chapter 4 we examine the general concept of structure and its distinguishing features in different types of systems. In keeping with an earlier point that modern science has shifted from concern for relatively stable substance and "qualities" to analysis of a more shifting structure in the relations of parts, we focus on the particularly fluid nature of the structure of sociocultural systems and the thin conceptual line between this "structure" and what is called "process." The perspectives of information theory and cybernetics on structure and process are investigated in conjunction with an attempt to sketch the foundations for a generalized model of the morphogenic or structure-elaborating process seen to operate in complex adaptive social systems, starting with conceptualizations of the "act" and the basic interaction process.

Building on a dynamic and fully interactive or transactional conception of human association underlying the notion of "social structure," we attempt to organize, in the fifth chapter, a number of considerations regarding the continuous structuring, destructuring and restructuring characteristic of the sociocultural system. A "morphogenic" model of society is suggested, built on a number of theoretical and empirical studies that have appeared in recent years, and which—we argue—are moving in a direction closely corresponding to, or highly compatible with, the modern systems perspective we are outlining.

Considerations of the nature of the macrostructures of sociocultural systems leads us to see more clearly the inadequacies of the current "consensus" model and its relatively static conception of "institutions," "social control," and social "order" and "disorder." In the sixth and last chapter we are concerned to suggest how a cybernetic, rather than an equilibrial or homeostatic, model of society can inform the concepts of social control, social order, and disorder. This leads us 1) to draw on current conceptualizations of the systemic process of deviance generation—an excellent example of the modern systems approach (whether consciously recognized or not) , and 2) to discuss in some detail current problems in the conception of power and authority, legitimacy, and processes of group goal-seeking and decision-making. Although we note the dangers involved in an overly simplistic application of the cybernetic conception of feedback control, "self-regulation" and "self-direction," we argue that it may have potential as an organizing tool helping us pull together the large number of strands of subgroup and societal policy formulation and execution.

The greater part of current discussion of systems in sociology is embarrassingly naive and out of date in the light of modern systems research in other disciplines. Though there is a fair amount of superficial (and often incorrect) use of the newer terminology (it is almost *de rigueur* to mention "boundary-maintenance," input-output, "cybernetic control" (*sic*), feedback, and the like), the underlying conceptions show little advance over the mechanical equilibrium model of earlier centuries. In a similar manner, the organic models have backed off only a little from the cul-de-sacs of the Social Darwinian era of organic and organismic analogies: "societies" still have "needs" and face "problems" of maintaining their given (institutionalized) structure that are met by built-in, automatic "homeostatic" mechanisms; or social classes represent a natural selection out of a competitive struggle in which the "fittest" or "most highly qualified" rise, more or less automatically to the top, to fill the positions functionally essential to the societies' "survival."

That one or the other of these models should underlie theorizing in the early stages of scientific sociology when little was clearly known about the sociocultural system is understandable enough. But the attempt to merge both the mechanical and organic models in the same theoretical framework, as is done today, is not only questionable in view of their many points of incompatibility, but retrograde in view of modern advances in sociology. These advances should have alerted us to the possibility that the sociocultural level of systems is structurally and dynamically unique and not fundamentally comparable to these other types of systems, despite some point of similarity. The development of modern systems theory in other fields in the last two or three decades provides a new perspective and basic principles pointing to a more appropriate sociocultural system model that sociological theory cannot afford to ignore.

Such are the themes that will be pursued in this chapter.

social system models 2

THE MECHANICAL MODEL

Pitirim A. Sorokin has provided us with an admirable survey of the development of the "mechanistic school" of sociology, and we shall borrow heavily from it.[1] With the rapid advance of physics, mechanics, and mathematics in the seventeenth century men turned to an interpretation of man, his mind, and society in terms of the same methods, concepts and assumptions, partly in rejection of the less palatable teleology, vitalism, mysticism, and anthropomorphism of other views. Thus, the "Social Physics" of the 17th century arose, whereby man was regarded as a physical object, a kind of elaborate machine, whose actions and psychic processes could be analyzed in terms of the principles of mechanics. In "social mechanics," society was seen as an "astronomical system" whose elements were human beings bound together by mutual attraction or differentiated by repulsion; groups of societies or states were systems of balanced oppositions. Man, his groups, and their interrelations thus constituted an unbroken continuity with the rest of the mechanistically interpreted universe. All were based on the interplay of natural causes, to be studied as systems of relationships that could be measured and expressed in terms of laws of social mechanics.

The physical concepts of space, time, attraction, inertia, force, power —which must be recognized as anthropomorphisms originally borrowed from everyday human experience—were borrowed back in their new connotative attire and applied to man and society. Thus we find conceptions of *moral or social space* in which social events occur; *position* in social space, and a *system of social coordinates* defining man's position in it; social processes as results of the "gravitation" or *attraction* and *inertia* of individuals and groups, the latter regarded as a *system in an equilibrium* of *centrifugal* and *centripetal forces*. Social organization, power and authority were resultants of the *"pressures"* of "social *atoms*" and "molecules": hence arose "social statics" or a theory of social equilibrium analogous to statics in physical mechanics, and "social dynamics" involving motion or change as a function of time and space expressible by various mathematical curves.

In Sorokin's view, almost all subsequent "social physics" in the eighteenth and the first half of the nineteenth centuries was but a variation of the seventeenth-century attempts, which made valuable contributions to social and psychological science. The second half of the nineteenth century, however, showed symptoms of a revival, though usually

---

[1] Pitirim Sorokin, *Contemporary Sociological Theories* (New York: Harper & Row, Publishers, 1928), Chap. 1.

without acknowledgments to the seventeenth. The men involved include H. C. Carey, A. Bentley, T. N. Carver, and Pareto. Their systems were built on such concepts as "fields of force," "transformation of energy," and "social entropy." Most of them gave "only a series of superficial analogies, based on invalid interpretations of mechanical concepts." The "rational mechanics" of Pareto, a trained engineer, however, is in a different class. He avoided the more specious analogizing, and utilized only the more general mechanical principles that seemed to apply to social phenomena on the methodological or heuristic levels. Thus, we have at base the concept of "system," of elements in mutual interrelations, which may be in a state of "equilibrium," such that any moderate changes in the elements or their interrelations away from the equilibrium position are counterbalanced by changes tending to restore it.

It is this conception that has been taken over almost unchanged by many contemporary sociologists, notably George C. Homans, and Talcott Parsons (both influenced by Henderson at Harvard).[2] Before them, and after Pareto, the idea of society as a "system" of interrelated parts with a boundary, and usually tending to maintain an equilibrium, was explicitly entertained by N. Bukharin, P. Sorokin, F. Znaniecki, and K. Lewin, among others.

Many social scientists referred to society or the group as a "social system" without, however, taking a wholly mechanistic view—in fact, like MacIver, placing an opposite emphasis on the mentalistic factors. Thus, in discussing cause as a "precipitant," MacIver offers an early preview of conceptions and difficulties much to the fore in social system theory a quarter century later:

> . . . we mean by "precipitant" any specific factor or condition regarded as diverting the pre-established direction of affairs, as disrupting a pre-existing equilibrium, or as releasing hitherto suppressed or latent tendencies or forces. The presumption is that a system is operating in a manner congenial to its self-perpetuation, until something intervenes; that a system is relatively closed, until something breaks it open. That 'something' is then a precipitant.
>
> This conception is one of the ways in which we seek to understand the problem of continuity and change. We postulate a social law roughly corresponding to the physical law of inertia, to the effect that every social system tends to maintain itself, to persevere in its present state, until compelled by some force to alter that state. Every social system is at every moment and in every part sustained by codes and institutions, by traditions, by interests. If a social order or any social situation within it suffers significant change we think of some insurgent or invading force, breaking as it

2 Lawrence J. Henderson, *Pareto's General Sociology* (Cambridge, Mass.: Harvard University Press, 1935) ; George C. Homans and C. P. Curtis, *An Introduction to Pareto* (New York: Alfred A. Knopf, Inc., 1934) . For an interesting alternative view of the equilibrium analogy, see R. Furth, "Physics of Social Equilibrium," *Advancement of Science*, 8 (1952) , 429–34.

were this 'inertia,' the *status quo*. The simplest form of the concept is that which we considered in the previous section, where change is thought of as the disturbance of a persistent equilibrium. The defect of that concept was not its postulate of an equilibrium, but its unwarranted assumption that a single type of equilibrium, determined by relatively simple forces, was fundamental and permanent so that any change affecting it was incidental, alien, or extraneous. It is more in keeping with the historical record to think in terms of a constant tendency towards equilibrium, beset always, even in simple or primitive society and still more obviously in the higher civilizations, by forces threatening to unbalance or disrupt it. So the nature of the equilibrium is itself forever changing.[3]

The tenacity and duration of an assumed equilibrium have gradually been diminished in the conceptions of some equilibrium theorists. That is, a given equilibrium is taken to be only a temporary, ephemeral state, as in the above MacIver quote or in what Homans now calls a "practical equilibrium" which behavior "no doubt temporarily and precariously, sometimes achieves."[4]

It is sometimes claimed that the concept of equilibrium is only a heuristic device, but it is never made clear just what heuristic function it performs. Thus, Parsons argues correctly that to study social change we need some reference point from which change occurs.[5] He then turns to both an assessment of the given structure at the starting point of analysis and an appeal to the equilibrium and inertia concepts. But it is not at all clear why an assessment of the structural and dynamic state at the start does not alone suffice as a reference point, without introducing "equilibrium" and "inertia." Furthermore, when Parsons goes on to admit change-forces *endogenous* to the system, we part company with anything recognizable to the student of classical mechanics. As others have noted, to say that internal system forces tend toward equilibrium but in fact may lead to change is a contradiction in terms.[6]

The equilibrium theorist, to support his appeal to that concept, typically points out that there are, in any society, sets of more or less common norms, values, expectations, and definitions of the situation supported by sanctions of one kind of another. However, he equally typically fails to mention that every society of any complexity also has quite stable sets of alternative, diverse, deviant, or counter norms, values, etc., as well as a vast area of ambiguities and uninstitutionalized "collective" behavior

---

3 Robert M. MacIver, *Social Causation* (New York: Harper Torchbook, 1964), pp. 172–73.

4 George C. Homans, *Social Behavior: Its Elementary Forms* (New York: Harcourt, Brace & World, Inc., 1961), p. 114.

5 Talcott Parsons, "Some Considerations on the Theory of Social Change," *Rural Sociology*, 26 (1961), 219–39.

6 See Barrington Moore, Jr., "Sociological Theory and Contemporary Politics," *American Journal of Sociology*, 61 (1955), 107–15.

of all shades and degrees. These can only be swept under the theoretical rug by definitional fiat: they are residual, or not really part of the system at all. But by this time, the argument has been reduced to word-play.

In sum, it becomes increasingly clear that mechanical and sociocultural systems are very different types of systems with basically different organizing principles and dynamics. Continued appeal to the former to understand the latter only postpones the search for other more appropriate and useful conceptualizations.

Such are the more common sense arguments against equilibrium theory in sociology. In the course of the book, more systematic considerations will be unfolded.

THE ORGANIC MODEL

The story of organic analogizing in social thought is an often-told one. The use of the organic metaphor is literally ancient history, but serious scientific usage is usually traced back only to Herbert Spencer and such followers as Lilienfeld, Worms, and Schäffle. Like the rise of the mechanical model in an era of physical science advances, the organic model of society was inspired by the advances in biology to which Spencer contributed.

Further discussion requires at this point that we distinguish between the "organismic" analogy and the more general "organic" model. Biological systems exist, of course, on more than one level: the organization and dynamics of the individual organism differ from those of a collection of organisms making up species or ecological systems. Many of the followers of Spencer exploited to extremes the organismic analogy, searching out the social analogue of the heart, brain, circulatory system, and the like. Spencer himself, however, was more cautious and appealed to more generalized principles of similarity.

> Here let it once more be distinctly asserted that there exist no analogies between the body politic and a living body, save those necessitated by that mutual dependence of parts which they display in common. Though, in foregoing chapters, sundry comparisons of social structures and functions to structures and functions in the human body have been made, they have been made only because structures and functions in the human body furnish familiar illustrations of structures and functions in general. The social organism, discrete instead of concrete, asymmetrical instead of symmetrical, sensitive in all its units instead of having a single sensitive centre, is not comparable to any particular type of individual organism, animal or vegetal.[7]

7 Herbert Spencer, *Principles of Sociology*, 3rd ed. (New York: Appleton-Century-Crofts, 1897), Part 2, p. 592.

It is, then, the general principle of "mutual dependence of parts" which makes society like an organism, but it also should be noted that this criterion applies equally to a mechanical system. We mention this because it has become common in current sociology to claim this principle as the central distinguishing feature of functional analysis, when, in fact, as our discussion of the mechanical model shows, it was central to seventeenth-century "social physics" and remains so in mechanical equilibrium models. Spencer rejected the inorganic realm as a basis of comparison with the "social aggregate" and sought further reasons for likening the relations among parts of society to those among parts of a living body.

But from one point of view it was an especially unfortunate decision of Spencer and others to liken society to the individual organisms rather than to the species, for many of the contradictions in their position stem from the failure to distinguish biological levels of organization. (This is probably due in part to the still persisting reluctance to accept ecological aggregates as "entities" or systems in the same sense as organisms—a topic we shall discuss in a later chapter.) With the benefit of hindsight, we might find this decision—made in the Darwinian era—as rather surprising, for after all, Darwin's theory concerns *species* and phylogeny, not *individuals* and physiology. Though we are not opting for the organic analogy, it would make more sense to say, for example, that societies are like species in that both conservation *and* change of structure are characteristic features under certain conditions; that neither species nor societies "die" as do organisms; and, as Lester Ward pointed out, that the struggle in evolution is not for "survival" (of individual organisms) *per se,* but more fundamentally, a "struggle for structure."[8] Colin S. Pittendrigh has noted that biologists themselves have stumbled over this problem:

> The clichés of struggle and survival, even for the professional biologist, have focused attention on secondary aspects of the historical process whereby genetic information accumulates. They have focused it on individuals—and it should be on populations; they have focused it on the avoidance of death (perpetuation of the individual) —and it should be on reproduction (perpetuation of the genotype) .[9]

The particular level of biological organization that is chosen as the basis for a model of society determines (or may be determined by) whether we see society as preeminently cooperative or basically conflictual. If so-

---

[8] Lester Ward, *Pure Sociology* (New York: The Macmillan Company, 1903) , p. 184.

[9] Colin S. Pittendrigh, "Adaptation, Natural Selection, and Behavior," in *Behavior and Evolution,* ed. Anne Roe and George Gaylord Simpson (New Haven, Conn.: Yale University Press, 1958), p. 397.

ciety is like an organism, then its parts cooperate and do not compete in a struggle for survival, but if society is like an ecological aggregate, then the Darwinian (or Hobbesian) model of competitive struggle is more applicable. Spencer took the first alternative:

> All kinds of creatures are alike in so far as each exhibits cooperation among its components for the benefit of the whole; and this trait, common to them, is a trait common also to societies. Further, among individual organisms, the degree of co-operation measures the degree of evolution; and this general truth, too, holds among social organisms.[10]

As we know, this is the basis for Spencer's "militaristic-industrial" typology of societal evolution.

On the other hand, Social Darwinism is most widely known for its opposite emphasis: the "natural" and inevitable rise of the "fittest" individuals in the competitive social struggle. The model is now the species, not the individual. Thus, the current controversy in sociological theory over the conflict as against the consensus model has its reflection in the dual aspects of the biological model so confusingly intermingled by social theorists.

One of the clearer lights cutting through the fog and all but demolishing Social Darwinism was the work of the biologist-sociologist, Lester Ward. In speaking of the analogy between the "individual organism" and the "social organism," Spencer had asserted a "community in the fundamental principles of organization" between them. Ward—and modern systems theory—see through this half-truth to the fundamental *differences in principles of organization* between sociocultural systems on the one hand and organisms and phylogenetic systems on the other. Ward's emphasis on knowledge (attaining) processes, his insights into the "struggle for structure," and his principles of "difference of potential" and of "synergy" ("the systematic and organic working together of the antithetical forces of nature" to produce organization) are in the mood of modern systems theory.[11]

Present-day functionalism in sociology represents the modern version of the biological model. But whereas the Social Darwinists, as suggested above, swung to the phylogenetic model to emphasize the competitive struggle theme, the functionalists—who today typically emphasize "order," cooperation and consensus—utilize the organismic model as the supreme example of the close cooperation of parts conserving a relatively fixed structure within close limits of deviation. Thus Parsons, in his functional analysis of social change, after representing the social system as tending to maintain a relatively stable *equilibrium* by way of continuous processes

---

10 Spencer, *Principles of Sociology.*
11 Ward, *Pure Sociology,* especially Chaps. 10 and 11.

which "neutralize" endogenous and exogenous sources of variability that would change the structure if proceeding too far, then gives an *organismic* illustration of *homeostasis*: temperature regulation in animals.[12] In addition to the indiscriminate equation of the equilibrium and homeostasis principles,[13] it should be noted that the implication logically to be drawn is that if the temperature of the animal were *not* kept within limits it would change its structure—which of course it does, in a rather Pickwickian sense. The basic point here is that whereas mature organisms, by the very nature of their organization, cannot change their given structure beyond very narrow limits and still remain viable, this capacity is precisely what distinguishes sociocultural systems. It is a major adaptive advantage, in the evolutionary scheme, of this latter level of organization. A model of society that does not bring this principle to the fore is doomed to sterility and eventual extinction. The newer systems perspective, we argue, makes ample room for appreciation and analysis of the mechanisms making such morphogenesis possible.

Cannon, we note, coined the term "homeostasis" for biological systems to avoid the static connotations of equilibrium, and to bring out the dynamic, processual, potential-maintaining properties of *basically unstable* physiological systems.

> When we consider the extreme instability of our bodily structure, its readiness for disturbance by the slightest application of external forces . . . its persistence through many decades seems almost miraculous. The wonder increases when we realize that the system is open, engaging in free exchange with the outer world, and that the structure itself is not permanent, but is being continuously built up again by processes of repair . . .
>
> The constant conditions which are maintained in the body might be termed *equilibria*. That word, however, has come to have fairly exact meaning as applied to relatively simple physico-chemical states, enclosed systems, where known forces are balanced. The coordinated physiological processes which maintain most of the steady states in the organism are so complex and so peculiar to living beings . . . that I have suggested a special designation for these states, *homeostasis*. The word does not imply something set and immobile, a stagnation. It means a condition—a condition which may vary, but which is relatively constant.[14]

In dealing with the sociocultural system, however, we jump to a new system level and need yet a new term to express not only the *structure-maintaining* feature, but also the *structure-elaborating* and *changing* feature

---

12 Parsons, "Some Considerations."

13 This failure of discrimination is fairly common; see for example, Alex Inkeles, who goes even further and sees the equilibrium model as simply a special version of the organic structural-functional approach, in *What Is Sociology?* (Englewood Cliffs, N.J.: Prentice-Hall, Inc., 1964), pp. 37–38.

14 Walter B. Cannon, *The Wisdom of the Body* (rev. ed.), New York: W. W. Norton & Company, Inc., 1939), pp. 20, 24.

of the inherently unstable system, i.e., a concept of morphogenesis. The notion of "steady state," now often used, approaches or allows for this conception if it is understood that the "state" that tends to remain steady is not to be identified with the *particular structure* of the system. That is, in order to maintain a steady state the system may have to change its particular structure. C. A. Mace recognizes this distinction and argues for an extension of the concept of homeostasis.

> The first extension would cover the case in which what is maintained or restored is not so much an internal state of the organism as some relation of the organism to its environment. This would take care of the facts of adaptation and adjustment, including adjustment to the social environment . . . the second extension would cover the case in which the goal and/or norm is some state or relation which has never previously been experienced. There is clearly no reason to suppose that every process of the homeostatic type consists in the maintenance or restoration of a norm. There is no reason whatever to suppose that the process always begins in a state of equilibrium which is then disturbed . . . there are, at any rate, many cases in which we require the concept of homeostasis to be extended so that it may apply not only to the restoration of an equilibrium but also to the discovery of new *equilibria*.[15]

And Karl Deutsch, in his critique of the organic model, points out that the concept of homeostasis is too narrow, and only a special case of the learning and growth processes characteristic of open, adaptive systems:

> . . . homeostasis is not a broad enough concept to describe either the *internal restructuring* of learning systems or the combinatorial findings of the solutions. It is too narrow a concept because it is change rather than stability which we must account for.[16]

The functionalist's appeal to the organismic analogy further drives him to overemphasize the more stable, overdetermined, and supported normative aspects of the social system at the expense of other, equally important aspects without which dynamic analysis is impossible. This is apparently due to the search for the social equivalent of the organism's relatively fixed structure, against which the biological functionalist can assess normality and abnormality, health and disease, and seek out automatic, homeostatic maintenance mechanisms. Thus, for the Parsonian the social system is all but synonymous with the dominant, institutionalized part of the social structure. In Parsons' article we have been citing, appeal is made to a stable structure as a reference point for change, but in due course this becomes *the* structure of the system and is defined as the "in-

---

15 C. A. Mace, "Homeostasis, Needs and Values," *British Journal of Psychology*, 44 (1953), 204–5.

16 Karl W. Deutsch, in *Towards a Unified Theory of Human Behavior*, ed. Roy Grinker (New York: Basic Books, Inc., Publishers, 1956), pp. 161–62.

stitutionalized patterns of normative culture." Stable "institutionalization," in turn, is defined in terms of stable norms, actors' motivational
commitment to "institutional expectations" (apparently those of the official establishment), commonly accepted "definitions of the situation,"
and integration into the larger governing normative system. Such a framework leaves us at a loss as to how to deal with those many important
variant, deviant, or alternative structures or subcultures that constitute
part of the *given structure* of a complex social system but do not meet
Parsons' criteria for institutionalization. How do we deal with the historical fact of change occurring due to the clash of different relatively
stable structures or subcultures within the system? Though the selection
of some reference frame for the study of change is essential, it is a risky
business and must involve well-specified, valid methodological reasoning
if one aspect of the system structure is selected over others *as the aspect
that "homeostatic" mechanisms are, over all, tending to maintain.*

The notion of "functional prerequisites" is also most appropriate as an
organismic analogue. There is a relatively fixed normal structure with
well-defined limits such that the conditions of persistence can be defined
within that degree of precision. On the phylogenetic level, where change
of structure is a condition of viability, the conditions of persistence must
be more broadly defined relative to possible environmental changes, and
a broader latitude of structures meeting these conditions seems permis-
sible. On the sociocultural level, too, there is no specific structure that is
alone viable and normal for every society. And not only may structure
change as a response to pressures on viability, but the internal limits of
structural compatibility seem greater than functionalists want to permit,
though certainly with outer bounds. For, just as human personality can
harbor fairly great incompatibilities in ideas, beliefs, attitudes, and ideologies, while operating quite effectively, so can and do sociocultural systems embrace wide diversities and incompatibilities while remaining
amazingly persistent over long periods. In effect, the specification of conditions essential for the persistence of any society (especially if we do not
specify the environmental conditions it must meet) can tell us little about
the particular structures it will develop to satisfy them. Granted that persisting societies are meeting the requirements at or beyond the minimum
level, the function concept itself provides no criteria for judging the
widely varying levels and structural procedures *within* the viable range.
Thus, the reproduction rate of a society cannot remain for long below the
replacement rate if the society is to be maintained, but the reproduction
rate may be just at the replacement level, moderately above it, or it may
be explosive. The repercussions of these three possibilities may obviously
be very different for the society in question. The same can be said of the
other requisites: the question of adequacy is to be assessed on other
grounds that constitute the center of most sociological interest. As S. F.
Nadel stated in his unsurpassed critique of functionalism:

. . . there is maladjustment as well as adjustment; the function concept only poses the question of adequacy but does not settle it beforehand. Only of society in the abstract can we say that it is integrated, and only of culture at large, that it leads to survival. Concrete societies weaken, disintegrate, or show symptoms of 'social pathology'; and concrete cultures may be full of frustrations and threats to survival. In their analysis, then, subservience to function means an attempted, varying, and often problematic adequacy. 'Functionalist' anthropology is apt to lose sight of this corollary and to speak about social facts 'having' such-and-such 'functions' as though these were self-sufficient truths. Yet if we simply aimed to show that exogamy facilitates cooperation, myths buttress codes of behavior, and religion helps towards social equilibrium, we should be implying that these modes of behavior fulfill the given necessities (under the given conditions) in the most adequate manner possible, and that any society having exogamy and the rest is to that extent an ideal society. Clearly, such a presumption of adequacy cannot be defended.[17]

In the next chapter we shall have occasion to discuss functionalism as a method of explanation in comparison to "causal," logico-meaningful, and modern systems research methods. We conclude here, as in the previous section, that the model in question is singularly inappropriate for more than superficial sociocultural system analysis. More systematic discussion will be presented below.

THE PROCESS MODEL

Before turning to a comparative analysis of the widely divergent pictures of the social system drawn by two contemporary theorists, each using the mechanical model (and in one case, also the organic model), we should not leave the implication that no other models or perspectives have been of significance in sociology. In particular, mention should be made of the "process" model, which was a predominant point of view in American sociology of the early twentieth century under the leadership especially of the "Chicago school," including, in particular, Albion W. Small, G. H. Mead, R. E. Park and E. W. Burgess, who in turn were stimulated by such German sociologists as G. Simmel and L. von Wiese. This perspective was not systematically developed, perhaps, to a state warranting the label of model; also, it drew much of its inspiration from aspects of the organic analogy, and even found room for the equilibrium concept on occasion, though opposed to it in principle. We are particularly concerned to make the point here, however, that the process view has gone a long way toward seeing through the weaknesses of the mechanical and organismic models for society, and is very congenial to —even anticipative of—basic principles of cybernetics.

---

17 S. F. Nadel, *Foundations of Social Anthropology* (New York: Free Press of Glencoe, Inc., 1951) , pp. 375–76.

In essence, the process model typically views society as a complex, multifaceted, fluid interplay of widely varying degrees and intensities of association and dissociation. The "structure" is an abstract construct, not something distinct from the ongoing interactive process but rather a temporary, accommodative representation of it at any one time. These considerations lead to the fundamental insight that sociocultural systems are inherently structure-elaborating and changing; for some, the terms "process" and "change" were synonymous. Put in terms of our earlier discussion, societies and groups continually shift their structures as adaptations to internal or external conditions. Process, then, focuses on the actions and interactions of the components of an ongoing system, such that varying degrees of structuring arise, persist, dissolve, or change.

Perhaps the first names we think of in the context of such a perspective are those of Marx and Engels, with their view of history as a dialectic process whereby new structures arise out of conditions immanent in previous ones. The radical opposition of this conception to the mechanical equilibrium framework has been forcibly stated by Barrington Moore, Jr.:

> For a Marxist it is almost as difficult to conceive of a situation returning to a state of maximum harmony as it is for an equilibrium theorist to conceive of a self-generating cycle of ever fiercer struggle culminating in destruction.[18]

(We could, however, substitute "process theorist" for "Marxist" in this statement.)

Strongly influenced by the process view of Marx was the important pioneering American sociologist, Albion W. Small. His emphasis on the social process saw the role of "interests," their conflict and adjustments, as keys to a truly dynamic sociology.

> Human experience composes an associational process . . . association becomes an accelerated process of differentiation or permutation of interests within the individual, of contacts between individuals and the groups into which they combine. Incidental to this pursuit of purposes, and to the process of adjustment between persons which results, individuals enter into certain more or less persistent structural relationships with each other, known in general as "institutions," and into certain more or less permanent directions of effort which we may call the social functions. These social structures and functions are, in the first instance, results of the previous associational process; but they no sooner pass out of the fluid state, into a relatively stable condition, than they become in turn causes of subsequent stages of the associational process . . .[19]

Near the turn of the century Small argued, with special clear-sightedness, that

---

18 Moore, "Sociological Theory," p. 112.

19 Albion W. Small, *General Sociology* (Chicago: University of Chicago Press, 1905) , pp. 619–20.

> The central line in the path of methodological progress in sociology is marked by the gradual shifting of effort from analogical representation of social structures to real analysis of social processes.[20]

(It can be safely conjectured that Small would have been rather disappointed with the turn of theoretical events at mid-century.) This was an important viewpoint for many social thinkers earlier in this century, possibly as part of the trend in physical science and philosophy toward a process view of reality developing from the work of such people as Whitehead, Einstein, Dewey, and Bentley. Such views apparently had little impact on those of recent decades who have developed the more dominant structure-oriented models of current sociology, but it seems clear that, with or without the aid of the essentially process-conscious general systems approach, a more even balance of process with structure in the analysis of sociocultural systems is gradually regaining lost ground.

C. H. Cooley, making similarly selective use of the organic model, focused—in his *Social Process*—on the "tentative process," involving inherent energy and growth as the dynamic agents, with ongoing "selective development" set in motion by the interaction of "active tendencies" and surrounding "conditions." He argued that for the social process, "that grows which works" is a better phrase than natural selection or survival of the fittest, since "it is not so likely to let us rest in mechanical or biological conceptions."

R. E. Park, with his recognition of the central importance of communication, kept the notion of process in the foreground whether analyzing the forms of interaction or the foundations of social ecology. Instead of Small's or Cooley's concept of *"the* social process," Park developed more inductively his classification (or continuum) of the many social processes operating in society. Perhaps it was his journalistic experience that led him to emphasize events rather than structures. In any case, all structures represented for him the temporary end results of processes of interpersonal accommodations, adjustments, and conflicts. As Bogardus put it, in Park's view "the world of life is full of strife and resultant accommodations and temporary equilibriums. Social equilibrium is in itself expressive of temporary accommodations."[21]

There are other process theorists who must be mentioned. The leaders of the so-called "formal" school were highly influential. Though Simmel and others focused on "forms" of interaction, their emphasis was always on the interaction as process rather than on the "forms," and

---

[20] *Ibid.*, p. ix. We might add here that Talcott Parsons' initial major work *The Structure of Social Action* must be seen as an important contribution to this progressive shift of effort. As others have noted, however, he has tended to backtrack in his later works, by stressing the structure at the expense of the action.

[21] Emory S. Bogardus, *The Development of Social Thought,* 4th ed. (New York: David McKay Co., Inc., 1960) , p. 567.

though the systematics of Leopold von Wiese and Howard Becker developed in great detail a classification of action *patterns,* it gave equal attention to *action* patterns. For W. I. Thomas, all social becoming was a product of continual interaction between individual consciousness and objective social reality, a view recently reinforced by Znaniecki. And at least one unbroken thread in this vein, continuing from the early part of the century, is the Dewey–Mead perspective referred to as social interactionism. A reviewer of a recent collection of social interactionist essays was "reminded throughout of the continuous character of socialization, of the complexity and fluidity of interaction when it is viewed as a process rather than as the mere enactment of social forms . . ."[22]

To this partial list, we can add only sketchily a few of the more recent arguments for the process viewpoint. The anthropologists, for example, have become acutely concerned with this issue in the last few years. G. P. Murdock seems to be echoing Small when he says:

> All in all, the static view of social structure which seeks explanations exclusively within the existing framework of a social system on the highly dubious assumption of cultural stability and nearly perfect functional integration seems clearly to be giving way, in this country at least, to a dynamic orientation which focuses attention on the processes by which such systems come into being and succeed one another over time.[23]

At about the same time, Raymond Firth, in the second of two presidential addresses before the Royal Anthropological Society devoted to this same topic stated:

> The air of enchantment which for the last two decades has surrounded the 'structuralist' point of view has now begun to be dispelled. Now that this is so, the basic value of the concept of social structure as an heuristic tool rather than a substantial social entity has come to be more clearly recognized.[24]

Soon after appeared the late S. F. Nadel's penetrating work, *The Theory of Social Structure,* which had been preceded by an early recognition and serious consideration of the significance of the new cybernetic point of view represented by his feedback analysis in "Social Control and Self Regulation."[25] This perspective is used effectively in the later work

---

[22] Melvin Seeman, review of *Human Behavior and Social Process: An Interactionist Approach,* ed. Arnold M. Rose, *American Sociological Review,* 27 (1962), p. 557.

[23] George P. Murdock, "Changing Emphasis in Social Structure," *Southwestern Journal of Anthropology,* 11 (1955), p. 366.

[24] Raymond Firth, "Some Principles of Social Organization," *Journal of the Royal Anthropological Institute,* 85 (1955), p. 1.

[25] S. F. Nadel, *The Theory of Social Structure* (New York: Free Press of Glencoe, Inc., 1957).

as a basis for a critique of the equilibrium model, with its emphasis on the "complementarity of expectations" to the relative neglect of the several other crucial types of associative *and dissociative* social interrelationships considered equally important in earlier sociology. Nadel's book as a whole explores the thesis that structural analysis is not, and should not be treated as, static analysis: "Social structure as Fortes once put it, must be 'visualized' as 'a sum of processes in time.' As I would phrase it, social structure is implicitly an event-structure . . ."[26] And in concluding he reiterates his argument:

> . . . it seems impossible to speak of social structure in the singular. Analysis in terms of structure is incapable of presenting whole societies; nor, which means the same, can any society be said to exhibit an embracing, coherent structure as we understand the term. There are always cleavages, dissociations, enclaves, so that any description alleged to present a single structure will in fact present only a fragmentary or one-sided picture.[27]

As a final example in anthropology, we should mention the cogent argument of Evon Z. Vogt that the two concepts of structure and process must be integrated into a general theoretical model. As did Nadel, structure is falsely conceived as static, and change as pathological. Rather must we pose the primacy of change, considering structure to be the way in which moving reality is translated, for the observer, into an instantaneous and artificial observation. Social and cultural structures are only the intersections in time and space of process in course of change and development.[28]

Among sociologists, a perennial critic of the structural conception of the group is Herbert Blumer. Blumer has argued that it is from the process of ongoing interaction itself that group life gets its main features, which cannot be adequately analyzed in terms of fixed attitudes, "culture," or social structure, nor can it be conceptualized in terms of mechanical structure, the functioning of an organism, or a system seeking equilibrium, ". . . in view of the formative and explorative character of interaction as the participants judge each other and guide their own acts by that judgment."

> The human being is not swept along as a neutral and indifferent unit by the operation of a system. As an organism capable of self-interaction he forges his actions out of a process of definition involving *choice, appraisal,* and *decision* . . . Cultural norms, status positions and role relationships

---

26 *Ibid.,* p. 128.

27 *Ibid.,* p. 153.

28 Evon Z. Vogt, "On the Concept of Structure and Process in Cultural Anthropology," *American Anthropologist,* 62 (1960) , 18–33.

are only *frameworks* inside of which that process of formative transaction goes on.[29]

Highly structured human association is relatively infrequent and not the prototype of human group life. In sum, institutionalized patterns constitute only one conceptual aspect of society, and they point to only part of the ongoing process. (And, as we argue later, they must be seen to include deviant and maladjustive patterns; for conceptual clarity and empirical relevance, "institutionalization" should probably not be taken to imply only "legitimacy," "consent," and ultimately adaptive values.)

As a final footnote to our sketch of the process view, it should be noted that personality theorists too seem to be repudiating the static view of personality. Thus, Gordon Allport, looking at personality as an open system, says:

> To be sure, it is an incomplete system, manifesting varying degrees of order and disorder. It has structure but also unstructure, function but also malfunction. As Murphy says, 'all normal people have many loose ends.' And yet personality is well enough knit to qualify as a system—which is defined merely as a *complex of elements in mutual interaction.*[30]

In contrast to such views, we need only recall the many critiques pointing to the incapacity or awkwardness of the Parsonian type of framework before the facts of process, "becoming," and the great range of "collective behavior."[31]

We suggest at this point that conceptions such as Blumer's, a continuation of the perspective of many neglected earlier sociologists and social psychologists, constitute a view that is now pursued by many under the rubric of "decision theory." For earlier antecedents it should be enough to mention W. I. Thomas's "definition of the situation," Znaniecki's "humanistic coefficient," Weber's *"verstehen,"* Becker's "interpretation," and MacIver's "dynamic assessment."[32] Again, the Parsonian scheme in its major emphasis represents a break from this focus. As Philip Selznick argued:

---

[29] Herbert Blumer, "Psychological Import of the Human Group," in *Group Relations at the Crossroads,* ed. Muzafer Sherif and M. O. Wilson (New York: Harper & Row, Publishers, 1953), pp. 199–201.

[30] Gordon W. Allport, *Pattern and Growth in Personality* (New York: Holt, Rinehart & Winston, Inc., 1961), p. 567. See also his "The Open System in Personality Theory," in *Personality and Social Encounter: Selected Essays* (Boston: Beacon Press, 1960), Chap. 3.

[31] See, for example, Alvin W. Gouldner, "Some Observations on Systematic Theory: 1945–55," in *Sociology in the United States of America,* ed. Hans L. Zetterberg (Paris: UNESCO, 1956), especially pp. 39–40.

[32] An excellent early introduction to sociological aspects of what is now called "decision theory" may be found in Robert M. MacIver, *Social Causation,* Chaps. 11 and 12.

> A true theory of social action would say something about goal-oriented or problem-solving behavior, isolating some of its distinctive attributes, stating the likely outcomes of determinate transformation . . . In Parsons' writing there is no true embrace of the idea that structure is being continuously opened up and reconstructed by the problem-solving behavior of individuals responding to concrete situations. This is a point of view we associate with John Dewey and G. H. Mead, for whom indeed, it had significant intellectual consequence. For them and for their intellectual heirs, social structure is something to be taken account of in action; cognition is not merely an empty category but a natural process involving dynamic assessments of the self and the other.[33]

It can be argued, then, that a refocusing is occurring *via* "decision theory," broadly conceived, whether elaborated in terms of "role-strain" theory; theories of cognitive dissonance, congruence, balance, or concept formation; exchange, bargaining, or conflict theories, or the mathematical theory of games. The basic problem is the same: how do interacting personalities and groups define, assess, interpret, *verstehen,* and act on the situation?

THE PARSONS AND HOMANS MODELS

In the present section we shall try to pull together some of the threads of the earlier sections and show a little more systematically how the mechanical and organic models have been used in recent sociology. This will involve a brief outline of the Parsonian mechanical-organic framework, incorporating the more important of the many recent criticisms made of it. A comparison will then be made with the equilibrium model of Homans. Our main point in these critical sketches is to show the diametrically opposing theoretical implications that can be drawn depending on how one uses seemingly similar concepts or models that are inadequate to their task. However, we shall argue that Homans conclusions are so different because his conceptualization is closer to the spirit of modern systems theory than to that of the traditional equilibrium model from which it was presumably derived.

The Parsonian Equilibrium–Function Model

The tedious job of adding yet another to the many critiques of the Parsonian framework must contend with its loose conceptual structure. Though some of the critiques are only the crudest of caricatures, the fact that the framework is not a close-knit postulation system of well-

---

[33] Philip Selznick, "Review Article: The Social Theories of Talcott Parsons," *American Sociological Review,* 26 (1961) , 934.

defined and consistently used concepts invites such treatment. The present sketch can only pretend to portray characteristic emphases rather than concise and consistent principles: the critical analyst of Parsonianism soon learns that statements can be found in that work which seemingly refute almost any critical point made against it.

Parsons has always been deeply concerned with the concept of "order," and he and Shils define the notion of "system" in its terms:

> The most general and fundamental property of a system is the interdependence of parts or variables. Interdependence consists in the existence of determinate relationships among the parts or variables as contrasted with randomness of variability. In other words, interdependence is *order* in the relationship among the components which enter into a system.[34]

Under this definition, we should note, "order" in society can embrace not only legitimized institutional patterns and processes, but also deviance, subcultural alternatives, persistent conflict, systemically structured collective behavior, and the like—as long as they can be seen to be functions of the "determinate relations among the parts" of the system rather than random incidents. We must also note here, however, a quite different meaning given to the concept of "order" later on in the same work:

> Order—peaceful coexistence under conditions of scarcity—is one of the very first of the functional imperatives of *social systems*.[35]

We point out this difference of meaning because it lies at the root of much of the difficulty and ambiguity of the Parsonian framework, pointing as it does to neutral causal relations on the one hand, and normative, or evaluative relations on the other.

As we have seen, Parsons and Shils go on to postulate that "this order must have a tendency to self-maintenance, which is very generally expressed in the concept of equilibrium."[36] The second meaning of "order" is clearly implied. An additional central property is the tendency of the social system to maintain equilibrium within certain boundaries relative to an environment (everything not part of the system), a property held to be very similar to the biological concept of homeostasis. Also in keeping with the biological model is the concept of functional imperatives: the constituent conditions and empirically necessary preconditions of ongoing systems set by the facts of scarcity in the object situation, the nature of the organism, and the realities of coexistence.

It is taken as a fundamental assumption by Parsons that the main-

---

[34] Talcott Parsons and Edward A. Shils, eds., *Toward a General Theory of Action* (Cambridge, Mass.: Harvard University Press, 1951) , p. 107.

[35] *Ibid.*, p. 180.

[36] *Ibid.*

tenance of an established state of a social system is non-problematic, that the tendency to maintain the interaction process is the "first law of social process," akin to the mechanical law of inertia. It is then asked what classes of tendencies *not* to maintain this interaction there are. First, new members coming into the system must acquire through learning their conforming role-orientations, since they are not inborn. Secondly, since learning is not always adequate in view of the existing social situation, there arise "tendencies to *deviance,* to depart from conformity with the normative standards which come to be set up as the common culture."[37] These two main sources of deviance thus present the social system with "problems" of control, since, if tolerated, they will tend to change or disintegrate the system. The system thus "meets" these problems through its "mechanisms of control:" mechanisms of socialization and mechanisms of social control thus work hand in hand with mechanisms of defense and adjustment in the personality system to motivate actors to conformity with the given system of expectations, counteract deviance and other strains in the system to bring it back to the given state, and maintain the initial equilibrium. By way of example, possibilities of disequilibrium, it is asserted, arise from the fact that non-empirical ideas are not always common to all members of a collectivity, as they need to be in order to maintain stability. These possibilities are reduced by mechanisms of control—mechanisms of "enforcement" of uniformity and stability in beliefs. "Traditionalism" and "authoritative enforcement" are two major types.

Finally, if the system's mechanisms of control do not work adequately, the system changes its state or disintegrates. In other words, the system either works or it does not, and in either case we analyze the situation by focusing on the mechanisms of control.

Often noted by critics is the ambiguous status of "deviance" in Parsons' social system. Although he clearly recognizes in many places that structured deviance, tensions, strains, etc. are determinate, *integral parts* of a social system, nevertheless somewhere along his line of exposition the "system" comes to be identified, as we saw earlier, with the dominant, legitimized, institutionalized structure, or at least with those characteristic structures that *do not include* patterned strains or structured deviance and disorder. And the concept of "institutionalized deviance" now widely recognized in one form or another by many sociologists, could be a contradiction in terms for Parsons.

In contrast, it can be argued that in dealing with a social system, or with *any* system, on a scientific level, deviance is a *normative,* or anthropocentric, concept that is *relative* to some arbitrarily selected reference

---

37 Talcott Parsons, *The Social System* (New York: Free Press of Glencoe, Inc., 1951) , p. 206.

point. For example, in the solar system astronomers found slight "deviations" of the planetary orbits from the perfect ellipse, due primarily to the interactions between planets themselves. But these "deviations" are only subjectively interpreted as such, that is, relative to the human observer who arbitrarily selects a reference frame (perfect ellipse) and compares reality to it. But in physical theory, the "deviations" are as much a part of the total system as the elliptical path itself, and the system of forces at work allow for no distinction. In the case of the social system, the issue is thus whether conformity and order, on the one hand, and deviance and disorder, on the other, are to be considered on a par as system characteristics or products. If the answer is "yes," then we need to balance "mechanisms of control" or conformity with an equally ardent search for and analysis of "mechanisms" of deviance and disorder. In both cases, the "mechanisms" arbitrarily focus on aspects of the system, with no difference in status, and both would seem important points of attack on the realities of society.

If it is correct to say that a given (or established) state of a social system at any time embraces all the determinate relations of parts including both what we call "conformity" patterns and what we call "deviant" patterns, then Parsons' following statement is clearly one-sided:

> An established state of a social system is a process of complementary interaction of two or more individual actors in which each conforms with the expectations of the other (s) in such a way that alter's reactions to ego's actions are positive sanctions which serve to reinforce his given need-dispositions and thus to fulfill his given expectations.[38]

Doesn't the established state also include structured non-complementary interaction in which each frustrates the expectations of others, and so forth? Or again:

> A social system is always characterized by an institutionalized value system. The social system's first functional imperative is to maintain the integrity of that value system and its institutionalization. This process of maintenance means stabilization against pressures to change the value system . . . The tendency to stabilize the system in the face of pressures to change institutionalized values through cultural channels may be called the "pattern maintenance" function . . . Motivational tensions, arising from strains in any part of the social situation or organic or other intrapersonal sources, may threaten individual motivation to conformity with institutionalized role expectations. Stabilization against this potential source of change may be called "tension management."[39]

---

38 *Ibid.,* pp. 204–5.

39 Talcott Parsons and Neil J. Smelser, *Economy and Society* (New York: Free Press of Glencoe, Inc., 1956), pp. 16–17.

We can accept this as far as it goes, but where are the counterpoints? There are equally tenable assumptions and propositions to be made, such as:

> An established state of any complex society includes structured non-complementary interaction (e.g., organized conflict, competition, and so forth) in which each actor frustrates the expectations or goal seeking of others.

> A social system is always characterized by multiple and contradictory value systems and their many shades of interpretation in concrete action and interaction.

> A first imperative of a relatively orderly, need-satisfying and stress-free social system is the nurturing of nonpathological deviation and variety as the basic source of the continued critical examination and considered change of the institutionalized structures and value-interpretations.

> The tendency to change the system in the face of pressures to conserve the traditional institutionalized value-interpretation through cultural channels may be called the "pattern renovating" function.

> Motivational tensions arising from conformity pressures in any part of the social situation or other sources may threaten individual motivation to question the integrity of the value system and to innovate with respect to institutionalized role expectations, thus helping preserve a disfunctional sociocultural structure. Innovation against this potential source of preservation of an inadequate structure may be called "creative tension release."

And so forth. An exercise such as this at least points up the ease with which we can allow vague terminology and its many implicit connotations to inject ambiguity, if not bias, into our intended theoretical propositions. Finally, our argument would seem to make the following strategy of questionable value:

> . . . for the social system as well as the personality we will *not* be concerned with the problem of the maintenance of given states of the social system *except where there are known tendencies to alter those states.* (Parsons' emphasis) [40]

If a given state of a social system *always contains* tendencies to alter that state, and Parsons often says that it does, then maintenance is perennially problematic. We can speak of the "law of inertia" only when there is no source of change within the system itself. Here is a fundamental difference between a closed system and an open one, which will be discussed more fully later on.

---

[40] Parsons, *The Social System*, p. 204.

Looking closely at Parsons' scheme we see that his conserving orientation is built tightly into the model. The boundary of the system is defined in terms of "constancy patterns" that are tied up to a harmonious set of common norms and values, mutually supporting expectations, and the like. Equilibrium, in turn, is defined in terms of the boundary-maintaining system of constant, harmonious, mutual, common, reciprocal, complementary, stabilized, and integrated patterns. In a word, the "system" here excludes, or includes only residually, structured strains and deviant patterns which, however, we know very well may be constant, mutual, and reciprocal, within themselves and to a great extent in relation to the dominant structure (recall, for example, William F. Whyte's study of the rackets in *Street Corner Society*).

It should be pointed out that essentially these criticisms were directed against the Parsonian scheme almost two decades ago by important theorists, but without apparent impact. Thus, Theodore Newcomb, in his "Discussion" of Parsons' early statement of his theoretical position, argued:

> My major proposed re-arrangement has to do with two of his 'Divisions' of sociological theory: 'the theory of motivation of institutional behavior' and 'the theory of motivation of deviant behavior and the problem of social control.' The distinction of these two sorts of motivation seems to me of the kind which Kurt Lewin would call phenotypical rather than genotypical. In terms of social psychology . . . there seems to me no important difference between motivated roles which are conforming and those which are not.
>
> From a psychological point of view, the process of learning to respond in certain ways to other people is the same whether this end result is a conforming or a deviant role. In either case the process is one of goal-directed behavior involving perception, performance, thought and affect. The goal toward which behavior is directed while institutionally prescribed roles are being acquired is not necessarily 'to acquire the prescribed role.'[41]

Much of the discussion concerning the place of deviance in the social system could be repeated for the status of "collective behavior" relative to institutionalized structures. It might be argued that any dynamic analysis must focus equally on systemic sources (or "mechanisms") of collective behavior. Such an approach would at least recognize that system patterns fall on a continuum from the "institutionalized" to the nearly unstructured, and that many forms of presumably "legitimized" patterns lie closed to the area of collective behavior—for example, many power structures and shifts of regimes in many nations illustrate this continuum.

On the basis of our all too brief discussion we may now attempt to summarily list more explicitly the major problems in the Parsonian

---

[41] Theodore Newcomb, "Discussion," *American Sociological Review*, 13 (1948), 168–69.

model, which we shall then use as points of comparison with the Homans model.

1. The social system of determinate relations comes to include only, or primarily, those determinate relations making up an "institutionalized" dominant structure of conformity to role expectations. This dominant structure is thus taken as the fixed point of reference against which other structures or latent consequences are seen as potentially disruptive. These latter pose "problems" of control (functional imperatives) for the "system" (that is, the dominant institutional structure) which must be met if the system is to be maintained or conserved. In this way, the "social system" comes to be narrowed down to embrace only *certain* determinate relations—those of presumably "peaceful coexistence," or Parsons' alternate definition of "order."

2. This means that deviance and strains of various kinds are residual in the model since they are not given full-fledged status as integral parts of the system. Such deviance or strains, whether they are manifested in diffuse neurotic symptoms, in delinquent and criminal behavior, in partially or fully organized social movements, or ideational innovation, must be lumped together and treated as disfunctional for the system.

3. The question arises whether the postulated "law of social statics" or "social inertia" is applicable to a dynamic system *within* which forces or pressures to change exist as integral elements. It would seem to make sense only when such pressures are considered external to the system, as Parsons often does in the case of his "system." We may agree here with his own observation that the law of "inertia" "is certainly contrary to much of the common sense of the social sciences . . ."[42]

4. The Parsonian model is rife with anthropomorphism and teleology. The system "seeks" equilibrium, it has "problems" and "imperatives" of control, it has "systemic needs." Parsons is always careful to enclose such terms in quotes, and explicitly pays lip service to the dangers involved. But unfortunately, as the history of science shows, this is not enough to cover the full price that we may eventually have to pay for using such notions for their presumably heuristic value. Strictly speaking, even for systems characterized in terms of "goal-seeking," there is abundant support from cybernetic analysis for the view that teleological terms such as "functional imperative" are entirely redundant, given an adequate definition of the system we are dealing with.

5. The postulated "mechanisms of control" are quite one-sided. We may grant the use of the concept of "mechanism" as valid and valuable: it refers to an arbitrarily isolated part of a total system that is itself treated as a system in order to judge its relevance (in terms of possible alternative outcomes of the mechanism) for the total system. What Par-

---

[42] *The Social System*, p. 205.

sons actually does, however, is to isolate out his mechanisms of control and judge their relevance, not to the *total* system, but to that part represented by the dominant or legitimized structure that he has taken as a fixed point of reference. It then follows that all other structures or tendencies to structural change are deviant or disfunctional and to be counteracted by the mechanisms. To correct this one-sidedness and be consistent with the realities of a social system, it would seem necessary to take the structured strains and structured deviance as an integral part of the system and a fixed point of reference and ask what mechanisms may be isolated out that tend to maintain *these* structures. The answer would lead straight to the crucial problems of power, ideology and propaganda, vested interest, and the like. We note, in fact, that in his discussion of social change, Parsons gives this last concept a central role, but he finds no place for it in his theoretical model; (perhaps this fact is related to his pessimistic tone in discussing the current possibilities of a theory of change). In sum, we note that the model leads only to a consideration of such mechanisms as those of defense, adjustment, and deviance control, all aimed at adaptation of the *actor* to a given dominant structure, with no consideration given to the historically obvious mechanisms that adapt or change the system structure to accommodate the actor and maintain the total system.

6. It follows that, as in the case of the related concept of deviance, the Parsonian model has grave difficulty in dealing with social change, since the latter tends also to be seen as residual—something that happens to the system when the relationships and mechanisms dealt with by the model break down. This often seems to imply that the sources of change are always external to the system, though the model is explicitly declared to allow endogenous change.

It might be suggested that Parsons' chapter on change in *The Social System* is much more insightful and far-reaching than strict adherence to his model would ever allow. In particular, the role of ideas or belief systems is given a prominent place in the former, but finds little room in the model since, for Parsons, ideas not "consonant" with the dominant social structure are deviant and inhibited by the mechanisms of control.

7. Finally, at the root of much of the difficulty with the Parsonian model is the fact that it is built after a melange of the biological structure-function model and a mechanical equilibrium model. It is significant that the biological and mechanical models break down for the social system at just those points where Parsons' model is weakest and most subject to criticism. a) In an organismic system we do have a relatively fixed structure that is normal for the species at a given time. b) This normal biological structure provides us with quite definite criteria against which to assess deviant or malfunctional structures and processes. c) As such tendencies toward deviance from the normal structure arise (due pri-

marily to external causes such as disease, extremes of weather, and so forth) , automatic homeostatic mechanisms of "control" come into play to counteract them and conserve the normal structure. d) When these fail the organism disintegrates (dies) and fuses into the environment.

A social system, however, does not have any such fixed, normal structure which, if changed beyond narrow limits, leads necessarily to the system's "death." In contrast to an organismic system, social systems are characterized primarily by their propensity to *change their structure* during their culturally continuous "lifetime." Parsons thus stretches the organismic model beyond its limits when he confines himself to the use of an existing fixed structure as a point of reference for assessing the "functional imperatives" of a social system. Such imperatives might well have reference to the very possibilities that a system in general can exist (for example, *any* system regardless of its particular internal structure must make provisions for food, shelter, reproduction, and so on) , but as any anthropology or history text makes clear, there is no one particular or "normal" internal structure that alone satisfies these imperatives. Although there are certainly limits within which the features of a social system structure may vary and still remain compatible enough for system maintenance, we can argue that these limits, for a social system compared to an organism or mechanical system, may be relatively broad. And it is within these limits that most sociologically interesting questions are posed.

Homans' Equilibrium Model

It is of great interest to note that Homans' model,[43] though similarly based on the concept of equilibrium derived from Pareto, is constructed in terms of principles and assumptions diametrically opposite those listed in the foregoing summary. We may thus analyze it in terms of these same seven points.

1. For Homans the system is consistently defined in terms of the determinate, reciprocal interrelationships of *all* its parts, regardless of the particular structure in which these interrelations are manifested. (The basic parts or elements are activities, interaction, sentiments, and norms.) Thus, the interrelations of the elements are manifested now as a family structure, now as a work or as a community structure. There is no attempt to take any of these structures as fixed, privileged points of reference.

2. This means that deviance is an integral part of the system, explicable in terms of the determinate mutual relations of the elements. For example, the social system developed in the Bank Wiring Room

---

[43] George C. Homans, *The Human Group* (New York: Harcourt, Brace & World, Inc., 1950) .

(Chapter 3) was analyzable into two main cliques, each of which was deviant in its behavior relative to the other. Although a work norm constituted part of the total system (or group), the mutual relations between the elements were such that if a man departed from his *existing degree* of obedience to the norm (in some cases quite deviant), other changes in the system of relations brought him back to *that degree*. Thus, stresses and strains may be an integral part of the system (manifesting themselves by way of the particular organization of sentiments, interaction patterns, activities, and norms), and constitute—along with the consensual normative structure—a self-maintaining equilibrium.

3. For Homans the maintenance of a given pattern or structure is problematic, even a "miracle." Why is custom customary? Why do recurrences recur? These are the Protean questions for Homans. Established patterns of conformity, *or deviance,* are not automatically self-sustaining, and regularity persists because departure is met by resistance. Nor is resistance mere inertia. Rather, it consists in the way the elements of the system are interrelated: a change in one element results in a change in others that counteract it and bring it back to its original state. A system in which this occurs is said to be in equilibrium. A social system is a configuration of dynamic forces; sometimes the configuration is in balance and a steady state is maintained. Sometimes it is out of balance and continuing change occurs.[44]

4. Not every state of a system is in equilibrium nor does a system "seek" equilibrium. Furthermore, a system does not have "problems," and structures do not arise because they are "needed" by the system—because they are "functional imperatives"—but *because there are forces producing them,* forces manifested in the nature of the elements of the system and their mutual relations. Structures may disappear for the very same reason.

5. The system *is* the social control, it does not "impose" a control. Social control is implicit in the relationships of elements of the system; it is the process by which, if a man departs from his existing degree of obedience to a norm, other changes result in bringing him back to that degree (if the system is in equilibrium and control is thus effective). The "controls" are nothing but the relations of mutual dependence, not a separate element of organization, nor a "function" the group performs. Furthermore, intelligence and ideas take part in social control and thus have a place in the system: intelligence enables one to "see," before taking action, the relations between interdependent elements of the system, and thus to act on this insight and avoid harmful consequences. This in turn permits the concept of "authority" to be located in the system. If an order given by a leader is accepted by a member and controls his activities in the group, the leader is said to have authority for that member; this

44 *Ibid.,* p. 282.

implies that the authority of an order always rests on the willingness of the person to whom it is addressed to obey it. But effective leadership, control, or authority implies that the mutual relations of a group are such that the group process does a great deal to see to it that the individual chooses rightly, that is, any "wrong" choices set in operation forces that bring them back to what are considered right by the group.

6. In studying social change we discover nothing new in the relationship between the elements of behavior. We see only how a change in the value of one or more of the elements (for example, an increase or decrease) effects changes in others.

In dealing with change Homans considers both processes of growth or elaboration of structures ("adaptive evolution") and processes of disorganization and disintegration of structures ("anomie"). In doing so, he distinguishes in the total system two analytically separable systems, the "external" and the "internal," and relates them in terms of the concept of feedback. The external system refers to the relations between sentiments, activities, interactions, and norms viewed as responses by members to the necessities of surviving in an environment. The internal system refers to the elaborations of these elements and their relations that simultaneously arise out of the external system and feed back to it and to the system as a whole. These two analytically separate systems are defined relatively, and are mutually dependent. The feedback that occurs between the two may be favorable *or* unfavorable to the continued existence of one or the other or both. For example, as the internal system develops out of the external, there may result a particular division of labor (for example, a growth of cliques based on differentiation of activities or social distinctions), a scheme of interaction that comes to act as a system of communication where this was minimal or nonexistent in the external system, and social control that is self-imposed and supports a set of norms that have arisen. It is the elaboration of this surplus of structures leading to new activities and new reactions to the environment that gives the social system room for adaptive evolution.

On the other hand, in the case of structures already elaborated, a change in one or more elements of the external system may lead to a decrease in the quantitative or qualitative value of elements in the internal system. These internal effects may then feed back to the external system to accelerate still further the process of change. Unless this process is checked in some way, the mutual relations of the system break down in a spiral of positive feedback and the system as such becomes disorganized and may disintegrate or split into separate fragments.

Consciously directed change may become a problem for a leader or leaders (not a "problem" for the "system" as such), and this problem is one of manipulating the elements or relations between elements of the system so that any departure from the goal-path is met by changes counteracting the departure. (Note that this does not necessarily imply manipulation of the *members* of the system, but may mean manipulation of the existing *structure* of relations such that what the members want to do also happens to be what is required if the system is to remain a system.)

7. Finally, Homans rejects the biological structure-function model in attacking its basic methodological underpinnings. Especially does he criticize the notion of survival of society as too hazy to be useful unless it is very clearly and concretely specified. In fact, he suggests that the idea of survival or continuity in functional theory can be made rigorous only if survival is redefined as equilibrium. And he has stressed that systems do not "seek" this condition, nor is every system in this state.

Though Homans' model avoids much of the difficulty and ambiguity of the Parsonian system, its own weakness seems to lie precisely in the mechanically derived notion of equilibrium. Homans tells us that *if* a system is in equilibrium we may expect certain consequences to follow, but he can provide us with no basis for assessing *whether or not* a system *is* in equilibrium—for defining the *conditions under which* it is or is not in equilibrium. Since equilibrium is defined operationally in terms of the actual consequences of a system's being in this state, we need criteria that are independent of these empirical consequences. But as Homans' model leaves us now, we can only wait and see what happens and then say that the system must have been in or not in equilibrium, *ex post facto*.

This, however, is not the heart of the difficulty, for Homans knows very well—having stated it several times—that the system he is talking about is an *open* one, in interaction with an environment, such that *an irreversible shift of system states is an inherent characteristic*. His recognition of this is made in terms of his distinction between the "external system" and the "internal system."[45]

> Assuming that there is established between the members of a group any set of relations satisfying the condition that the group survives for a time in its particular environment, physical and social, we can show that on the foundation of these relations the group will develop new ones, that the latter will modify or even create the relations we assumed at the beginning, and that, finally, the behavior of the group, besides being determined by the environment, will itself change the environment.[46]

> Social life is never wholly utilitarian: it elaborates itself, complicates itself, beyond the demands of the original situation. The elaboration brings changes in the motives of individuals . . . But the elaboration also means changes in their activities and interactions—changes, in fact, in the organization of the group as a whole.[47]

---

[45] *Ibid.*, Chaps. 4 and 5.
[46] *Ibid.*, p. 91.
[47] *Ibid.*, p. 109.

Society does not just survive; in surviving it creates conditions that, under favorable circumstances, allows it to survive at a new level. Given half a chance, it pulls itself up by its own bootstraps. How can we account in any other way for the emergence of a civilization from a tribe? . . .

We have argued, for instance, that the Tikopia family has to have some division of labor and some chain of command. To the extent that we have 'explained' the existence of these features of group life by the assumption that the group could not survive without them, we have been functionalists. But in our study of the build-up and feedback of the internal system, we have considered . . . the efficient causes of these features. That is, we have shown some of the processes that create or modify the group characteristics we assumed at the beginning . . . But the feedbacks are not all favorable, and the social distance between father and son, or, more generally, between persons of different social rank, may be a source of possible conflict and failure of communication.[48]

We quote Homans extensively here to make two concluding points. First, he effectively argues not only that the organic nature of society goes far beyond anything conceived by the functional anthropologists, but that it goes far beyond anything that could possibly be confined within a mechanical equilibrium model. Mechanical equilibrium systems do not *elaborate structures,* do not *create new and more complicated relations,* do not *manifest efficient causes playing into the hands of final ones,* do not *pull themselves up by their own bootstraps* to new levels of survival. They are closed and entropic systems. Social systems are not. At one point Homans had used the analogy of the gasoline engine, but he did not fail to recognize that

. . . there is one great difference between describing the gasoline engine and describing the group. With the gasoline engine we show how the later events in the cycle create the very conditions we assumed in the beginning, whereas with the group we shall show that the later events in the cycle may modify the conditions we assumed in the beginning. We shall have to allow scope for emergent evolution.[49]

Secondly, Homans argues with his characteristically eloquent simplicity for the modern systems approach, even utilizing some of its basic vocabulary. For this approach, too, is concerned to translate final causes into efficient ones involving internal communications and feedbacks, and to discover the conditions under which relatively transient "steady states" give way to new "steady states" on a different level of structural complexity. In his work a decade or so later, Homans comes to speak of a "practical equilibrium," "in order to avoid the almost mystical arguments that have encrusted the latter word in social science." He continues:

48 *Ibid.,* pp. 272–74.
49 *Ibid.,* p. 94.

Nor do we assume that if a change from practical equilibrium does occur, behavior necessarily reacts so as to reduce or get rid of it. There is no homeostasis here: no belief that a group acts like an animal body shaking off an infection. Should some groups under some circumstances behave this way, there is no evidence that they do so always. Nor do we, like the so-called functional sociologists, simply assume that equilibrium exists and then use it to try to explain why the other features of a group or a society should be what they are. If a group is in equilibrium, they say, then its behavior *must* exhibit certain other features. For us, on the other hand, specific effects must follow from specific causes, but more than that we do not ask of the behavior of any group; there is no more *must* about it. Practical equilibrium, then, is not a state toward which all creation moves; it is rather a state that behavior, no doubt temporarily and precariously, sometimes achieves. It is not something we assume; it is something that within the limits of our methods we observe. It is not something we use to explain the other features of social behavior; it is rather something that, when it does occur, is itself to be explained by these other features.[50]

It is clear that Homans has left both the classical equilibrium model and the organismic functional model far behind in the evolution of his theoretical conception of the sociocultural system. We shall have occasion to discuss later his disappointing appeal to a reductionist psychologism—a giant-step down from his earlier systems approach.

THE GENERAL SYSTEMS PERSPECTIVE

As has been suggested, modern systems theory, though seemingly springing *de novo* out of the last war effort, can be seen as a culmination of a broad shift in scientific perspective striving for dominance over the last few centuries. This scientific world-view, product of a constant dialectic between conceptions of physical and those of biological science, have led away from concern for inherent substance, qualities, and properties to a central focus on the principles of *organization per se,* regardless of what it is that is organized. Stephen Toulmin and June Goodfield, tracing the historical development of matter-theory, tell the story of the long struggle to bridge the theoretical gap between organic and inorganic matter.[51] One of those who took a bold leap forward was de la Mettrie, the eighteenth-century physiologist, whose treatise *Man a Machine* was published in 1747. "By a sweeping generalization," Toulmin and Goodfield suggest, "de la Mettrie sketched the bold outlines of a new system of physiology: one in which the key concept was 'organization'."[52] For

---

50 *Social Behavior: Its Elementary Forms*, 113–14.

51 Stephen Toulmin and June Goodfield, *The Architecture of Matter* (New York: Harper & Row, Publishers, 1962).

52 *Ibid.*, p. 315.

eighteenth-century physiologists were faced with a basic dilemma stemming from a presupposition underlying matter-theory:

> namely, the presupposition that the raw material of Nature must, intrinsically, be *either* animate *or* inanimate. If, on the one hand, matter was essentially brute, mechanical and insensible, the consequences were clear: no assemblage constructed solely out of matter could be anything but brute, mechanical and insensible—as Descartes had declared animals to be. If that were so, the very idea of a *conscious machine* must be a contradiction in terms: nothing composed of matter alone would be capable of thinking or feeling, and mental capacities (perhaps vital properties also) must spring from some distant, non-material ingredient.[53]

But de la Mettrie, alone among his colleagues, escaped the dilemma by rejecting this fundamental supposition.

> Matter was in itself neither organic nor inorganic, neither living nor dead, neither sensible nor insensible. The difference between these states or properties of material things sprang, not from the intrinsic natures of their raw materials, but from the different ways in which these materials were *organized*.[54]

However, de la Mettrie could offer little solid evidence for his point of view. "Just what was 'organized,' and how, and in what ways this 'organization' was maintained and transmitted from generation to generation: on these subjects he was necessarily silent."[55] The details had to be filled in by the gradual accumulation of research and theory.

The struggle continued between mechanistic and vitalistic conceptions, but with periodic efforts to mesh the two by such men as Claude Bernard in the nineteenth century, who explained the regulating mechanisms of the animal machine "on principles which have been fully exploited only in *twentieth-century* machines—the principles underlying thermostats, electronic controls and servo-mechanisms."[56] The story from then on is recent, if not current history: it is an account of the final efforts of those who held the organic or holistic view in biology advancing a "new vitalism" against the cruder mechanistic biology, culminating in the current fusion of both organicism and mechanism in cybernetics and general systems theory.[57]

---

53 *Ibid.*, p. 317.

54 *Ibid.*, p. 318.

55 *Ibid.*

56 *Ibid.*, p. 334.

57 See Ludwig von Bertalanffy, *Modern Theories of Development* (New York: Harper & Row, Publishers, Torchbook ed., 1962), and *Problems of Life* (New York: Harper & Row, Publishers, Torchbook ed., 1960); Morton Beckner, *The Biological Way of Thought* (New York: Columbia University Press, 1959); and G. Sommerhoff, *Analytical Biology* (London: Oxford University Press, 1950).

The outlines of this most recent chapter in the history of science are instructively sketched in a paper on organization theory by Anatol Rapoport and William J. Horvath.[58] In recent decades it came to be fully appreciated by such men as Whitehead that the growing problems of "organized complexity" could not be adequately studied within the approach of classical physics. The answer lay rather in the direction of the organic holism of biology, whose procedures differed from those of classical physics by their emphasis on 1) teleological "explanation," and 2) the heavy utilization of classification and categorization. Though modern biology and physics approach one another more closely today, we can still argue that the methods of biology offer more to the study of organized complexity as long as we can show how the older biological view now fits into more modern modes of analysis. The key concept of organized complexity—defined as a collection of entities interconnected by a complex net of relations—is to be distinguished from 1) "organized simplicity"—a complex of relatively unchanging components linked by a strict sequential order or linear additivity, without closed loops in the causal chain; and from 2) "chaotic complexity"—a vast number of components that do not have to be specifically identified and whose interactions can be described in terms of continuously distributed quantities or gradients, as in statistical mechanics.

Rapoport and Horvath go on to suggest that two classes of conceptual tools were needed to extend "systematic rigorous theoretical methods" to the organized complexity of the holist. Both of these derive from the older biological methods of teleology and taxonomy. 1) The old teleology has been made respectable by cybernetics, which appeals directly to physical laws and the principles governing the construction of networks of causal relations, including closed-loop "feedbacks," which made possible an acceptable operational definition of goal-seeking behavior without true teleology. 2) The distinction between machines with and without the feedback loops that make for goal-seeking is a *topological* distinction, definable in terms of graph theory, a branch of topology. The causal relations shown as directed segments, describe the system as a directed graph with cycles, such that complex behavior is precisely defined. This principle had been suggested by McCulloch and Pitts in 1943 in their demonstration of the isomorphism between symbolic logic and network theory. Topology, argue Rapoport and Horvath, can be seen as a "taxonomic" branch of mathematics—qualitative rather than quantitative, and whose theorems have an all-or-none flavor; they assert that something does or does not exist, is or is not possible, rather than express functional relations between variables that may assume a continuum of

---

[58] Anatol Rapoport and William J. Horvath, "Thoughts on Organization Theory," *General Systems,* 4 (1959) , 87–91.

values. These two interrelated conceptual tools—cybernetics and topology —are thus seen as two disciplines which, along with a third cornerstone— the "theory of decisions," will "be at the foundation of that branch of science which deals with 'organized complexity,' that is, organization theory."[59]

In sum, then, the modern systems approach aims to replace the older analytic, atomic, Laplacian technique with a more holistic orientation to the problem of complex organization. In the view of W. Ross Ashby, the centuries-old strategy of varying one factor is now of use only when the system is fairly simple; when it becomes complex we can only appeal to a special strategy that has been developing perhaps since the work of R. A. Fisher in the 1920's and leads up to current information theory and cybernetics. The way *not* to approach a complex system, Ashby says,

> . . . is by analysis, for this process gives us only a vast number of separate parts or items of information, the results of whose interactions no one can predict. If we take such a system to pieces, we find that we cannot reassemble it.

Not only that, but the old view that the current state of a complex system is simply a function of its initial conditions is no longer tenable, for the complex, open system, though determinate, "changes so that, as time goes on, its state is characterized more by the experiences that have come to it than by its state initially."[60]

The lessons of this brief history of science seem of great significance for sociology, though their application has barely begun. The modern systems approach should be especially attractive to sociology because, in sum, it promises to develop:

1. A common vocabulary unifying the several "behavioral" disciplines;

2. A technique for treating large, complex organization;

3. A synthetic approach where piecemeal analysis is not possible due to the intricate interrelationships of parts that cannot be treated out of context of the whole;

4. A viewpoint that gets at the heart of sociology because it sees the sociocultural system in terms of information and communication nets;

5. The study of *relations* rather than "entities," with an emphasis on process and transition probabilities as the basis of a flexible structure with many degrees of freedom;

6. An operationally definable, objective, non-anthropomorphic study of purposiveness, goal-seeking system behavior, symbolic cognitive processes, consciousness and self-awareness, and sociocultural emergence and dynamics in general.

---

59 *Ibid.*, 90.

60 W. Ross Ashby, "The Effect of Experience on a Determinate Synamic System," *Behavioral Science*, 1 (1956) , 35–42.

These are large promises and must be taken with reservations, for they only point in the direction in which the hard work lies. We conclude our comparison of the various models with the following generalized diagram of what seems to us the crucial distinctions. (Figure 2-1.)

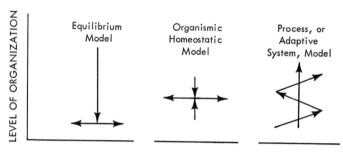

FIGURE 2-1

The equilibrium model, strictly speaking, is applicable to types of systems which, in moving to an equilibrium point, typically lose organization, and then tend to hold that minimum level within relatively narrow conditions of disturbance. Homeostatic models apply to systems tending to maintain a given, relatively high, level of organization against ever-present tendencies to reduce it. The process, or complex adaptive system, model applies to systems characterized by the elaboration or evolution of organization; as we shall see, they thrive on, in fact depend on, "disturbances" and "variety" in the environment.

We turn, in the next chapter, to an elaboration of the adaptive system model and its major differences from lower-level systems models, such as those based on equilibrium and homeostasis.

We shall not, in this chapter, indulge to any great extent in the sport of defining the general concept of "system" in formal terms. Our main emphasis will be on the differences among the major types of systems specified in terms of their structural arrangements and dynamics, and on the methodological problems of analysis they raise.

The kind of system we are interested in may be described generally as a complex of elements or components directly or indirectly related in a causal network, such that each component is related to at least some others in a more or less stable way within any particular period of time.[1] The components may be relatively simple and stable, or complex and changing; they may vary in only one or two properties or take on many different states. The interrelations between them may be mutual or unidirectional, linear, nonlinear or intermittent, and varying in degrees of causal efficacy or priority. The particular kinds of more or less stable interrelationships of components that become established at any time constitute the particular structure of the system at that time, thus achieving a kind of "whole" with some degree of continuity and boundary. Also, we are mainly interested in systems within which some process is continually going on, including an interchange with an environment across the boundary. It is generally agreed that when we deal with the more open system with a highly flexible structure, the distinction between the boundaries and the environment becomes a more and more arbitrary matter, dependent on the purpose of the observer.

---

[1] A good statement of the concept of "system" may be found in Arthur D. Hall and R. E. Fagen, "Definition of Systems," *General Systems,* 1 (1956), 18–28.

systems 3

SYSTEMS AND ENTITIES

In fact, it is becoming clear that we cannot make a neat division of those things that are and those that are not systems; rather, we shall have to recognize varying degrees of "systemness." And if we also recognize that the "substances" or "entities" that the various scientific disciplines study—nuclear "particles," atoms, molecules, solar systems, cells, organs, organisms, ecological communities, societies—are all subsumable under a definition of system, then we seem forced to accept the notion of varying degrees of "entitivity." If we continue to think in terms of "real substances" this does not seem to make much sense, for how can there be degrees of "substance"? But if substances or entities represent systems whose characteristics or properties are due to a particular *organization* of lower-level components, and if we admit of varying degrees of organization, the mystery disappears. For we can understand that it is the *organization* that ceases to exist or is formed when, for example, a nuclear particle is "annihilated" and another "created," or water is broken down into hydrogen and oxygen or table salt built up from sodium and chlorine atoms, or a living cell dies and becomes nothing but its constituent molecules while a new living cell is synthesized from such constituents, or a social group dissolves into its constituent individuals as another is created out of previously unrelated persons.

Thus, if social groups are not "real entities" then neither are individual organisms, organs, cells, molecules or atoms, since they are all "nothing but" the constituents of which they are made. But this "nothing but" hides the central key to modern thinking—the fact of *organization* of components into systemic relationships. When we say that "the whole is more than the sum of its parts," the meaning becomes unambiguous and loses its mystery: the "more than" points to the fact of *organization,* which imparts to the aggregate characteristics that are not only *different* from, but often *not found in* the components alone; and the "sum of the parts" must be taken to mean, not their numerical addition, but their unorganized aggregation.

What we have led up to is a way of viewing the hoary problem of sociological nominalism *vs.* realism. Herbert Spencer, facing the question of the nature of this thing called "society," offered a criterion for an "entity" which is also basic to the concept of system.

> Until we have decided whether or not to regard a society as an entity; and until we have decided whether, if regarded as an entity, a society is to be classed as absolutely unlike all other entities or as like some others; our conception of the subject matter before us remains vague.
> It may be said that a society is but a collective name for a number

of individuals . . . But . . . it is the permanence of the relations among component parts which constitutes the individuality of a whole as distinguished from the individualities of its parts.[2]

Though acceptable, Spencer's statement requires several comments. First, we cannot take too literally the criterion of *"permanence* of the relations," for although some stability is necessary to constitute a persisting system, we have to allow for the possibility that aspects of a system's structure may change from time to time or even continuously without the dissolution of the system itself. Secondly, the question of whether society is absolutely unlike or like some other entities cannot be taken to imply a black or white distinction, for we can probably always find both similarities and differences between any two systems. Spencer argued cogently that since the constant relations among its parts make society an entity, then between a society and any other entity "the only conceivable resemblance must be one due to parallelism of principle in the arrangement of components."[3] He then went on to draw the analogy between society and organism, with the consequences noted in the previous chapter. The grounds for his jump from society to organism, however, were not very solid, and modern systems theory is now in a position to advance his line of reasoning in a more acceptable direction.

Generally speaking, we might say that the modern concepts of system and organization are now taking over the duty of the overworked and perhaps retiring concept of the "organic." This concept, along with that of mechanical equilibrium, has performed the essential job of bringing the social scientist to full recognition of the fact that the parts of society are not independent, that society is to some degree an interrelated whole. But further advance required that we come to appreciate the important ways in which society differs from the organic or the mechanical.

An important shift of focus occurred with the growing recognition of the fact that, while phenomena of widely differing kinds are wholes constituted by a more or less permanent relations of parts, a crucial distinguishing feature is *the particular nature of those relations.* After Spencer, it became clearer and clearer that whereas the relations of parts of an organism are physiological, involving complex physico-chemical *energy* interchanges, the relations of parts of society are primarily psychic, involving complex communicative processes of *information* exchange, and that this difference makes all the difference.

As Becker and Barnes have noted,[4] the shift from the "organismic"

---

[2] Herbert Spencer, *Principles of Sociology*, 3rd ed. (New York: Appleton-Century-Crofts, 1897) , p. 447.

[3] *Ibid.*, p. 448.

[4] Howard Becker and Harry E. Barnes, *Social Thought from Lore to Science*, 3rd ed., 2 (New York: Dover Publications, Inc., 1961) , 688–92.

view to the later "organic" view gradually led such students as Schäffle, Tarde, and Worms to the psychosocial perspective of "mental interactionism," developed in illuminating detail by Baldwin, Cooley, and G. A. Mead. It was only after their analysis of the nature and dynamics of the psychic interrelations of the components that the underlying nature of the wholeness of society, which even Durkheim comprehended but vaguely, was understood to a point where a truly fundamental resolution of the so-called Hobbesian problem of order and disorder became possible. Their insight was summed up in the notion that the individual is truly social and society truly psychical. Thus it was no longer a question of the individual *vs.* society; it was no longer relevant to ask how group unity or societal order is possible when we only experience discrete individuals. The answer emerging was that society's "individuals" are *not* discrete. What is discrete to the human observer's limited sensory apparatus is simply the physical organism. The behaving individual—the psychological person—is essentially an organization that is developed and maintained only in and through a continually ongoing symbolic interchange with other persons. Some of these interchanges become repetitive and expected in certain situations—and we then refer to a "structure" of relatively stable social interrelationships comprising organizations and institutions. It is these psychosocially developed and supported webs of communicative interrelations of varying degrees of permanence that give society some degree of wholeness, or make it an "entity" in its own right, to be studied by techniques and perspectives different from those used in studying the entity called "the individual."

It is not necessary to trace the often tedious and unrewarding nominalist-realist argument. What is of interest to us is the recent transition of the question from one of either–or to the problem of *degrees* of wholeness or unity, *degrees* of integration, *degrees* of "entitivity" or "systemness." The psychologist Donald T. Campbell, in a recent paper to which our discussion is already indebted, argues that it is methodologically improper to assume axiomatically that the social groups we are studying constitute entities or systems. This is, rather, an hypothesis to be tested. To this end he addresses himself to the general psychological problem of how we perceive entities. He argues that:

> The natural knowledge processes with which we are biologically endowed somehow make objects like stones and teacups much more "real" than social groups or neutrinos, so that we are offended by the use of the same term "real" to cover both instances . . . Two sources of the feeling can be suggested. First: according to certain objective criteria to be discussed below, groups are in most instances less "solid," less multiply confirmed, of less sharp boundaries, less "hard." Second, and most important, we have evolved in an environment in which the identification of certain middle-sized entities was both useful and anatomically possible. As a product of this evolutionary process we have the marvelously effective mechanism of

vision, which, within a limited range of entities, analyzes entitativity so rapidly and vividly that all other inferential processes seem in contrast indirect, ponderous, and undependable. More important, the visual process is so powerful and seemingly direct that we usually do not stop to notice the inferential steps involved in it and the nature of the clues employed. My proposal is that we look to the empirical clues of entity used in the visual perception of middle-sized physical entities and then employ these clues in the analysis of social aggregates as entities.[5]

Campbell then goes on to set forth a number of criteria of "entitativity," derived in part from Wertheimer's principles of perceptual organization, which lead discrete elements to be perceived as parts of a whole. Among these are: proximity, similarity, common fate, and "pregnance" or completed boundary. To the principles of Gestalt psychology are added criteria determined by 1) "reflection or resistance to intrusions of external energy, matter, or diagnostic probes (for example, for groups, the sentry's challenge, indoctrination procedures, or permeability), and 2) internal diffusion, transfer, or communication rates and boundaries. Campbell recognizes, however, that some of these criteria may be relatively superficial or less essential when it comes to social groups or societies. But his analysis in general should go a long way in breaking down the naive epistemology underlying much of social science.[6]

We shall not take up here the question of exact specification and measurement of degrees of systemness, organization, or "entitativity." Current statistical techniques of association, correlation and variance analysis, and the like, can be considered, of course, crude measures of these. However, the problem of specifying and measuring the degree of organization or structure seems solvable in principle by such techniques as those of information theory and graph theory, though the era of their application to social organization has barely begun. We shall have occasion to look more closely at the concept of "structure" and its relation to the concept of "information" in the next chapter.

COMPARATIVE SYSTEMS

We turn now to a more detailed consideration of the nature of the organization characterizing and differentiating types of systems. Our purposes are

---

5 Donald T. Campbell, "Common Fate, Similarity, and Other Indices of the Status of Aggregates of Persons as Social Entities," *Behavioral Science*, 3 (1958), 17.

6 See also Ralph W. Gerard, "Entitation, Animorgs, and Other Systems," in *Views on General Systems Theory*, ed. Mihajlo D. Mesarović (New York: John Wiley & Sons, Inc., 1964), Chap. 8.

1. To probe somewhat deeper into the intricacies of analysis of the nature of organization—beyond the mere interdependence of parts which characterizes any system;

2. To promote a deeper appreciation of the differences between the organization and dynamics of mechanical, organic, and sociocultural systems;

3. To introduce some key conceptions of modern systems analysis.

Since the types of systems we discuss here represent only three points along a series of possible system levels, our generalizations will only approximate any particular empirical system. And especially in the case of the mechanical system, our model is sometimes the man-made Machine enthroned in the eighteenth and nineteenth centuries, the prototype often being the clock, rather than natural physical systems. The Machine in this context will refer to the pre-cybernetic type, without deviation-regulating feedback loops. But to represent a system in equilibrium, our model may be a collection of gases or other substances at different temperatures, pressures, or concentrations, interacting in isolation from other influences long enough to reach an equilibrium state.

System Parts: Simple to Complex

The *nature of the parts* or components of a mechanical system are, typically, relatively simple in their own structure, stable, and not appreciably or permanently affected by being part of the system. By contrast, as we proceed up through the organic and sociocultural levels the components that are interrelated become more complex in their own organization, more and more unstable (more easily subject to change by small forces), and more fundamentally alterable by the workings of the system of which they are a part. These features, of course, are all prerequisite to the very development of higher levels of organization.

Systemic Relations: Energy Links to Information Links

The *nature of the relations* among components varies importantly along many dimensions for different types of system. In mechanical systems of the machine type the interrelations are typically narrowly restricted, with very few degrees of freedom in the behavior of the components. The structure of the system is rigid, and we have an example of what Rapoport calls "organized simplicity."[7] In the typical equilibrium system of particle mechanics we find conditions at the opposite extreme, "chaotic complexity."[8] There are so many degrees of freedom in the relations of com-

---

[7] Anatol Rapoport and William J. Horvath, "Thoughts on Organization Theory," *General Systems*, 4 (1959), 89.
[8] *Ibid.*

ponents that states of the system can only be specified statistically, and there is little or no stable structure.

Organic and sociocultural systems are examples of "organized complexity."[9] As we proceed up the various levels, the relations of parts become more flexible and the "structure" more fluid with process as the set of alternative behaviors open to the components increases. Whereas the relations among components of mechanical systems are a function primarily of spatial and temporal considerations and the transmission of energy from one component to another, the interrelations characterizing higher levels come to depend more and more on the transmission of *information*—a principle fundamental to modern complex system analysis (which we shall discuss in greater detail in the next chapter). Though "information" is dependent on some physical base or energy flow, the energy component is entirely subordinate to the particular form or structure of variations that the physical base or flow may manifest. In the process of transmitting information, the base or carrier energy may change in many ways—as in the production and reproduction of phonograph records—but the structure of variations in the various media remains invariant over the carrier transformations. This structured variation—the marks of writing, the sounds of speech, the molecular arrangement of the genetic code substance DNA, etc.—is still only raw material or energy unless it "corresponds" to, or matches in some important way, the structure of variations of other components to which it may thereby become dynamically related. A person speaking a language foreign to a companion is emitting only noise or vibrating energy as far as the latter is concerned, because there is no mapping of the structured variety of the vocal energy with the repertoire of meaningful sounds structured in the mind of the companion. If the latter did understand the language, however, and the information spoken was, "Look out, a car is coming at you!" —the very small amount of vocal energy would trigger off a large amount of energy in the companion who is acting as the receiving system.[10]

Thus, "information" is not a substance or concrete entity but rather a *relationship* between sets or ensembles of structured variety—to put it very generally. The implications of this shift from energy flow to information flow as a basis for the interrelations of components in higher level systems, are of central importance in distinguishing the nature and behavioral capabilities of the latter, as against lower-level systems. Thus, a minute amount of structured energy or matter from one component

---

9 *Ibid.*

10 A more pertinent example for the social researcher is the central methodological problem of mapping the researcher's scientifically oriented cognitive structure into the research subject's common-sense mapping (interpretive understanding) of the structured variety of the external situation of action. This example is suggested by the extensive discussion of the problem in Aaron V. Cicourel, *Method and Measurement in Sociology* (New York: Free Press of Glencoe, Inc., 1964).

of a higher system is able to "trigger" selectively a large amount of activity or behavior in other components in the system, at the same time overcoming limitations of temporal and spatial proximity as well as availability of energy. The components of systems thus become more autonomous in certain respects while still maintaining intimate and more intricate interrelation with one another. The structure of the system becomes more and more "fluid" as it merges with process—the communication process which is its predominant feature. At the higher ecological, social, and sociocultural system levels, the component individuals need come into physical contact in the manner of mechanical systems only or principally in sexual union and physical combat.

Interactions among components mediated by the selective "triggering" of information flows are possible, of course, only because 1) the system components are themselves organized and relatively unstable, or "sensitive," or in "tension," such that they react easily to a small influence of the correct type (or code) and can release much larger amounts of bound energy than that embodied in the triggering signal; and 2) each of the alternative behaviors open to the system components have somehow become associated with one of the structural arrangements embodying the information code.[11]

Donald M. MacKay is one of the small number of systems theorists who have tackled the question of *semantic* information from the perspective of modern information theory,[12] and his work enlightens our present discussion. He begins by suggesting that so little progress is being made on the semantic side of information theory because of a failure to study the communicative process within a wide enough context to embrace, not only the channel and the nature of the signals flowing through it, but the terminal sender and receiver as goal-directed, self-adaptive systems. In a manner that strongly suggests the pioneering work of G. H. Mead (see Chapter 4), MacKay then conceptualizes an organism as a system with a repertoire of basic acts that, in various combinations, make up its behavior.

> In order that its behavior should be adaptive to its environment, the selective process by which basic acts are concatenated requires to be *organized* according to the current state of the environment in relation to the organism. There are various ways of picturing this need. In its most basic terms, we may regard what is required as equivalent to a vast constantly changing matrix of *conditional probabilities* . . . determining the relative probabilities of various patterns (and patterns of patterns) of behavior in all possible circumstances. More economically, we can think of it as the setting up of a hierarchic structure of organizing 'sub-routines' to determine these

---

11 We shall discuss information theory and its relation to organization theory in more detail in the next chapter.

12 Donald M. MacKay, "The Informational Analysis of Questions and Commands," in *Information Theory: Fourth London Symposium,* ed. Colin Cherry (London: Butterworth & Co., Publisher, Ltd., 1961) .

conditional probabilities, interlocked in such a way as to represent implicitly the structure of the environment (the world of activity) with which the organism must interact. For many purposes we may reduce it to the filling-out of a world-map, ready to be consulted according to current needs and goals.

Whatever our thought-model, it is clear that unless the organism happens to be organized exactly to match the current state of affairs, *work* must be done to bring it up to date: work, not only in a physical, but in a *logical* sense. This 'logical work' consists in the adjusting and moulding of the conditional-probability structure of the organizing system: the formation, strengthening or dissolution of functional linkages between various basic acts or basic sequences of acts. The total configuration of these linkages embodies what we may call the total 'state of readiness' of the organism. Some of them will of course have purely vegetative functions that do not concern us. What does interest us is the total configuration that keeps the organism matched to its field of purposive activity, and so implicitly represents (whether correctly or not) the features of that field. For brevity, let us call this the *orienting* system, and the corresponding total state of readiness the orientation of the organism.[13]

Within this conceptual framework, MacKay then goes on to define information, meaning, and communication, in a generalized way that we believe to be especially congenial to, and an important theoretical underpinning for, the social interactionist perspective in sociology.

Information can now be defined as that which does logical work on the organism's orientation (whether correctly or not, and whether by adding to, replacing or confirming the functional linkages of the orienting system) . Thus we leave open the question whether the information is true or false, fresh, corrective or confirmatory, and so on . . . The *meaning* of an indicative item of information to the organism may now be defined as its selective function on the range of the organism's possible states of orientation, or for short, its *organizing function* for the organism. It will be noted that this too is a relation . . .

A solitary organism keeps its orienting system up to date in response to physical *signs* of the state of the environment, received by its sense organs. This adaptive updating of the state of orientation we call *perception*. We can regard *communication* as an extension of this process whereby some of the organizing work in one organism is attempted by *another organism*. Normally this means that the receiving organism is induced to adapt itself in response to physical signs that are perceived as *symbols*— as calling for orienting (or other) activity over and above that which constitutes their perception as physical events.

The logical starting point for a semantic theory of communication would therefore seem to be the analysis of the organizing functions that are 'extensible' in this way from one organism to another.[14]

---

13 *Ibid.*

14 *Ibid.*, pp. 470–71. We can only suggest here the analytical significance of such an abstract systems formulation for the contemporary developments in linguistic analysis associated with such names as Noam Chomsky, Dell Hymes, Ward Goodenough, Floyd Lounsbury, and so forth. It would seem that the great complexities and subtleties of the sociology of language structure and use require a "metalanguage" with this kind of potential.

Though oriented particularly toward the human, adaptive level, this conceptualization is broad enough to embrace the various evolutionary levels of the process of communication of information, from the genetic, biochemical information processes directing the formation or maintenance of organic structure, through tropistic and instinctual matchings with the environment, to individual learning and cultural accumulation processes. The key underlying notions in all cases, to be discussed in more detail later are: 1) the matching of two or more sets of structured things or events; and 2) the selectivity thus made possible on the action of a subset of one by a subset of another. In a real sense, then, information can "represent" structure or organization, and thus can preserve it, transmit it over space and time, and change it. The evolution of levels leading up to the sociocultural system show greater and greater dependence on indirect, arbitrary, or symbolic communication linkage of components and less and less on substantive and energy linkages, until at the sociocultural level the system is linked almost entirely by conventionalized information exchange, with *process* overshadowing any rigid substantial structure such as is found at organismic levels.

From Closed to Open Systems

The transition from mechanical systems to adaptive, information-processing systems is closely related to the transition from the relatively *closed* to the *open* type of system. That a system is *open* means, not simply that it engages in interchanges with the environment, but that this interchange is *an essential factor* underlying the system's viability, its reproductive ability or continuity, and its ability to change. As L. J. Henderson was at great pains to point out in his book, *The Fitness of the Environment,* the environment is just as basic as the organic system in the intimate system-environment transactions that account for the particular adaptation and evolution of complex systems.[15] In fact, of course, the system and its environment make up sub-parts of a wider system which often must be treated on its own level. Indeed, this is a key principle underlying the field or transactional approach.

The typical response of natural, closed systems to an intrusion of environmental events is a loss of organization, or a change in the direction of dissolution of the system (although, depending on the nature and strength of the intrusion, the system may sometimes move to a new level of equilibrium). On the other hand, the typical response of open systems to environmental intrusions is elaboration or change of their structure to a higher or more complex level. This is due to factors discussed above: the environmental interchange is not, or does not long remain, random or

---

15 Lawrence J. Henderson, *The Fitness of the Environment* (New York: The Macmillan Company, 1915).

unstructured, but rather becomes selective due to the mapping, or coding, or information-processing capabilities (that is, its adaptiveness) inherent in this type of system. This is true whether the system is the lowliest biological organism or a complex sociocultural system. And as we proceed up the system levels we find the systems becoming more and more open in the sense that they become involved in a wider interchange with a greater variety of aspects of the environment, that is, are capable of mapping or responding selectively to a greater range and detail of the endless variety of the environment. At the sociocultural level the details of the natural environment become subordinate to the social, gestural, symbolic environment which is now mapped and responded to selectively in greater detail as the basis of group life.

The important distinction between open and closed systems has often been expressed in terms of "entropy": closed systems tend to increase in entropy—to "run down"; open systems are "negentropic"—tending to decrease in entropy, or to elaborate structure.[16] To apply the concept of equilibrium to open systems is to miss this important distinction.

System Tension

As we noted earlier, the source of action and interaction of the parts of mechanical systems is expressed in the physical concept of energy, whereas in complex, adaptive systems raw energy plays a less and less important role as it gives way to a more complex form of organized and directed motive force that we refer to as the inherent "irritability of protoplasm," tension or stress in animals, and psychic energy or motive power in men. "Tension," in the broad sense, of which "stress" and "strain" are manifestations under conditions of felt blockage, is ever present in one form or another throughout the sociocultural system— sometimes as diffuse, socially unstructured strivings, frustrations, enthusiasms, aggressions, neurotic or normative deviation; sometimes as clustered and minimally structured crowd or quasi-group processes, normatively constructive as well as destructive; and sometimes as socioculturally structured creativity and production, conflict and competition, or upheaval and destruction. As Thelen and colleagues put it:

1. Man is always trying to live beyond his means. Life is a sequence of reactions to stress; Man is continually meeting situations with which he cannot quite cope.

2. In stress situations, energy is mobilized and a state of tension is produced.

---

[16] See Erwin Schrödinger, *What Is Life?* (London: Cambridge University Press, 1945) ; and Leon Brillouin, "Life, Thermodynamics, and Cybernetics," *American Scientist,* 37 (1949) , 554–68.

3. The state of tension tends to be disturbing, and Man seeks to reduce the tension.

4. He has direct impulses to take action . . .[17]

Thus it can be argued that, far from seeing any principle of "inertia" operating in complex adaptive systems, with "tension" occurring only occasionally or residually as a "disturbing" factor, we must see some level of tension as characteristic of and vital to such systems though it may manifest itself as now destructive, now constructive.

Feedback and Purposive Systems

Given the open, negentropic, information-processing nature of complex adaptive systems, we still need a more exact delineation of the mechanisms whereby these systems come to behave in a characteristic manner so different from physical systems—a manner usually expressed by the concept of "purposive." It is generally agreed among systems theorists that a basic principle underlying these purposive, or goal-seeking mechanisms is embodied in the concept of *"feedback."*[18] The notion of feedback is seen as finally removing the ancient mysticism associated with teleology by redefining it in operationally respectable terms. As Anatol Rapoport has argued, the trend is definitely toward explanation in terms of "efficient" causes operating here and now, and not of "final" causes (or future events, system "requirements," or ultimate functions). Today we can treat "purpose" causally in the former sense of forces acting here and now; if we can build a model of purposefulness, we can explain it.[19]

The concept of feedback has now been vulgarized, and is very often equated simply with any reciprocal interaction between variables. As a principle underlying the goal-seeking behavior of complex systems, however, it involves much more than that. As used here, it applies particularly to an open system:

---

[17] Herbert A. Thelen, "Emotionality and Work in Groups," in *The State of the Social Sciences,* ed. Leonard D. White (Chicago: University of Chicago Press, 1956), pp. 184–86. Such a conception also underlies the pragmatism or social behaviorism of William James, John Dewey, and G. H. Mead.

[18] Arturo Rosenblueth, Norbert Wiener, and Julian Bigelow, "Behavior, Purpose, and Teleology," *Philosophy of Science,* 10 (1943), 18–24; Arturo Rosenblueth and Norbert Wiener, "Purposeful and Non-Purposeful Behavior," *Philosophy of Science,* 17 (1950), 318–26; W. Ross Ashby, *An Introduction to Cybernetics* (London: Chapman & Hall, Ltd., 1956); C. W. Churchman and R. L. Ackoff, "Purposive Behavior and Cybernetics," *Social Forces,* 29 (1950), 32–39. For a critical review, see Richard Taylor, "Comments on a Mechanistic Conception of Purposefulness," and "Purposeful and Non-Purposeful Behavior: A Rejoinder," *Philosophy of Science,* 17 (1950), 310–17, 327–32.

[19] Anatol Rapoport, in *Toward a Unified Theory of Human Behavior,* ed. Roy Grinker (New York: Basic Books, Inc., Publishers, 1956), Chap. 17.

1. Whose characteristic features depend on certain internal parameters or criterion variables remaining within certain limits;

2. Whose organization has developed a selective sensitivity, or mapped relationship, to environmental things or events of relevance to these criterion variables;

3. Whose sensory apparatus is able to distinguish any deviations of the systems' internal states and/or overt behavior from goal-states defined in terms of the criterion variables;

4. Such that feedback of this "mismatch" information into the system's behavior-directing centers reduces (in the case of negative feedback) or increases (in the case of positive feedback) the deviation of the system from its goal-states or criterion limits.

Even the simple thermostat meets these basic requirements: it is a system of components open to one aspect of the environment, and contains: 1) A criterion variable representing the particular temperature setting selected, 2) An element sensitive to the temperature of the surrounding air such that 3) The system responds to deviations of the air temperature on either side of the setting by 4) Turning on or off the heating component such that the deviation is reduced (hence, an example of negative feedback) . We shall refer to simpler closed causal loops, lacking in internal variables, as "pseudo-feedback" loops.

Feedback-controlled systems are referred to as goal-*directed,* and not merely goal-*oriented,* since it is the deviations from the goal-state itself that direct the behavior of the system, rather than some predetermined internal mechanism that aims blindly. The significance of feedback control for complex systems can be partially expressed by a comparison of "pre-cybernetic" machines with modern servomechanisms. In the former, the designer had to attempt to anticipate all the contingencies the machine was apt to meet in performing its task, and to build counteracting features into the design; the modern machine, however, uses these very contingencies themselves as information which, fed into the machine, directs it against them. The great gain in capabilities is easily understood in these terms.

Of particular interest to us here in dealing with the evolution of complex adaptive systems is the development of more and more complex criterion-testing subsystems. Our concern is not so much with homeostatic mechanisms, which may or may not be made more comprehensible by translation into feedback terms, but rather with mechanisms that direct system behavior. These latter mechanisms run the gamut from tropistic, instinctual, and reflexive feedback testing mechanisms, to learned, conscious, symbol-actuated subsystems, to the mechanisms of social planning. It may be questionable whether all mechanisms on each of these levels involve true feedback, but it seems clear that higher levels of control, from cortical learning on, can only be adequately understood in terms of complex, often higher order feedback transactions.[20]

A growing number of psychologists, leaning on the feedback concept, have been attacking with force the basic underpinnings of traditional psychology, namely, the reflex arc and the behavioristic Stimulus-Response conceptions, as inadequate to explain the learning and functioning of higher organisms. Thus, Charles W. Slack, among others, has pointed out the cogency of John Dewey's 1896 critique of the concept of the reflex arc in the light of cybernetics and of recent experiments that have finally tested the concept in gross behavior. He shows that, as Dewey argued, we cannot define a "stimulus" as independent of the subject on whom it acts, and in fact we do not know what the stimulus, *or* the response, is without a good understanding of the total feedback transaction, which involves the experimenter's manipulations, the subject's internal goals, and the interactions of the subject with the situation.[21] For, as we have seen in discussing the information theoretic view of "meaning," what is relevant to an organism and its behavior is not simply some external event, or solely some internal state, but rather the transaction whereby certain aspects of the external "stimulus" are "sampled" by the organism and matched against selected internal states. The "meaning" of the stimulus is not something "in" it, or something "in" the organism, but the *relationship* between the two: in MacKay's terms, it lies in the "selective function" or "organizing function"[22] of aspects of the stimulus for the organism and its behavior. Carrying this view to its logical conclusion, we must say that "meaning" is *generated* during the total transaction and ceases to exist when the transaction is terminated. Though such a conception may apply equally to rat and human, there is an important difference. Because of his capacity to manipulate symbols and his self-awareness, the human can "rehearse" a total transaction entirely on the covert level, and hence can continually generate meaning and meaningful behavior apart from the concrete events symbolized. It is perhaps for this reason that we, not quite correctly, think of persons as carrying "meaning" around in their heads.

In the spirit of the newer perspective, theorists such as O. H. Mowrer, Charles E. Osgood, and Donald T. Campbell have launched new attacks on the problem of specifying the mechanisms involved in the various stages of the complex cognitive processes underlying this total transaction, which involves environmental events, perception, learning, thinking, deciding, and motor responses. Whether their approach is neo-behavioristic, neurological, or subjectivistic (or is called "subjective be-

---

20 See, for example, Derek H. Fender, "Control Mechanisms of the Eye," *Scientific American*, 211 (July, 1964).

21 Charles W. Slack, "Feedback Theory and the Reflex Arc Concept," *Psychological Review*, 62 (1955), 263–67.

22 MacKay, "The Informational Analysis," pp. 470–71.

haviorism," as is the recent stimulating work of Miller, Galanter and Pribram) ,[23] the old fear of peering too closely into the psychological "black box" is abating considerably. And what is being found appears more and more clearly to be analyzable as a highly flexible and efficient information processing servosystem.[24] The gap between stimulus and response is opening wide to make room for the multi-stage mediating processes that alone can account for the differences in behavior between interacting billiard balls and interacting adaptive systems. Fundamental contributions to a specification of these mediating processes have been made by the basic research of such cyberneticians as Norbert Wiener, McCulloch and Pitts, Bertalanffy, Ashby, Neumann, and others.[25]

Other areas of psychology benefiting from the concept of feedback include those of stress, conflict, and disorganization, as represented by the work, for example, of Geoffrey Vickers and of Notterman and Trumbull.[26] Sociology, however, has yet to feel the impact of modern systems research. The little that has been written of sociological relevance by non-sociologists has not, for the most part, been presented in terms directly applicable to the field. The little that has been done with a cybernetic orientation by the sociologically minded will be discussed later. However, Karl W. Deutsch has provided a very useful discussion of the advances in social system analysis provided by the concept of feedback as contrasted with the notions of equilibrium or homeostasis. His views also add substantially to our earlier critique of these latter concepts as used in sociology, and will be presented briefly here. For Deutsch, feedback

> . . . is a more sophisticated notion than the simple mechanical notion of equilibrium, and it promises to become a more powerful tool in the social sciences than the traditional equilibrium analysis.[27]

---

[23] See George A. Miller *et al.*, *Plans and the Structure of Behavior* (New York: Holt, Rinehart & Winston, Inc., 1960) .

[24] See also Omar K. Moore and Donald J. Lewis, "Purpose and Learning Theory," *The Psychological Review*, 60 (1953) , 149–56; David Kretch, "Dynamic Systems as Open Neurological Systems," *The Psychological Review*, 57 (1950) , 345–61; and D. O. Hebb, *The Organization of Behavior* (New York: John Wiley & Sons, Inc., 1949) .

[25] For example, Warren S. McCulloch and Walter H. Pitts, "A Logical Calculus of the Ideas Immanent in Nervous Activity," *The Bulletin of Mathematical Biophysics*, 5 (1943) , 115–33; W. Ross Ashby, *Design for a Brain* (London: Chapman & Hall, Ltd., 1952) ; and John von Neumann, "The General and Logical Theory of Automata," in *Cerebral Mechanisms in Behavior: The Hixon Symposium*, ed. Lloyd A. Jeffress (New York: John Wiley and Sons, Inc., 1951) , pp. 1–31.

[26] Geoffrey Vickers, "The Concept of Stress in Relation to the Disorganization of Human Behavior," in *Stress and Psychiatric Disorder*, ed. J. M. Tanner (Oxford: Blackwell Scientific Publications, Ltd., 1959) , pp. 3–10; Joseph M. Notterman and Richard Trumbull, "Note on Self-Regulating Systems and Stress," *Behavioral Science*, 4 (1950) , 324–27.

[27] Karl W. Deutsch, "Mechanism, Teleology, and Mind," *Philosophy and Phenomenological Research*, 12 (1951) , 185–222. Quote is on p. 198.

In Deutsch's view, to say that a social system is in equilibrium implies that: 1) it will return to a particular state when disturbed; 2) the disturbance is coming from outside the system; 3) the greater the disturbance the greater the force with which the system will return to its original state; 4) the speed of the system's reaction to disturbance is somehow less relevant—a sort of friction, or blemish having no place in the "ideal" equilibrium; 5) no catastrophe can happen within the system, but once the equilibrium is disturbed, almost nothing can be said of the future of the society. Such equilibrium theories, Deutsch points out, are based on the very restricted field of "steady state dynamics," and are not well suited to deal with transient events, to predict the consequences of sudden changes. "Altogether, in the world of equilibrium theory, there is no growth, no evolution, no sudden changes, no efficient prediction of the consequences of 'friction' over time."[28]

Feedback theory, on the other hand, does not push "friction" into the background, but can deal specifically with the "lag" and "gain" between impinging events. Large "lag" can be conceptualized as a swing away from common goals so far before feedback correction occurs that only violent reaction, for example, revolution, can bring the social system back to a more viable, goal-oriented state. A full appreciation of the role and nature of feedback permits a relatively objective attack on the problem of assessment and correction of the "lag" in the system.

Deutsch further promotes our conception of feedback by suggesting the kinds of information required to "steer" a society, the kinds or levels of feedback underlying system effectiveness, and the successive levels of purpose thereby made possible. For effective "self-direction" a sociocultural system must continue to receive a *full flow* of three kinds of information: 1) information of the world outside; 2) information from the past, with a wide range of recall and recombination; and 3) information about itself and its own parts. Three kinds of feedback, which make use of these types of information, include: 1) *goal-seeking*—feedback of new external data into the system net whose operational channels remain unchanged; 2) *learning*—feedback of new external data for the *changing of these operating channels themselves,* that is, a change in the structure of the system; and 3) *consciousness,* or "self-awareness"—feedback of new *internal* data via secondary messages, messages about changes in the state of parts of the system itself. These secondary messages serve as symbols or internal labels for changes of state within the net. Finally, four successively higher orders of purposes can be recognized: 1) seeking of immediate satisfaction; 2) self-preservation, which may require overruling the first; 3) preservation of the group; and 4) preservation of a process of

---

28 *Ibid.*

goal-seeking beyond any one group. These orders of purpose, of course, require successively higher–order feedback nets.[29]

These suggestions of course, need extensive development but may serve here to make the point that, whereas the concept of "equilibrium" is restricted to descriptions of steady states, the cybernetic view is based on full dynamics, including change of state as an inherent and necessary aspect of complex system operation. In particular, it can be seen that cybernetics offers to restore the problem of purpose to a fuller share of attention, and even to help us make a much needed distinction between the attainment of actual external goals, and the reduction of goal-drive merely by internal readjustment that provides an ersatz satisfaction (or short-circuit), such as scapegoating, drug addiction, or other so-called "mechanisms of control." In Deutsch's view, more complex, goal-changing, feedback conceptions take this distinction into account.

Donald T. Campbell has suggested a hierarchy of "knowledge processes" found at the different evolutionary levels of complex adaptive systems.[30] Their brief consideration may further serve to broaden our perspective on adaptive systems and strengthen our sense of the continuity of such systems as they lead up to the sociocultural level, at the same time sensitizing us to the important differences in their organization and dynamics.

The most basic lower-level processes that permit adaptive systems to "map" into themselves some of the environmental variety, i.e., gain practical knowledge of the world, are: 1) *genetic mutation and selective survival*—of those systems most effectively matching the environment, and 2) *bisexuality and heterozygosity*—which, in combination with the first, make possible more rapid adjustments to environmental changes.

The levels above these, Campbell suggests, are more readily recognizable as "knowledge processes": 3) *blind trial and error problem solving*, such as that of paramecia and Stentor or W. Ross Ashby's "homeostat"; 4) *learning*—the retention of adaptive response patterns for subsequent use, thus cutting short the trial and error process for familiar problem situations; 5) *perception*—visual exploration of potential behavior alternatives, substituting for overt exploration; 6) *observational learning*—characteristic of social animals, who learn from observing the outcomes of another exploring animal, thus profiting from the potentially fatal experiences of another; 7) *imitation*—the acquisition of a model for behavior by perception of another's behavior; 8) *linguistic instruction*—about the nature of the world and of correct responses to it; 9) *thought*—whereby potential behavior is symbolically rehearsed against a learned model of the environment; and 10) *social decision making*—in

---

29 *Ibid.*, 201.

30 Donald T. Campbell, "Methodological Suggestions from a Comparative Psychology of Knowledge Processes," *Inquiry,* 2 (1959), 152–82.

which the observations of many persons are pooled into a single, more adequate model of the environment.

The essential similarity between the inductive processes of natural selection in evolution and those of trial-and-error learning (noted, incidentally, as early as 1900 by J. M. Baldwin) is seen by Campbell as "perhaps the key insight in this whole reorganization of perspective on knowledge processes."[31] The further implications of such a perspective are discussed later.

Morphostasis and Morphogenesis

The various features of complex adaptive systems sketched so far —openness, information-linkage of the parts and the environment, feedback loops, goal-direction, and so forth—provide the basic conceptual elements that underlie the general features characteristic of systems referred to as "self-regulating," "self-directing," and "self-organizing." These concepts all point to the fact that the behavior of complex, open systems is not a simple and direct function of impinging external forces, as is the case with colliding billiard balls or gravitational systems. Rather, as open systems become more complex there develop within them more and more complex mediating processes that intervene between external forces and behavior. At higher levels these mediating processes become more and more independent or autonomous, and more determinative of behavior. They come to perform the operations of: 1) temporarily adjusting the system to external contingencies: 2) directing the system toward more congenial environments; and 3) permanently reorganizing aspects of the system itself to deal perhaps more effectively with the environment. The "self" in "self-regulation," "self-direction," and "self-organizing" points, of course, to these mediating processes, though we tend to use the term "self" in its full sense only on the human level. However, the perspective we are taking argues that an understanding of the mediating processes on lower system levels should help us understand their nature and workings on the higher level: sharp discontinuities are not to be found.

Some of the connotations of these concepts of "self-regulation" and the like are misleading, whether applied to modern machines, men, or groups, since the tendency is to overemphasize the independence of the internal system at the expense of situational or environmental variables. For this reason it might be profitable to utilize more neutral terms for the two basic processes of interest to us here, namely, *morphostasis* and *morphogenesis*. The former refers to those processes in complex system-environment exchanges that tend to preserve or maintain a system's given form, organization, or state. Morphogenesis will refer to those processes which tend to elaborate or change a system's given form, structure, or state. Homeostatic processes in organisms, and ritual in sociocultural

---

[31] *Ibid.,* 156 ff.

systems are examples of "morphostasis"; biological evolution, learning, and societal development are examples of "morphogenesis."

We have already discussed morphostatic processes in dealing with equilibrium, homeostasis, and negative feedback. These conserving, deviation-counterbalancing processes have come to be emphasized in the literature at the expense of structure-elaborating, deviation-promoting processes that are central to an understanding of higher level systems such as the sociocultural. Just as the concept of negative feedback has provided insight into the mechanisms underlying homeostatic processes, the concept of positive feedback provides insight into the mechanisms underlying structure-building, or morphogenesis. Magoroh Maruyama has recently argued very effectively the case for greater concern with the latter.

> By focusing on the deviation-counteracting aspect of the mutual causal relationships . . . the cyberneticians paid less attention to the systems in which the mutual causal effects are deviation-amplifying. Such systems are ubiquitous: accumulation of capital in industry, evolution of living organisms, the rise of cultures of various types, interpersonal processes which produce mental illness, international conflicts, and the processes that are loosely termed as 'vicious circles' and 'compound interests': in short, all processes of mutual causal relationships that amplify an insignificant or accidental initial kick, build up deviation and diverge from the initial condition.[32]

Maruyama gives as one example the development of a city in an agricultural plain. A farmer starts a farm at some chance spot on the homogeneous plain. Other farmers are attracted and follow suit. Someone opens a tool shop, someone else a food stand, and gradually a village grows. The village facilitates the marketing of crops and attracts more farms. The increased activity and population necessitates the development of industry, and the village becomes a city.[33]

One of the many evolutionary examples is the adaptation of varieties of a species to colder and colder climates. In the beginning some mutants are enabled to live at a somewhat colder temperature than normal for the species. They move to a colder climate, where further mutations occur. Some of these are unfit for the colder climate and die off, but other mutants can stand even colder surroundings than their parents and move to a still colder climate. This deviation-amplifying process continues until some limit is reached.

Many sociocultural examples in the sociocultural realm could also be given. Besides the above processes of growth or adaptive structural change, there are the often nonadaptive processes such as those embodied in Myrdal's "vicious circle" theory of racial discrimination, whereby initial prejudice generates those personal and social characteristics of

---

[32] Magoroh Maruyama, "The Second Cybernetics: Deviation-Amplifying Mutual Causal Processes," *American Scientist,* 51 (1963), 164–79. Quote is on p. 164.

[33] *Ibid.,* 165–66.

Negroes that are then seen to justify further discrimination which, in turn, aggravates further the Negroes' condition.[34] Another example is the process by which the malfunctioning of bureaucratic organizations may occur. March and Simon have traced out, in *Organizations*, a model of Robert Merton's theory of bureaucracy which, in simplified form, starts with the demand for control made on the organization by upper management. This demand takes the form of an emphasis on the reliability of behavior of lower level administrators, operationalized in terms of accountability and predictability of behavior. This, in turn, leads to a rigid adherence to rules and mutual defense of members' positions. But this creates difficulties in administrator-client relations, which lead to a felt need for defensibility of individual action. The net effect of client pressure on lower and higher officials is to tighten further the top official emphasis on reliability, thus closing the positive feedback loop leading back to a more rigid adherence to rules and a more vigorous defense of status. In sum, deviation from the goal of satisfying clients tends to reinforce the very factors creating the deviation.[35]

As Maruyama points out, there are a number of methodological implications to be drawn from the consideration of these morphogenetic processes. The classical principle of causality held that similar conditions produce similar effects, and consequently dissimilar results are due to dissimilar conditions.[36] Bertalanffy, in analyzing the self-regulating, or morphostatic, features of open biological systems, loosened this classical conception by introducing the concept of "equifinality."[37] This holds that, in ontogenesis for example, a final normal adult state may be reached by any number of devious developmental routes. Morphogenetic processes, however, go even further and suggest an opposite principle that might be called "multifinality":[38] similar initial conditions may lead to dissimilar end-states. Thus, two cultures developing in very similar ecological environments may end up with very different sociocultural systems. In the example of city growth, Maruyama suggests that if a historian should try to find the "cause" of the city's growth in that particular spot he will be unable to do so either in terms of the initial homogeneity of the plain or the decision of the first farmer.

> The secret of the growth of the city is in the process of deviation-amplifying mutual positive feedback networks rather than in the initial condition

---

34 Gunnar Myrdal, *An American Dilemma* (New York: Harper & Row, Publishers, 1944), pp. 75–78.

35 James G. March and Herbert A. Simon, *Organizations* (New York: John Wiley & Sons, Inc., 1958), pp. 37–41.

36 Myrdal, *An American Dilemma.*

37 Ludwig von Bertalanffy, *Problems of Life* (New York: Harper & Row, Publishers, Torchbook ed., 1960), pp. 142 ff.

38 This concept is perhaps implied in the biological notion of "equipotential."

or in the initial kick. This process, rather than the initial condition, has generated the complexly structured city. It is in this sense that the deviation-amplifying mutual causal process is called "morphogenesis."[39]

Such considerations provide a more precise and basic methodological rationale for the transactional approach to the study of complex adaptive systems. For example, the classical approach to the study of delinquent or criminal behavior was to look either at personality or at the environing situation. We now, however, can appreciate more fully the possibility that some deviation-amplifying transaction operating between the personality system and the situation has *generated* the deviant outcome. The initial conditions in either the personality or the situation may or may not be relevant or causally dominant.[40]

A partial generalization of the morphogenic process is suggested in Maruyama's discussion of the biologist's puzzlement over the fact that the amount of information stored in the genes is much too small to specify the detailed structure of the adult individual. The puzzle can be resolved if we find that it is not necessary for the genes to carry all the detailed information, but rather that it suffices for them to carry *a set of rules to generate the information.* This can be conceptualized, for example, in terms of rules specifying the general direction and amount of cellular growth in terms of the immediate spatial and cellular environment of the growing tissues; the details are then generated by the *interactions* of the cells, tissues and other limiting boundaries and gradients. Thus, though the total process is deterministic, it is not possible or necessary to specify in the initial condition whether, for example, a particular part of an embryo is to become eye-tissue or skin tissue. In Maruyama's words:

> The amount of information to describe the resulting pattern is much more than the amount of information to describe the generating rules and the positions of the initial tissues. The pattern is generated by the rules and by the *interaction* between the tissues. In this sense, the information to describe the adult individual was not contained in the initial tissues at the beginning but was generated by their interactions.[41]

This principle applies equally to the sociocultural system. There is not enough information, knowledge, or decision-making power when simply summed over all the relevant individuals or groups to account for the full-blown complex organization, the metropolitan agglomeration, the body of scientific theory, or the developed religious dogma. The sociocultural pattern is generated by the rules (norms, laws, and values— themselves generated in a similar manner) *and by the interactions* among

---

39 M. Maruyama, "The Second Cybernetics," 166.

40 We shall discuss the generation of social deviance as a morphogenic process in more detail in the last chapter.

41 *Ibid.,* 174.

normatively and purposively oriented individuals and subgroups in an ecological setting. Full understanding and explanation can appeal, alone, neither to early history nor common human characteristics (initial conditions), nor to final structure and functions. Attention must finally be paid to the interactions generated by the rules, seen as only limiting frameworks of action; to the new information, meanings, and revised rules generated by the interactions; and to the more or less temporary social products that represent the current state or structure of the ongoing process. Only one-sided, highly selective observation and conceptualization could lead us to see a principle of "social inertia" or a predominance of morphostatic processes operating in the sociocultural realm. In Chapter 5, we shall examine some new directions in current sociological thinking that build their analysis and theories around morphogenic rather than morphostatic processes.

AN ABSTRACT MODEL OF MORPHOGENESIS

The conceptualizations of morphogenic processes suggested by Campbell, Maruyama, and others,[42] have paved the way for the emergence of a highly generalized paradigm of morphogenesis or evolution applicable, in principle, to all complex system levels. Such a paradigm warrants careful consideration as a framework providing for a deeper penetration not only into the mechanisms underlying the evolution of organization, but into the meaning of evolution itself as a scientifically definable process. Just as modern systems theory promises to rescue "purpose" from metaphysical disrepute, so may it help to restore the reviving concept of sociocultural evolution to the center of respectable scientific concern.

Since the paradigm we shall outline below is so highly generalized, we shall begin with a brief definition of the basic concepts to be used.

The *environment,* however else it may be characterized, can be seen at bottom as *a set or ensemble of more or less distinguishable elements,* states, or events, whether these discriminations are made in terms of spatial or temporal relations, or properties. Such distinguishable differences in an ensemble may be most generally referred to as *"variety."*

The relatively stable "causal," spatial and/or temporal relations between these distinguishable elements or events may be generally referred to as *"constraint"*: most events are determinately as-

---

42 See J. W. S. Pringle, "On the Parallel Between Learning and Evolution," *Behavior*, 3 (1951), 174–215.

sociated with other events. If the elements are so loosely related that there is an equal probability of any element or state being associated with any other, we speak of "chaos" or complete randomness, and hence, lack of constraint. But our more typical natural environment is characterized by a relatively high degree of constraint, without which the development and elaboration of adaptive systems (as well as "science") would not have been possible.

When the internal organization of an adaptive system acquires features that permit it to discriminate, act upon, and respond to aspects of the environmental variety and its constraints, we say that the system has mapped part of the environmental variety and constraints into its organization. Thus, a subset of the ensemble of constrained variety in the environment, transmitted *via* various channels, results in a selective activation of the structure of the receiving system, which has become isomorphic in certain respects to the original variety. The system thus becomes *selectively related* to its environment both on its sensory and motor sides. It should be added that two or more adaptive systems, as well as an adaptive system and its natural environment, may be said to be interrelated by more or less constrained variety in the same way (for example, as in "socialization").

In these terms, then, the paradigm underlying the evolution of more and more complex adaptive systems begins with the fact of a potentially changing environment characterized by constrained variety and an adaptive system or organization whose persistence and elaboration to higher levels depends upon a successful mapping of some of the environmental variety and constraints into its own organization on at least a semipermanent basis. This means that our adaptive system—whether biological, psychological, or sociocultural—must manifest 1) some degree of "plasticity" and "sensitivity" or *tension* vis-a-vis its environment such that it carries on a constant interchange with environmental events, acting on and reacting to them; 2) some source of mechanism providing for *variety*, to act as a potential pool of adaptive variability to meet the problem of mapping new or more detailed variety and constraints in a changeable environment; 3) a set of *selective* criteria or mechanisms against which the "variety pool" may be sifted into those variations in the organization or system that more closely map the environment and those that do not; and 4) an arrangement for *preserving and/or propagating* these "successful" mappings.[43]

It should be noted, as suggested above, that this is a *relational* per-

---

[43] Campbell, "Methodological Suggestions."

spective, corresponding closely with the current conception of "information," viewed as the process of selection, from an ensemble of variety, of a subset which, to have "meaning," must match another subset taken from a similar ensemble. Communication is the process by which this constrained variety is transmitted in one form or another between such ensembles, involving coding and decoding such that the original variety and its constraints remain relatively invariant at the receiving end. If the source of the communication is the causally constrained variety of the natural environment, and the destination is the biological adaptive system, we refer to the Darwinian process of natural selection whereby the information encoded in the chromosomal material (for example the DNA) reflects or is a mapping of the environmental variety, and makes possible a continuous and more or less successful adaptation of the organism to the environment. If the adaptive system in question is a (relatively high level) psychological or cortical system, we refer to "learning," whereby the significant environmental variety is transmitted via sensory and perceptual channels and decodings to the cortical centers where, on the basis of selective criteria (for example, "reward" and "punishment") related to physiological and/or other "needs" or "drives," relevant parts of it are encoded and preserved as "experience" for varying periods of time, and may promote adaptation. Or, on the level of the symbol-based sociocultural system, where the more or less patterned actions of individuals and groups are as crucial a part of the environment of other individuals and groups as the non-social environment, the behavioral variety and its more or less normatively defined constraints is culturally encoded, transmitted, and decoded at the receiving end by way of the various familiar channels and intragroup processes, with varying degrees of fidelity. In time, again by a selective process—now much more complex, tentative, and less easily specified—we note the selective elaboration and more or less temporary preservation of some of this complex social and physical variety in the form of "culture," "social organization," and "personality structure."

On the basis of such a continuum of evolving, elaborating, levels of adaptive systems (we have only pointed to three points along this continuum), we could add to and refine our discussion of the differential characteristics of the various levels of systems. Thus, we note that as the adaptive systems develop from the lower biological levels through the higher psychological and sociocultural levels we can distinguish: 1) The varying time span required for exemplars of the adaptive system to map or encode within themselves changes in the variety and constraints of the environment. A phylogenetic time scale is required for genetic and tropistic or instinctual neural systems; an ontogenetic time scale for higher psychological or cortical systems; and in the sociocultural case, the time span may be very short—days—or very long, but complicated by the fact that the relevant environment includes both intra- and inter-societal variety and constraints as well as the variety of the natural environment (with the latter becoming progressively less determinant). 2) The greatly varying degrees of fidelity of mapping of the environment into the adaptive system, from the lower unicellular organisms with a very simple repertoire of actions on and reactions to the environment, through the complex of instinctual and learned behaviors, to the ever-proliferating more refined and veridical accumulations of a sociocultural system. 3) The progressively greater separation of the more refined stored information from purely biological processes, as genetic information is gradually augmented by cortically imprinted information and finally by entirely extrasomatic sociocultural depositories. Thus our understanding of the significance of "culture" is deepened by recognizing both its developmental continuity with psychological and biological "information" processes and its qualitative differences.

One point that requires much more discussion may be briefly mentioned here. This is the apparent discontinuity we may see in the transition from the nonhuman adaptive system to human society. (The insect society and the rudimentary higher animal society make for much less than a clean break.) As we progress from lower to higher biological adaptive systems we note, as a general rule, the gradually increasing role of other biological units of the same as well as different species as part of the significant environment. The variety and constraints represented by the behavior of these units must be mapped, as well as that of the physical environment. With the transition from the higher primate social organization to the full-blown human, symbolically mediated, sociocultural system, the mapping of the subtle behaviors, gestures, and intentions of the individuals making up the effective social organization become increasingly central, and eventually equals or even overshadows, the mapping of the physical environment.[44] The new, demanding requirements of coordination, anticipation, expectation, and the like within an increasingly complex *social* environment of interacting and interdependent others—where genetic mappings were absent or inadequate—prompted the fairly rapid elaboration of relatively new features in the social system. These included, of course: 1) the ever-greater conventionalizing of gestures into true symbol; 2) the development of a "self," self-awareness, or self-consciousness out of the symbolically mediated, continuous mirroring and mapping of each person's own behaviors and gestures in those of ever-present others (a process well described by John Dewey, G. H. Mead, Cooley, and others); and 3) the resulting ability to deal in the present with the predicted future as well as the past and hence to manifest conscious goal seeking, evaluating, self-other relating, norm-referring behavior. In

---

44 As we shall see later, the social psychology of G. H. Mead and others was concerned with tracing out the social interactional process whereby this "mapping" of gestures and intentions of others takes place.

cybernetic terminology, this higher level sociocultural system became possible through the development of higher order feedbacks such that the component subsystems became able to map, store, and selectively or normatively act toward not only the external variety and constraints of the social and physical environment, but also their own internal states. To speak of self-consciousness, internalization, expectations, choice, certainty and uncertainty, and the like is to elaborate on this basic point. This transition, then, gave rise to the new adaptive level we refer to as sociocultural, which thus warrants scientific study in terms as distinct from a purely biological system as the analytical terms of the latter are from physical systems.

In the next two chapters we turn to a more detailed attempt to conceptualize in modern terms this process whereby complex sociocultural structures are built up and elaborated in terms of the lower level processes of symbolic action and interaction.

THE PROBLEM OF CAUSALITY IN SOCIAL THEORY

During most of the present century, sociology has devoted its energies to the establishment of basic propositions showing that one part or aspect of society is related to another part or aspect: religion is related to voting, solidarity is related to suicide, education is related to class, delinquency is related to group association, and so forth. A basic tool has been some simple statistical measure of association showing the relation between two, sometimes three variables. Moreover, the traditional techniques of measurement are based on a two-valued logic and tend to focus on attributes of elements of a system; as a result, they are not adapted to the full dynamics of system process, especially when feedback loops change initial parameters.[45]

Now that the groundwork has been laid, however, we have begun to ask much more complete questions and to seek to understand the more detailed mechanisms underlying the development, maintenance, and change of the established societal interrelationships. On the theoretical level, the notion of society as a *system* has been around for some time, but it has been unable—as we have tried to show—to carry us very far toward an adequate analysis of the more complex questions. It has rightly insisted that at least many parts of a social system are related to many other parts, but the theory—especially as interpreted by the functionalists —has failed to offer any program of research that does more than admonish us to go out there and trace the interrelations of all the parts or

---

[45] For a discussion of aspects of this problem see Cicourel, *Method and Measurement in Sociology.*

even more narrowly, to trace out the "consequences" of any part for any other part. And research methodology has hardly begun to think beyond relatively simple, traditional statistical techniques to the methods needed to get at a system of complexly interacting parts.

Our comparative sketch of the nature of the sociocultural system earlier in this chapter alerts us to the fact that a simple model of causation and correlation and its methodology is woefully inadequate in the face of complex adaptive systems. We now wish to conclude this chapter with a brief discussion of the ways in which relationships between variables have been conceptualized and the major theoretical orientations that have thus been built.

We are not primarily concerned here with the various types of (mathematical) functions relating two variables, but it is pertinent to call attention to them. Whereas our traditional methodological tools generally focus on or assume a simple linear relation, newer research is making clear the importance of other types of functions for an understanding of the dynamics of the development, maintenance, or change of social systems. One type of relation more and more frequently encountered is the special kind of nonlinear relation referred to as a *step function,* whereby a variable has no appreciable effect on others until its value has increased or decreased by some minimal increment. Consequently, research may fail to disclose any significant relationship even though a large potential interaction is in fact building up. A related kind of interrelation of variables involves the presence of *buffer mechanisms,* which delay the effects of a variable until some later point in a process. These two functions pose similar problems for the researcher. An especially important problem today involves the *primacy* of certain systemic variables over others, what might be called the problem of "methodological pluralism." We have overreacted against single-factor theories by assuming an equally radical "equality of effectiveness" of a plurality of factors. Thus, as Andrew Hacker has remarked, "Parsons' scheme has too many ideas which interact on a parity of causal significance."[46] But modern systems theorists have long recognized that just because a number of variables are interrelated in a systemic manner does not necessarily mean that each is of equal weight in producing characteristic states of the system: any systemic variable may run the gamut from insignificance to overwhelming primacy. Sociological discussions in this area will remain sophomoric until the principles of modern systems research are more widely ingested.

Important as these considerations are—in fact, just because they are so important—we must leave it to the expert methodologist to provide us with a much needed treatise on the research implications of modern (especially non-equilibrial) social systems analysis. We shall discuss below,

---

[46] Andrew Hacker, "Sociology and Ideology," in *The Social Theories of Talcott Parsons,* ed. Max Black (Englewood Cliffs, N.J.: Prentice-Hall, Inc., 1961) , p. 297.

rather, the more general ways in which social scientists have treated relations between variables or system parts, and the theoretical orientations built on them.

Traditional causal relations. The most common method of analyzing a given phenomenon X has been to relate it to *prior* phenomena, or "causes," *a, b, c* . . . , in a one-way causal linkage. If the prior events are proximal to the event being explained, we speak of "efficient causes"; if more distant, we speak of "historical causes."

Teleology or final cause. Here we attempt to analyze an event X in terms of its relation to *future* events (or purposes, functions, or consequences).

Reciprocal or mutual relations. Especially with the advent of the mechanical equilibrium model, the recognition of the importance of mutually interrelated events, variables, or system elements challenged the more simplified appeals to causality. For a period, an overreaction seems in fact to have occurred, associated with the claim that mutual interactionism completely replaces the older causality. However, moderation now seems to have set in, based on the recognition that (as is usually the case with new scientific theories) new perspectives usually refine and broaden older ones rather than replace them outright, such that the old come to be seen as special cases restricted in applicability. It can perhaps be argued that Robert M. MacIver's book, *Social Causation,* represents an attempt in social science to temper the claims of mutual interactionism to have done away with "causality" entirely. In any case, recognition of reciprocal relations among parts of a larger complex was an important early step in the direction of a thoroughgoing systems analysis. Or, to turn it around, early treatments of society or the group in terms of physical or mechanical system models led to the widespread recognition that the parts of society are not typically independent, but are mutually interrelated and constitute a whole, at least to some degree. This historical point needs emphasis, as suggested earlier, in view of the current attempt, often ingenuous, of many functionalists to claim credit for this insight or, indeed, to *define* functional analysis in terms of its emphasis on mutual relations of parts rather than, more correctly, its emphasis on final causes or consequences for the larger whole.[47]

Circular causal chains (pseudo-feedback). The concept of mutual relations of parts could not long remain a simple and undifferentiated one, since there are many subtypes to be recognized and analyzed. We have

---

[47] An earlier argument attempting to equate functionalism simply with good sociological analysis, or even with scientific analysis in general, was quite unsuccessful, largely because it failed to appreciate this point. See Kingsley Davis, "The Myth of Functional Analysis as a Special Method in Sociology and Anthropology," *American Sociological Review,* 24 (1959), 757–72.

pointed to the growing centrality of the concept of organization for modern science; underlying this concept is the understanding and analysis of the complex ways the parts of a whole are interrelated to produce the structure and dynamics of what we now call systems. Of particular importance are those kinds of mutual relations that make up what have been called circular causal chains: the effect of an event or variable returns indirectly to influence the orginal event itself by way of one or more intermediate events or variables. This kind of interrelationship of parts came to be recognized as a kind of building block of higher-level, adaptive, self-regulating systems, and a prototype of the kind of organization manifesting "purpose" or goal-seeking.

However, it becomes important to recognize that the simple circular causal chain is not to be identified with the true goal-directed feedback loop underlying the more advanced self-directing systems. Some examples of the circular causal chain are the re-equilibrating process in disturbed mechanical equilibrium systems, the chain reaction in nuclear fission, the ecological interrelations between population size and food supply, the "vicious circle" of racial discrimination, etc. These are not true "feedback" cycles in the cybernetic sense, inasmuch as there are no internal mechanisms which measure or compare the feedback input against a goal and pass the mismatch information on to a *control center* which activates appropriate system counter behavior. There is no "control" here, only a blind reaction of the original variable to the forces it has helped to create and which are now reacting back on it. It is this lack of a clear distinction between the pseudo-feedback of simpler, circular causal chains and true feedback control loops that helped create the controversy between the cyberneticians Rosenblueth, Wiener, and Bigelow, on the one hand, and the philosopher Richard Taylor on the other, concerning the definition of purposeful behavior and the question of whether cybernetic machines can be said to be purposeful in those terms.[48] The cyberneticians attempted to define purposeful behavior as that directed toward a goal, the goal being any feature of the environment with which the behaving object strives to attain a certain definite correlation. As Taylor correctly points out, from the observer's point of view, such a definition would appear to apply even to a rolling stone.[49] In a similar manner, we can argue that processes based on circular causal chains (for example, those underlying the evolution of lower living forms) , are only superficially similar to purposeful behavior. The correlations found between the behaving object and its environment are due to blind processes involving circular causal chains, untested by criteria other than sheer survival and reproducibility. It is only at the higher levels of evolution

---

[48] Rosenblueth, Wiener, and Bigelow, "Behavior, Purpose, and Teleology"; and Taylor, "Comments."

[49] Taylor, "Comments," pp. 311 ff.

or of cybernetic machinery that we find internal test parameters operating in accordance with signals or symbols standing for certain goal-
states, which alone make possible goal-directed, "purposeful" behavior. It
is the matching of external events or objects against these internal test
criteria that appears basic here, and fundamental to any satisfactory
answer to Taylor's well-taken argument. He insists that at least one significant and irreducible difference between human purposive behavior
and servomechanism behavior is the presumed fact that the latter can
never positively seek objects which are non-existent, such as Holy Grails.[50]
But once we recognize that purpose *must* involve some internal representation of a goal-state, and that it may lie in the future or even be non-
existent, Taylor's objection loses force and we must allow that servo-
mechanisms, as well as men, can seek to match the environment against
an internal representation for which there is no external counterpart.
The question of how that representation got into the system, whether it
was designed into the servomechanism or learned as a belief or motive
by the man, is a different question, one that should not prejudice the
problem of the purposiveness of the behavior *per se*. And, to reiterate our
main point, purposeful behavior involves true feedback loops, not just
simple, circular causal chains. Higher level systems had to wait for the
development of symbolically mediated internal representations and testing subsystems before true purposive behavior became possible.

True self-regulating *feedback loops*, then, constitute a higher level
of interrelations of parts, and underlie the complex organization and
dynamics of higher level adaptive systems. Here we have gone beyond
the kinds of interrelationships pertinent to mere aggregates of elements
or to closed equilibrial systems, and are now dealing with open systems
involving some degree of learning, purpose or goal-seeking, elaboration
of organization, or evolution in general.

FIGURE 3-1 *Relations Between Variables*

Each of these increasingly complex kinds of interrelationships of
elements shown in Figure 3-1 can be seen—without too much distortion
—as underlying one of the basic methodological orientations in sociology:
traditional causal analysis, functionalism, equilibrial system analysis,
and cybernetic systems analysis. We shall discuss each of these briefly.

---

50 Taylor, "Purposeful and Non-Purposeful Behavior," pp. 329–30.

Traditional causal analysis. One who views events as related primarily in terms of cause and effect sequences will use a more or less traditional kind of causal analysis as the basis of a theory or explanation of the phenomenon he is studying. If the causal chain goes relatively far back into the past, we refer to historical analysis; if the causal events are proximate to the phenomenon being explained we may speak of "efficient causes." Though traditional causal theory may be inefficient or ineffective, as we are arguing, when one is dealing with complex systems, and despite the fact that the systemic nature of society is widely accepted, causal analysis remains a hardy perennial of social science. For comparative perspective, two recent examples of this may be mentioned. Angus Campbell *et al.* have attempted to develop a systematic framework that provides a broad explanation of political voting behavior in the United States. Recognizing the many difficulties in the traditional concept of causality, they decided that

> Nonetheless, limiting the concept to refer to uniformities of sequence observed in time past, which may be expected in the absence of exogenous factors to hold in the future, remains useful to our inquiry.[51]

In order to make use of the information provided by different levels of explanation (for example, social and psychological) without confusion, and taking account of the particular problem they have chosen (that is, "to account for a single behavior at a fixed point in time . . . that stems from a multitude of prior factors"), they attempt to structure their theory in terms of a "funnel of causality."

> Events are conceived to follow each other in a converging sequence of causal chains, moving from the mouth to the stem of the funnel. The funnel shape is a logical product of the explanatory task chosen. Most of the complex events in the funnel occur as a result of multiple prior causes. Each such event is, in its turn, responsible for multiple effects as well, but our focus of interest narrows as we approach the dependent behavior . . . We progressively eliminate those effects that do not continue to have relevance for the political act. Since we are forced to take all partial causes as relevant at any juncture, relevant effects are therefore many fewer in number than relevant causes. The result is a convergence effect.[52]

By taking a cross section of the funnel at any point, it is imagined "that we can measure all events and states as they stand at the moment they flow through this plane," and thus that the congeries of variables would be more or less of the same "conceptual order" and should predict the dependent behavior perfectly, "provided that we know the necessary com-

---

[51] Angus Campbell *et al.*, *The American Voter* (New York: John Wiley & Sons, Inc., 1960), p. 21.

[52] *Ibid.*, p. 24.

bining laws"—that is, that we "understand the interaction of our system of factors at all cross sections that intervene."[53]

This theoretical strategy raises some important problems, especially the question of how far back one should attempt to explore the infinite regress of antecedent factors. The authors see two major approaches to this problem. The first is the "social" approach, which they view as more "historical" or genetic in its attempt to predict from points more remote in the funnel of causation. This approach seems to be identified in the authors' minds with the older Newtonian treatment of causality, which presumed action at a distance and connected widely separated events. The second, which they adopt, is the "attitudinal" approach, identified with Kurt Lewin's field theory, which views the field of events at any moment as a product of the field in the immediate neighborhood at a time just past. This is interpreted as "an appeal for initial measurement at cross sections of the funnel that lie very close to the dependent event, with 'historical' explanation proceeding backward in short steps."[54] Despite their recognition of the shortcomings of this approach, Campbell *et al.* feel that it has relatively high explanatory power for several reasons.

> First, the exogenous factors that can intervene are reduced to a minimum. Second, the use of attitudes restricts measurement to relevant conditions that are already personal, so that we do not have to take into account the conditions of communication that govern the transition from external events to personal events. Finally, and perhaps most important, events are observed after they have received their political translations, so that the conditions of uncertainty that surround prediction of the voter's interpretation of events are excluded from the system.[55]

Although there are many critical points to be made about this theoretical orientation, we shall only stop long enough here to suggest that, if society is truly a complex, adaptive system of psychological and social events that are interrelated in a web of communications and involve continual decision-making under conditions of uncertainty, then the strategy of the authors exemplified especially in the passage quoted immediately above may have the effect of stripping out of the way the very kinds of systemic considerations that alone could lead to deeper understanding and explanation.

A second example of current causal analysis, with a somewhat different twist, is the *Theory of Collective Behavior* of Neil J. Smelser. His strategy involves the use of what he calls the "value-added process" as a means of organizing the major causes—or "determinants," as he prefers to call them—of collective behavior into an explanatory model.

---

[53] *Ibid.*

[54] *Ibid.*, pp. 33–34.

[55] *Ibid.*, p. 34.

The major determinants are structural conduciveness, strain, crystallization of a generalized belief, precipitating factors, mobilization for action,
and social control.

We conceive the operation of these determinants as a value-added
process. Each determinant is a necessary condition for the next to operate
as a determinant in an episode of collective behavior. As the necessary
conditions accumulate, the explanation of the episode becomes more determinate. Together the necessary conditions constitute the sufficient condition for the episode. It should be stressed, moreover, that we view the accumulation of necessary conditions as an analytic, not a temporal process.[56]

Thus, for example, "Structural conduciveness," the first stage of
value-added, refers to the degree to which any structure permits a given
type of collective behavior . . ." Strain is also a necessary condition,
which ". . . can assume significance as a determinant, however, only
within the scope established by the prior conditions of conduciveness."[57]
A typical proposition in this scheme becomes, then, "Panic will occur if
the appropriate conditions of conduciveness are present *and* if the appropriate conditions of strain are present *and* if a hysterical belief develops, *and* if mobilization occurs, *and* if social controls fail to operate."[58]

Thus, whereas Campbell, *et al.*, visualize one funnel of causation,
Smelser's scheme might be seen as a series of connected funnels, the
event at the narrower end of one funnel constituting one of a number of
conditions necessary to the development of the next.

In the present context, however, the two schemes differ in more important respects. First, Smelser's strategy attempts to embrace *both* social and
psychological factors, and in a manner that does not seem inimical to
field theory. This suggests to us that it may be inept to identify field
theory with the analysis only of psychological variables and to view
"social" factors only as "historical" or "genetic" and widely separated, in
some causal sense, from current behavioral events. Secondly, and perhaps
most important, Smelser's strategy operates at least a little further toward
recognizing the systemic nature of social-psychological phenomena. It
does this by seeking out not only the determinants antecedent to the
phenomenon being explained, but also the effects generated by the
phenomenon which feed back by way of societal reactions (for example,
"social control") to determine whether it persists and develops further or
whether it aborts. However, Smelser's "value-added" model does not allow
full recognition of the complex, ongoing systemic process within which
any one of the so-called "necessary conditions" may in fact require for its
generation the presence of one, two, or all of the other "necessary conditions" to some degree—in a spiral, for example, of positive feedback. The

[56] Neil J. Smelser, *Theory of Collective Behavior* (New York: Free Press of Glencoe, Inc., 1963) , p. 382.

[57] *Ibid.*, pp. 383–84.

[58] *Ibid.*, p. 385.

"value-added" model implies an isolation of some of the various factors from one another, whether analytically or temporally, thus missing the important possibility that they are all in fact involved in a truly systemic process of emergence. (What we have in mind is similar to the systemic analysis of the generation of social deviance, which is discussed and diagrammed in Chapter 6.)

Mutual interactionism. Reaction against the causal principle was especially strong in the earlier part of this century under the leadership of the neo-positivists, who were impressed with the widespread evidence of the many reciprocal interrelations found in nature and particularly in equilibrial systems, and with the great success of mathematical equations in describing them. As Mario Bunge states it:

> . . . the traditional empiricist efforts to reduce causation to regular as-
> sociation, to the external juxtaposition of concomitant events, were re-
> placed, by some of the followers of Hume, by the attempt to substitute
> functional interdependence for causal dependence. This was especially the
> case with Mach, who, unlike most of his forerunners and followers, had a
> keen and somewhat romantic feeling for the diversity of nature and for the
> intimate interconnections existing among its different members and aspects
> . . . Mach proposed . . . that the mathematical concept of function be
> used as the precise scientific tool for reflecting interdependence. Mach
> showed thereby that by interdependence he did not mean *genetic* inter-
> relation but rather mutual dependence among existents, a static net of re-
> ciprocal dependences like that among the parts of a steel frame.[59]

This principle of mutual interactionism made its appearance in social science also, and is perhaps epitomized in the work of Pareto and of his one-time follower Homans, which we referred to earlier.

We wish to restate here our argument that, whereas this principle of interactionism has been of inestimable importance to sociology in emphasizing the interdependent nature of much of social life, it has overstated its case in identifying the concept of system with only the mechanical equilibrium type. In sum, though it is applicable to closed systems in equilibrium, it breaks down when it comes to open, adaptive systems, in which development, or change through time, is endemic. MacIver, in his valiant defense of the causal principle against what he called "mathematical limbo," saw this rather clearly, though he did not appreciate the modern systems principles at stake here:

> A functional equation is an admirable device to symbolize certain
> highly general or universal relationships under hypothetical conditions,
> where, for example, a number of determinate factors or forces are as-
> sumed to constitute the structure of a closed system in a state of equi-

---

[59] Mario Bunge, *Causality: The Place of the Causal Principle in Modern Science* (Cambridge, Mass.: Harvard University Press, 1959) , pp. 90–91.

librium. It has no relevance to a system that cannot be understood in terms of isolable factors or components. It has no application to a system the changes of which depend in any degree on the impact of factors lying outside it. It is incapable of expressing or even of indicating the nature of the changes that occur in any changeful order—which is practically the whole world of our experience. The relations it symbolizes are the concomitant variation of factors in a timeless order . . . In no sense does the mathematical function symbolize our experience of time, the irreversible order that moves from present to past, *from cause to effect* . . . It is a fine instrument for expressing the calculable elemental attributes of physical mechanics, but it is futile to seek to apply it to the processes, trends, and happenings of the complex time-bound constructs within which we have our being.[60]

No doubt the major difficulty with the principle of mutual interactionism, one which has done the most to reduce its import in current science, is its failure to allow that some variables or factors in the system may have primacy or priority over others. Translated into practical, or applied, terms, this means a lack of a point of application of purpose or planned effort. Quoting Bunge again:

> . . . most contemporary social scientists would be prepared to admit that interaction rather than causation is the prevailing category of determination in social matters. Yet nobody except (mathematical) functionalists, regards society as a muddle of reciprocal actions standing *all on the same footing*. The various social functions are usually acknowledged to rest *ultimately* upon work, upon material production, upon economics, just as the highest functions of the organism are *ultimately* dependent on the intake of food, oxygen, and heat . . .[61]

Some time ago Pitirim Sorokin, in a critique of the Marxian thesis of economic determinism, argued that the fault lay principally in the assumption of a one-sided causal relationship rather than a mutual relationism, and engaged in an extensive review of the research that supported the view that economic primacy was either conceptually unclear or not well supported empirically. But today the tide has turned, and we find Gouldner and Peterson, for example, engaging in similar research to demonstrate the principle of primacy, particularly in the realm of economic factors.[62] It is significant that their study was at least partly a reaction against current equilibrium system analysis in sociology.

Functional analysis. Whereas traditional causal analysis focuses on a time sequence of prior cause and present effect, and mutual interaction-

---

60 Robert M. MacIver, *Social Causation* (New York: Harper & Row, Publishers, 1964), p. 52.

61 *Causality*, p. 157.

62 Alvin W. Gouldner and R. A. Peterson, *Notes on Technology and the Moral Order* (Indianapolis: The Bobbs-Merrill Co., Inc., 1962).

ism appeals to a timeless or simultaneous state of related variables, functionalism focuses from present to future events, and seeks to understand or explain a present phenomenon in terms of its consequences for the continuity, persistence, stability, or survival of the complex of which it is a part. This, as we have argued, is its distinguishing feature (and not the notion of systemic interdependence of parts), and it is in these terms that it has been shown time and again to be inadequate. As Homans and other sociologists, as well as biologists, have convincingly argued, and logicians confirmed, *explanation* must always translate "functions" into "efficient causes" (that is, prior or current states of a system rather than presumed future effects) unless some presumption of *automatic* adequacy or self-regulation can be supported. And such a presumption would provide only a substitute explanation, in the case of physiological structures and their functions, because we understand so well the process of natural selection whereby such structures evolve. But this blind process of "genesis," as Lester Ward called it, is quite different from the social selective process of "telesis." When we note, for example, that a particular structure that has arisen in some modern industrial society seems to be playing a role in maintaining that society, we cannot appeal to any blind process of natural selection involving the turnover of many such societies; but neither can we presume, in most cases, that there has been true recognition and planning in the name of some "functional prerequisite." The only possible source of explanation, then, is in terms of the forces and mechanisms that were at work to produce the given structure; any appeal to universal "functional prerequisites" or "needs" of a social system remains gratuitous.

We have noted that functionalism, like mutual interactionism, has often been charged with the inability to deal with the causal priority of some parts of a system over others, and consequently, with an inability to handle problems of development or change. This deficiency has been related to the above-noted identification of functionalism with a limited emphasis on the more or less static interdependence of parts of society. These points are well illustrated in the following statement from Elman R. Service's work:

> One of the important aims of this book is to discuss in some detail the dependent relation of social structure to other parts of culture.
> This latter point is a way of talking about cause-and-effect, of discussing the developmental priority of some things over others. Structural-functional analysis, because it is not concerned with development through time, does not and cannot assign varying significances to the different parts of a culture—the parts are all interdependent in an apparently equivalent sense. As Meyer Fortes (1953) put it: 'There is no way of establishing an order of priority where all institutions are interdependent, except by criteria that cannot be used in a synchronic study; and synchronic study is the *sine qua non* of functional research.' The present work is evolution-

ary, not merely synchronic or functional; hence, we may be able to elicit some ideas about primary, or initiatory, features in culture as compared to consequences. We may be able better to distinguish factors relating to the origins of institutions from the functions, a procedure long ago proposed by Durkheim (1938, Ch. V) but little heeded since.[63]

The final point we should like to make about functionalism in the present context concerns its methodological treatment, or rather, lack of treatment, of the concept of purpose. Put in other terms, the question concerns the role of cognitive processes of decision-making as well as motives and interests, or sentiments, where we are trying to understand stability and change. As currently practiced, functionalism tends to focus primarily on so-called system "needs." The key problem of human purposes and decisions, central in earlier American sociology—as attested to by the concepts of *verstehen*, "dynamic assessment," "definition of the situation," "humanistic coefficient," "logico-meaningful," and the like—has become so lost that we now find pleas made for "Bringing Men Back In,"[64] or at least for a greater use of psychological factors as intervening variables in social explanation.[65]

This problem was a basic one in MacIver's study of social causation. We recall that in his classification of the various "Modes of the Question Why," MacIver recognizes the functional principle, but regards it as "properly relevant to the biological level" as the "Why of Organic Function." On the distinctively *social* level he distinguishes two major categories of the "causal nexus." The first is the social-psychological or "teleological nexus": "a mode of determination that is peculiar to beings endowed with consciousness, beings who are in some degree aware of what they are doing and who are in some sense purposive in doing it."[66] The three subtypes are the "Why of Objective," the "Why of Motivation," and the "Why of Design." The second type of nexus is one that is "explicitly social":

> The phenomena we are referring to are the social resultants of a great many individual or group actions directed to quite other ends but together conspiring to bring them about. It is thus that the social structure is for the most part created. We include here . . . the standards, customs, and cultural patterns that men everywhere follow. They do not foresee and then design these larger patterns . . . Nor do they create them by concerted action directed to one objective, as men co-operate to construct a machine. These patterns emerge instead from the conjuncture

[63] Elman R. Service, *Primitive Social Organization* (New York: Random House, Inc., 1962) , pp. 6–7.

[64] George C. Homans, "Bringing Men Back In," *American Sociological Review*, 29 (1964) , 809–18.

[65] Alex Inkeles, "Personality and Social Structure," in *Sociology Today*, ed. Robert K. Merton *et al.* (New York: Basic Books, Inc., Publishers, 1959) .

[66] MacIver, *Social Causation*, pp. 14–15.

of diverse activities directed to less comprehensive and more immediate ends.[67]

This nexus between social phenomena and a mass of individualized activities is given a distinctive place in MacIver's system of causation under the rubric of the "Why of Social Conjuncture."

It is highly instructive to contrast the current, simple distinction between "manifest" (conscious and intended) and "latent" (unconscious and unintended) consequences of human behavior along with the view that social structures persist because they satisfy social system "needs," on the one hand, with MacIver's conception of social structure and the role of purpose and "dynamic assessment," on the other. For most social patterns are a complex emergent product of both purposive and unintended consequences. When we *are* able to distinguish the two empirically, important questions remain. For examples, for *which* individuals and groups are the consequences intended, and for which unintended or unrecognized? We have already suggested, earlier in this book, that MacIver's chapters on the "dynamic assessment" constitute an important prolegomenon to the reviving concern with decision-making processes in social analysis. And, in fact, it is on this level—of the purposes and decisions of complexes of interrelated and interacting individuals and groups—that current research and theory is developing the important modern theories of tension, "role-strain," exchange or bargaining, and the like (although it is not thereby necessary to reduce analysis to a framework of radical methodological individualism as some have argued) .[68]

Modern systems analysis. We must certainly agree with MacIver's recent restatement of his belief that "the advancement of the social sciences (and, not least, that of sociology) depends to a great degree on a more thorough grappling with the exceedingly complex problem of the causation of social phenomena."[69] We argue that the most significant grappling occurring today is within the modern systems research movement, which is augmenting our traditional conceptions of causation to such a degree that it might be best, as many suggest, to avoid causal terminology altogether (though it would be misleading, if at all meaningful, to claim that the "causal principle" has been "overthrown") .

We have already seen how oversimplified are the old causal axioms, such as, "Whatever happens has a cause," or "Like causes, like effects," or "Where there is difference in the effect there is difference in the cause."

[67] *Ibid.,* pp. 20–21.

[68] For two recent, perceptive discussions of the problem of function and cause see Ronald P. Dare, "Function and Cause," *American Sociological Review,* 26 (1961) , 843–53; and Yonima Talmon, "Mate Selection in Collective Settlements," *American Sociological Review,* 29 (1964) , 491–508.

[69] MacIver, *Social Causation,* p. vii.

Modern systems research has suggested, rather, the concepts of "equifinality" and "multifinality," whereby different initial conditions lead to similar end effects, or similar initial conditions lead to different end effects. It has also demonstrated the inadequacy of traditional causal analysis to deal with such important phenomena as emergence, purpose or goal-seeking, self-regulation, adaptation, and the like.

In contrasting systems research with mutual interactionism, we have seen how the former transcends the static equilibrium reference of the latter in recognizing the very different problem of the complex open, adaptive system which depends not simply on mutual relations of parts, but on very particular kinds of mutual interrelations. In addition, the important problems of primacy of some parts over others and the varying degrees of connectedness of some parts of the system to others are made subject to analysis. Thus, Karl Deutsch suggests that one test of importance for determining whether some component of a system is more critical than another is the answer to the question, "Which part of the system gives you the maximum over-all change in system performance for the least change or smallest change in the subassembly structure?"[70]

Finally, in contrasting systems analysis with functionalism, we note that the concepts of teleology and purpose have been made respectable or precise by rendering them into "efficient causes," or more particularly, into specifiable mechanisms involving feedbacks. Furthermore, the groundwork has been laid for elucidating the conditions making for self-regulation, development, or disintegration—instead of assuming automatic regulation or "mechanisms of control" for any system we are dealing with. And the decision-making of learning, thinking, groups of individuals is given an important place as a psycho-social process that brings into conjunction previously unrelated events or conditions, by way of social action and transaction, to produce the current sociocultural structure. Thus, decision-making is seen as the exemplar, in the sociocultural system, of the general selective process occurring in every adaptive system, whereby variety is selectively organized and utilized for self-regulation and self-direction.

A brief but suggestive illustration of some of these points may be made in connection with the Midtown Manhattan Study of mental health, in which Leo Srole, *et al.*, started with a convergent view of causality that viewed sociogenic factors as leading to mental illness or health.[71] But the authors then recognized the importance of: 1) the possible reciprocal influences of the dependent variable back onto the independent variables, by way, for example, of the "choices" of individuals of their

---

70 In rinker, *Toward a Unified Theory*, p. 279.
71 Leo Srole *et al.*, *Mental Health in the Metropolis* (New York: McGraw-Hill Book Company, 1962) .

particular social environments, and 2) the possible "circular" or "spiral-ing" interactions of these related factors through time. Thus, there were now seen to be at least three categories of factors or variables to be taken into account: 1) the dependent variable—mental health or illness, 2) the "independent" factors—age, sex, ethnic origin, and so forth, 3) "reciprocal variables"—marital status, socioeconomic status, religion, rural-urban mi-gration. In commenting on these last four variables, the authors suggest that "Variations on all four may be self-determined, and as such may well be consequences rather than independent antecedents of mental health."[72] We note, then, that whereas any one of the approaches we have discussed might be used in such a study, only the modern systems approach promises to get at the full complexity of the interacting phenomena—to see not only the *causes* acting on the phenomena under study, the possible *conse-quences* of the phenomena, and the possible *mutual interactions* of some of these factors, but also to see the *total emergent processes* as a function of possible positive and/or negative *feedbacks* mediated by the *selective decisions,* or "choices," of the individuals and groups directly or indirectly involved. No less complex an approach can be expected to get at the com-plexity of the phenomena studied.

---

[72] *Ibid.,* p. 18.

The preceding chapter has presented a broad outline of some of the central principles of the modern systems approach, with only occasional and unsystematic reference to their implications for the analysis of sociocultural systems. The remaining chapters are devoted to the support of the major thesis of this book: that the modern systems perspective provides a theoretical framework for the socio-cultural system that is significantly more appropriate and adequate than the mechanical-equilibrium or organismic-functional models dominating much of current social science thinking.

The present chapter is divided into two sections. Section A will attempt to review in greater detail the abstract theory of or-ganization, or model of morphogenesis in complex adaptive systems, outlined in the last chapter. This will involve a closer look at the interlocking concepts of information, organization, meaning, un-certainty, selection, constraint, and the like. It is suggested that an information theoretic perspective provides conceptual tools empha-sizing the processual, rather than static, nature of sociocultural or-ganization.

Section B examines a number of conceptual models of social ac-tion and interaction, each complementing the others in contributing to a theory of the basic dynamics of the sociocultural morphogenic process. It is suggested that, on the one hand, these models of the basic interaction process demonstrate the relevance and suggest in-terpretations of the more abstract systems theory of organization by utilizing, whether implicitly or explicitly, its basic principles, and on the other hand, that the systems model has the potential to synthesize the interaction models into a coherent conceptual scheme —a basic theory—of the sociocultural process. We do not pretend to perform this coherent synthesis here, but merely to indicate the basic principles and some points of articulation between the several contributing models.

organization 4
and its genesis:
1–acts and interactions

In the succeeding chapters then, the central unifying theme is the attempt to outline the development of a model of the sociocultural system as a "complex adaptive system" in the sense discussed in the previous chapter. This development proceeds from the micro-level of the *act* and the basic symbolic *interaction* process (discussed later in this chapter) to the more or less stabilized interaction matrix referred to as the *role* and role dynamics, to the complex of roles contributing to the makeup of *organizations* and *institutions*.

ORGANIZATION AND INFORMATION

It should be of particular interest to us that the modern systems theorist links closely the generalized concept of organization to that of information and communication, because—as we have seen—the sociocultural system is to be viewed as a set of elements linked almost entirely by way of the intercommunication of information (in the broad sense) rather than being energy- or substance-linked as are physical or organismic systems. Although the modern perspective is of sufficient generality to embrace the more simple, and perhaps more common, view of organization as a rather static structure of rigidly linked parts, the more recent concern with complex adaptive organization has led to the notion of *contingency* as the important key. Thus Wiener, while working in the field of communications and probability theory, became convinced "that a significant idea of organization cannot be obtained in a world in which everything is necessary and nothing is contingent."

> Such a rigid world is organized only in the sense in which a rigidly welded bridge is organized . . . Organization we must consider as something in which there is an interdependence between the several organized parts but in which this interdependence has degrees. Certain internal interdependencies must be more important than others, which is the same thing as saying that the internal interdependence is not complete, and that the determination of certain quantities of the system leaves others with the chance to vary.[1]

In a similar manner, W. Ross Ashby argues that "The hard core of the concept is, in my opinion, that of 'conditionality.' As soon as the relation between two entities A and B becomes conditional on C's value or state, then a necessary component of 'organization' is present."[2]

Looked at from a slightly different point of view, that a set of ele-

---

[1] Norbert Wiener, *I am a Mathematician* (New York: Doubleday & Company, Inc., 1956), pp. 322–23.

[2] W. Ross Ashby, "Principles of the Self-Organizing System," in *Principles of Self-Organization*, ed. Heinz von Foerster and George W. Zopf (New York: Pergamon Press, 1962), pp. 255–56.

ments is organized implies that there are *constraints* operating between the elements such that only certain interrelations or interactions obtain between them, and not others. Thus, for Ashby, an essential idea underlying conditionality is that, of the product space of *possibilities* of interaction given by a set of elements, any *actual* organization of the elements is constrained to some *subset* of interactions. The converse of organization is *independence* of elements: if, for a given event at *A*, all possible events may occur at *B*, then there is no "co-relation," "interaction," or "communication" and thus no constraint over the possible *A-B* couples. In a word, "the presence of 'organization' between variables is equivalent to the existence of a *constraint* in the product-space of the possibilities."[3]

Besides "contingency" and "constraints," there is a third important concept underlying the explication of complex organization. This is implied in the quote from Wiener above, and involves the presence of some *degrees of freedom* in the interrelations of parts. Although there must be constraints between the interaction of elements, there must also be some free play within the confines of the constraints, or we have only a rigid organization, devoid of dynamics. A precise account of this requirement has been given by Jerome Rothstein. Given a set of elements, we can conceptualize a dynamic organization as one in which each element is associated with its own *set of alternative* couplings with other elements.

> Were there no freedom to choose from a set of alternatives, the corresponding element would be a static, passive cog rather than an active unit contributing to the organization in an essential way. Such an element can be called structural, as distinguished from the active or organizational element.[4]

Thus, conceptualizing the set of all possible interrelations of elements in a manner similar to Ashby's "product space," Rothstein enables us to visualize the whole range of varying degrees of freedom of an organization, from a mere aggregate of unrelated elements to a rigidly fixed structure. If there is zero coupling between the elements, we have a condition of zero organization. At the other extreme, if the coupling between elements is so strong that only one subset of couplings (only one "complexion") is possible, with no other alternatives for any element to "choose" from, organization is said to be maximal. All the elements are then "cogs" in a rigid structure.

> In general, the interactions in which the organization consists serve to narrow the ensemble of admissible complexions. These interactions are of the nature of correlations, couplings, constraints, orders, or instructions which restrict the choices available to a given element in accordance with

---

3 *Ibid.*, p. 257.

4 Jerome Rothstein, *Communication, Organization and Science* (Indian Hills, Colo.: Falcon's Wing Press, 1958), p. 35.

choices made from the ensemble of alternatives associated with other elements.[5]

On the basis of such considerations, Rothstein argues for the essential equivalence of the concept of "organization" and the "negative entropy" of modern information theory.

The following brief discussion of "information theory" is not aimed at an account of the statistical theory of signal variety, coding, and transmission over limited and noisy channels, but rather with the generalized logical framework for the discussion of symbolic intercommunication that this important work has helped to develop.[6] As Colin Cherry has well noted,

> The measure for H_n (average 'information') . . . from Wiener and Shannon, is applicable to the signs themselves, and does not concern their 'meaning.' In a sense, it is a pity that the mathematical concepts stemming from Hartley have been called 'information' at all. The formula for H_n is really a measure of one facet only of the concept of information; it is the statistical rarity or 'surprise value' of a source of signs.[7]

The same sort of thing should also be said about the terms "choice" and "uncertainty" that Shannon and Weaver and many other expositors have been using, since these psychological concepts are, at best, heuristic or pedagogic devices playing no role in the statistical theory, and at worst can cause a great deal of confusion and even mislead us into believing that the theory elucidates them.

Our purpose immediately below is to investigate the possibilities of information theory as a basis for developing the fundamentals of the concepts of "organization" and "meaning" (only briefly discussed in the last chapter) as basic to the study of social and personal organization taken up in the latter part of this chapter.

Information theory

The mathematical theory of "information" begins by supposing some *source* which is continually generating signals, symbols, or messages —most generally, what we have called *variety*—and some *receiver* who can

---

[5] *Ibid.*, pp. 35–36.

[6] We sometimes find "information theory" and "communication theory" used synonymously, but very often—especially abroad—the former is considered just one facet of the much broader study conducted under the latter designation. For detailed study of these areas the student is referred to the now easily available original paper of Shannon and the more popular account by Weaver in Claude E. Shannon and Warren Weaver, *The Mathematical Theory of Communication* (Urbana: University of Illinois Press, 1963), as well as to the broad treatment given in Colin Cherry, *On Human Communication* (New York: Science Editions, 1961) and to Cherry's extensive bibliography.

[7] *Ibid.*, p. 50.

put this variety to use. Thus, the generating source might be a set of traffic lights emitting a variety of colored signals, or a person speaking words or sentences. It is assumed that both the source and receiver have previously *mapped* or coded this variety to the same or similar referents, such that the messages may have meaning and relate to behavior; but of this the mathematical theory has nothing more to say.

It should be recognized at the start that the theory is a statistical one providing an *average* as an "information" measure dependent on the assumption of long sequences of "messages" generated by a Markov or other stochastic process such that they approach a stable frequency distribution of elements as the sequences approach infinite length (i.e., they are "ergodic"). The principle behind the measure is best introduced, however, by way of illustrations involving short sequences and little variety. Thus, let us imagine Paul Revere and his observer in the church tower near Boston with a pre-arranged code utilizing lighted lanterns to advise of the coming of the British. Let us complicate the original situation for the sake of exposition, and assume that Revere wanted information not only as to whether they were coming by land or by sea, but also whether the force was large or small, and whether it was approaching from a northerly or a southerly direction. There would then be eight possibilities for which signals would have to be provided: land–large–northerly; land–large–southerly; land–small–northerly; and so forth. In other terms, the variety in the environment that is of interest can take one of eight states. One possible way of transmitting the proper information might be for the observer to present a different number of lighted lanterns, one through eight, depending on which state materialized, with each number prearranged to match one of the states. On this basis, the measure of the amount of "information" necessary to specify the possible variety of the environment would be simply the raw number of possible states: H (the "information" measure) $= n$ (the number of different possible states) $= 8$. A little thought, however, suggests that it is not necessary to burn all that lantern oil. For it might be arranged that one lantern, say the first on the left, specify the land–sea dichotomy (say by being shaded either red or green, since on–off might not work too well), with a second one similarly specifying a large or small force, and a third on the right specifying northerly or southerly approach. Now we require only three lanterns, each taking one of two states. This dichotomous nature of each lantern represents the minimal unit of information specification—the yes–no or on–off unit, the "bit." The minimal amount of "information" now seen to be necessary to specify the 8 states is only 3 bits—which, not by accident, is the logarithm to the base 2 of 8. In a word, the formula for the information measure in such simple cases is $H = \log_2 n$.

The information measure of greater generality deals, however, not with a particular limited set of signals, but with a rate or average amount generated by a source if enough long sequences of signals or messages are transmitted. Different sequences will specify different amounts of variety, such that the average amount we can expect for any one message from the given source is expressed in the formula $H = -\sum_i p_i \log_2 p_i$, where p_i is the probability in the long run that the ith signal or message will occur. Thus, H in bits per message or per unit time (often called "entropy" because the formula, if not the principle, is nearly identical to that for entropy in thermodynamics) increases as the raw amount of variety in the ensemble of possible messages increases, but it is weighted by the relative frequency of occurrence of the various signals or messages making up the ensemble. If all elements are equally probable, H goes to a maximum; at the other extreme, if the probabilities of all elements but one are zero, then only the one can occur and the variety, and H, is zero. Also, constraints on the possible combinations of elements reduce the variety, and hence H. Thus our Paul Revere might have known that any force coming by sea would have to be small and any by land, large. This, in effect, would reduce the number of contingencies to 4, and only 2 lanterns would be required. Hence, the variety H is reduced to $\log_2 4 = 2$. It may be noted that H is thus related to statistical measures of correlation or contingency in common use, and can be regarded as a nonparametric measure of variance.[8] In sum, the "entropy" H of an ensemble of varying elements measures the amount of variation in the elements, their relative frequency of occurrence, and the amount of constraints, correlations, or interdependencies among them.

(If the rationale for the use of the log rather than the raw amount of variety is not entirely clear, it should be noted that the coding and transmission of information takes advantage of the spatial (or temporal or other classificatory) ordering of the elements. Thus, Paul Revere's specification of a left, a center, and a right lantern is as important in specifying the information as the number and color of the lanterns, just as is the spatial or temporal ordering of writing or speech for communicating information. This consideration is usually left implicit in most discussions of information theory.)

In developing his mathematical theory, Shannon went on to consider the case of another source of variety, "noise," introduced into the flow of variety from an information source, and the resulting difference between the output and the input ensemble of messages. His important theorems specified the conditions under which output fidelity could be

8 F. C. Frick, "The Application of Information Theory in Behavioral Studies," in *Psychology: A Study of a Science*, 2, ed. Sigmund Koch (New York: McGraw-Hill Book Company, 1959), 611–36; W. R. Garner and W. J. McGill, "Relation Between Uncertainty, Variance and Correlation Analyses," *Psychometrika*, 21 (1956), 219–28; W. J. McGill, "Isomorphism in Statistical Analysis," in *Information Theory in Psychology*, ed. Henry Quastler (New York: Free Press of Glencoe, Inc., 1955), pp. 56–62; and W. R. Garner, *Uncertainty and Structure as Psychological Concepts* (New York: John Wiley & Sons, Inc., 1962).

attained with minimal error despite the introduction of noise into the channel, conditions which involve the relative channel capacity, the introduction of sufficient redundancy into the messages, and their encoding in an efficient manner. We shall not follow out these ideas here, except where they are necessary to our discussion of the relation between "information" and "organization" noted earlier. In wondering about all the fuss raised by the introduction of information theory, George A. Miller was led to say:

> The reason for the fuss is that information theory provides a yardstick for measuring organization. The argument runs like this. A well-organized system is predictable—you know almost what it is going to do before it happens. When a well-organized system does something, you learn little that you didn't already know—you acquire little information. A perfectly organized system is completely predictable and its behavior provides no information at all. The more disorganized and unpredictable a system is, the more information you can get by watching it. Information, organization, and predictability room together in this theoretical house.[9]

We have noted Rothstein's attempt to express this in more precise terms by visualizing organization as a number of elements each associated with its own set of alternative interactions with other elements. Thus each element has some freedom of choice of interactions, but also some constraints. Any particular set of all the single choices made by each of the elements in the organization constitutes what Rothstein calls a "complexion." There are thus as many complexions in an organization as there are ways of selecting a representative from each set of alternatives. We thus have a situation logically equivalent to a typical information-theoretical ensemble of variety, and the information or "entropy" measure H can be used. If the elements of a presumed organization were in fact independent of one another, so that any element could interact with any other with equal probability, then we have a case equivalent to an ensemble of "messages" which are emitted from a source with equal probability and have no constraints between them. The "entropy" in both cases would be maximal, and "organization," intuitively felt to be the opposite of "entropy," would be zero—that is, there is complete "disorganization." In Rothstein's terms, the set of complexions here has an entropy that is merely the sum of the entropies of the individual sets of alternatives. At the opposite extreme, where only one complexion is permitted by the organization, the entropy of the potential set of complexions is zero, and organization is maximal.

Generally, however, in a dynamic organization we have a situation in between, and the entropy of the set of complexions is not zero, but is

---

[9] George A. Miller, "What Is Information Measurement?", *American Psychologist*, 8 (1953), 3–12. Quote is on p. 3.

less than the sum of the entropies of the individual sets of alternatives. On this basis, Rothstein offers a definition of the amount of organization:

> We define the amount of organization as the excess of this maximum possible value of the complexion entropy over the entropy of the set of complexions calculated with the correlations characterizing the organization taken into account. It is easy to see that organization measures how much information has been introduced into the ensemble of complexions because of the interactions.[10]

(In the last sentence we might prefer to say that organization measures the amount of *constraint* introduced into, or the loss of *variety* in, the ensemble of complexions due to the interactions. On the other hand, the original statement suggests that we see social organization as "bound information," where "information" is used broadly to imply common meanings, normatively defined roles, etc.) It can be seen that Rothstein's definition of organization is equivalent to the information-theoretical measure of "redundancy": this is simply one minus the ratio of the actual entropy of an ensemble of messages due to constraints among them, to the maximum for that ensemble without constraints.

Rothstein goes on to apply these notions to a "system" as "an organization with a function" (that is, task, program, behavior pattern, or objective). By a "function" he means a *mapping* of one set of alternatives called the input, into another set, called the output. Thus, a *measuring* system maps a set of states of an object of interest into the set of possible indications of the apparatus, or a *communication* system maps a set of messages from a source into a set at the destination, or a *transportation* system maps a set of starting points into a set of destinations. It is then suggested that:

> The entropy of the function is less than the sum of input and output entropies by the amount of organization introduced by the system. In order to perform its function, the system must have an entropy at least as great as that of its function.[11]

Thus we meet, in somewhat different form, Ashby's principle of "requisite variety," introduced in the last chapter: if a system or organization is to adapt to or control its environment, it must contain at least as much

---

[10] *Communication, Organization and Science*, p. 36. It is pointed out by two of my graduate students, John Walton and John Shiflett, that it would be difficult to specify the whole ensemble of possible complexions for many concrete social situations, so that the measure of the ratio of actual to possible alternative actions or interactions is operationally problematic.

[11] *Ibid.*, p. 37. See also Jerome Rothstein's "Information and Organization as the Language of the Operational Viewpoint," *Philosophy of Science*, 29 (1962), 406–11.

variety (or "entropy" or "freedom" of selection of alternatives) as there is in the environment to be controlled.

Shannon's treatment of the interaction of an information source and a "noise" source to produce a mixed output can be taken as the basis of an extension of the above model of organization to the case of two (or more) organizations interacting to produce a joint outcome. This can be conceptualized in terms of Figure 4–1, the Euler diagram of overlapping sets, suggested by G. A. Miller. Two collectivities (or groups, or societies) are represented by x and y. $H(x)$ and $H(y)$ represent the organization of interactions for each of the groups.

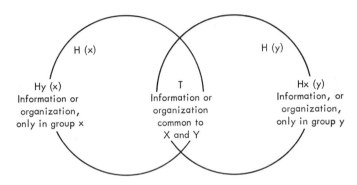

FIGURE 4-1

$Hy(x)$ and $Hx(y)$ represent the mutually incompatible or irrelevant interactions (or norms and values) for each of the organizations relative to the other. And T represents the amount of common or compatible organizational interactions generated by the two groups in contact. Thus the task or behavioral output of two interacting groups with widely differing sociocultural organizations would be expected to be confined to a relatively narrow common area (assuming the absence of total conflict), whereas groups with very similar organizations might be expected to mesh them, so that the output takes advantage of both the wider variety and the constraints afforded by the two together.

The social scientist should easily see both the great generality of such a model and the many points at which it articulates with social theory. We should not have to isue the caution, however, that the application of the *mathematical* theory here is restricted, although we have hardly begun to explore the possibilities as, for example, the psychologists have been doing for over a decade. We might also reaffirm our contention, at this point, that the *abstract model* we are dealing with is *not* mere analogizing or translating into new terms with no gain of comprehension. But that will have to be judged later, after a number of serious efforts have been made.

Empirical Illustration

We shall take a short break in the argument here to outline a suggestive illustration from the recent work of an anthropologist studying
the interpenetration of a number of culturally related, but independent
Indian patrilocal bands of Northern Baja California.[12] These bands were
strung out over a fair distance, but contact between them is possible.
Three mutually unintelligible languages were spoken in the area: Kiliwa,
Paipai, and Tipai. Each was subdivided into regional dialects, each linguistic group being relatively small and more or less localized in quite
different environmental settings, and with no extra-political integrations
among them. A rigid exogamy was practiced, with marriage forbidden
with known consanguineal relatives on either side. Each band thus varied
somewhat linguistically, faced somewhat different environmental problems, and had a somewhat different culture or "adaptive conceptual system." We note, then, that we have a situation closely equivalent to the
biological one of an ecological system with gradients of genetic interchange underlying such processes as speciation, hybridization, genetic
drift, and the like. From an information theoretic point of view we have a
number of ensembles of constrained variety acting as sources of continual
generation and transmission of symbol systems, with differential distribu-
tions of mappings or intercommunication among them. And from the
viewpoint of our abstract model of morphogenesis, we have a number of
overlapping open systems or complex adaptive organizations, in the
process of mapping into their sociocultural and psychic structures the
variety of their particular physical and social environments.

Because of the exogamy rule, marriage partners, mainly female, had
to be selected from non-relatives—which meant from relatively distant
bands. For the probability of selecting a partner from a contiguous band
was small since nearby bands consisted mainly of relatives who, even if far
removed genealogically, were barred by the extreme incest taboo. This
meant the importation into a band of a constant stream of females from
linguistically and culturally different bands, thereby introducing "variety" (if not "noise") into the band.

These bands, then, were made up principally of males speaking
one language and trained in one set of adaptive symbols, and many females speaking another language, or at least dialect, and trained in a different set of folkways. In the typical family, the children acquired—up to
a certain age—the language and cultural ways of the mother and other females (often differing among themselves), and later acquired the male

---

12 Roger C. Owen, "The Patrilocal Band: A Linguistically and Culturally Hybrid
Social Unit," *American Anthropologist*, 67 (1965), 675–90.

symbol system. Thus there was great variety within the band, the children varying from either parent under their bi-cultural and bi-lingual constraints, as well as diverging from other children in the band. The patrilocal band is thus characterized as a culturally and linguistically hybrid residence group, united by patrilineal consanguineal ties but not by ties of either common language or common culture.

Our abstract information–organization model suggests that, given such a situation, certain developments might be expected (depending, however, on sufficient knowledge of the important parameters, such as the stability or rate of change of the significant environments of the bands and the rates of symbol interchange between them. The modern probability theorist might wish to analyze the probable developments in terms of a set of transition probabilities generated by a Markov process.)

First, the continuous introduction of new symbol systems into the band by way of marriage partners provides a continually renewed "pool of variety" from which the band may draw, in adapting to or controlling the variety of the environment, should the latter (both social and physical) change enough to vitiate aspects of the existing cultural adaptations and/or lead to felt needs for different arrangements. Thus, Owen remarks:

> In regard to general evolutionary growth and change, the hybrid patri-local band would provide a highly adaptive structural type. Contained in any given population would be a diversified set of adaptive symbols derived from the females; to any situation of rigorous selective stress, there would be available a number of possible responses, thusly giving to the culturally hybrid band a high survival potential.[13]

Second, the general paradigm of the evolution of the complex, adaptive system, discussed in the last chapter, and the related information-theoretic discussion above of the interactions of two or more "organizations," may be seen to provide at least the beginnings of a general model of the evolution of sociocultural systems into ever larger, more structurally differentiated societal units. The interaction of a number of partly overlapping organizations or symbol-generating sources leads, at the output end of the transmission system, and under certain conditions, to the selective loss of incompatible or equivocal symbols, the diffusion of others, and the resultant convergence of the several organizations and symbol ensembles toward a more common symbol system and an amalgamated social organization. Thus, the increased survival potential of the patrilocal band, provided by the large variety pool, tends to increase the population density, which is recognized by many anthropologists as a prerequisite to cultural advancement. Roger Owen goes on to sketch the implications of this as follows:

_____

[13] In an earlier, unpublished version of the above-cited paper.

The structural concomitant of increased density, of course, would be to increase such things as intensity of linguistic communication and cultural
communication in general. This would act to lower regional dialectical
and cultural differences. A further effect of increased population density
would be to make available additional marriage partners from nearby residence groups. Within the band this would act to lower the degree of
linguistic and cultural dissimilarity between mates and, ultimately, the
development of sedentary, endogamous villages would bring about mat-
ings between individuals speaking precisely the same language and prac-
ticing a virtually identical culture.[14]

In sum, such a process leads to the next level of sociocultural integration,
the "tribal" level characteristic of the neolithic period—to use Elman
R. Service's evolutionary classification.[15]

It is hoped that this brief illustration, whatever else it may do, will
serve to reinforce the view—often voiced but not as often taken seriously
—that society is a communication system in a much deeper sense than
the common meaning of the term may imply.

Society: An Organization of Meanings

Having briefly treated the central aspects of the "signal transmission" side of "information theory" and the related concept of "organization," it remains to consolidate our understanding of the concept of
"meaning" and its relation to both of these. We have seen that "information theory" deals with events between a signal source and a receiver, but
not with the nature of these termini themselves and the conditions under
which the signals transmitted between them become "meaningful" information. The general framework of this theory has, however, stimulated
renewed concern with the problem of meaning. This framework emphasizes that "information," as a carrier of "meaning," is not an entity that
exists some place or flows from one place to another, but a *relation,* or
"mapping," between sets of structured variety, embodied—for our present
purposes—in goal-oriented adaptive systems and in their environments;
and that "communication" involves a *process of selection* from such sets.
In the last chapter we noted MacKay's conceptualization of an organism
as a set of basic acts which, in various combinations, make up behavior.
The adaptive behavior of such an organism involves a selective process
by which a subset of these basic arts are concatenated in such a way as
to match, according to some goal, the subset of constrained variety that
is the current state of the organism's environment. In the case of the human organism, these selective mappings are mediated by an ensemble of
symbols, and social behavior involves such symbolically mediated map-

---

14 *Ibid.*

15 Elman R. Service, *Primitive Social Organization* (New York: Random House,
Inc., 1962) .

pings between interactively coupled individuals. Thus, social interaction —which is meaningful interaction—implies some minimal commonness in the mappings of the individuals and their referent environments, symbol systems, and need states.

Such a view is well brought out, for example, in Rothstein's discussion of the methodology of operationism in science.

> The operational viewpoint makes the implicit assumption that observers performing the same operations will produce the same results. The word 'same' applied to different observers means that they can communicate, that they can agree on some things, and that these things therefore are interpersonal and thus objective. This is also implicit in the informational viewpoint, for it is implicitly assumed that common sets of alternatives can be defined for all observers. More precisely, one to one mappings can be defined between the sets of alternatives associated with each observer for all observers. By this we mean that objects exist to which we can give names, and people can use these names to communicate and agree that they refer to the same object.[16]

Many others, though intending to present the mathematical theory of "information" as a purely formal theory, in fact suggest this same sort of substantive (social psychological) interpretation, as did Shannon himself. Thus, F. C. Frick introduces the "basic theory" by discussing the insight that all information-conveying processes are basically *selection* processes, as, for example, speech.

> Alternatively, we need information only when we are faced with a choice of some sort. If I know the road to Boston, I do not need a route sign at the intersection . . .
> Thus, information and ignorance, choice, prediction, and uncertainty are all intimately related. On the other hand, complete ignorance or indeterminance also precludes information transmission. A lecture in German is not informative to a listener who does not understand German. There must be some degree of agreement, some sort of common language established between the information source and the receiver. Put somewhat more precisely: information processes are selection processes, but these selections must be made from a *specific* set of alternatives, and if the sequence of selections is to convey information, the possible choices must be known to the receiver . . .
> Within these bounds of complete knowledge and complete ignorance, it seems intuitively reasonable to speak of degrees of uncertainty. The wider the choice, the larger the set of alternatives open to us, the more uncertain we are as to how to proceed—the more information we require in order to make our decision . . . Our uncertainties are intimately tied up with probability estimates and if we are to fit our intuitive notions regarding information, we must consider not only the range of choices available but the probabilities associated with each.[17]

---

16 Jerome Rothstein, "Information and Organization," 410–11.
17 Frederick C. Frick, "Information Theory," in *Psychology: A Study of a Science*, 2, ed. Sigmund Koch (New York: McGraw-Hill Book Company, 1959), **614–15**.

Given this very general conception of "meaning," the problem becomes, how do such common meanings arise, and what is their relationship to the behaviors of individuals and groups. The answers we have to date are embodied in much of the work of this century in social psychology and sociology. In general, we find that meanings are generated in a process of social interaction of a number of individuals dealing with a more or less common environment. Once generated, they act in the capacity of selective functions underlying the decision-making processes that make possible (but do not guarantee) organized social behavior. Thus, social organization can be seen in terms of a set of common-meaning-based constraints in the ensemble of possible interactions of social units, a reduction in uncertainty of behaviors, or a set of "mappings" of behaviors and goal-states. Certain of these mappings, those that are stable enough or salient enough, come to be generalized as codes or rules or norms. But it is important not to confuse these rules, or norms, with the actual organizational process that they partly inform. For, as we saw earlier in dealing with the problem of morphogenesis, the concrete "organization" is a resultant both of actors following out rules *plus* the interactions of these actors with each other and with an environment whose constraints or exigencies are usually much too rich to be covered by the rules (or, there is too little selective information in the rules to specify or control the full variety of the interacting elements and their environment).

In the next section, we turn to conceptualizations of individual actions, interactions, and social organization, as they may be seen in this perspective.

ACTION AND INTERACTION: THE DYNAMICS OF MORPHOGENESIS

We have seen that, of the several models used to characterize society, the process model—especially as developed in this century under the name of social interactionism—is most congenial to, if not a forerunner of, the modern systems view we are exploring. Thus our exposition in this section will lean heavily on that perspective, especially as presented in the work of G. H. Mead and his followers, though we recognize that many other sources have contributed.

The "Act"

The process view of Dewey and Mead (who were very close at the University of Chicago) was very strongly and explicitly an evolutionary view, with the organism and the environment seen as intimately interdependent in what we now call a systemic manner. We do not find a mechanical stimulus–response relation, but a complex ongoing "act" within which the individual is an active agent with degrees of freedom, selectivity, or innovation mediating between external influences and overt behavior. The total *act* involves an "impulse," or problem-induced tension, or goal-in-view, as well as the person's selective perception and manipulation of the environment, such that each of these elements is defined or given meaning only in terms of the others. In Mead's terms,

> An act is an impulse that maintains the life-process by the selection of certain sorts of stimuli it needs. Thus, the organism creates its environment . . . Stimuli are means, tendency is the real thing. Intelligence is the selection of stimuli that will set free and maintain life and aid in rebuilding it.[18]

And likewise for the social act, a basic focus of social psychology:

> The social act is not explained by building it up out of stimulus plus response; it must be taken as a dynamic whole—as something going on—no part of which can be considered or understood by itself—a complex organic process implied by each individual stimulus and response involved in it.[19]

It is further explained that the social act is to be restricted to "the class of acts which involve the co-operation of more than one individual, and whose object . . . is a social object . . . The objective of the acts is then found in the life-process of the group, and not in those of the separate individuals alone."

Recognizing that "part of the act lies within the organism and only comes to expression later," Mead saw that

> . . . this approach is one of particular importance because it is able to deal with the field of communication in a way which neither Watson nor the introspectionist can do. We want to approach language . . . in its larger context of co-operation in the group taking place by means of signals and gestures. Meaning appears within that process.[20]

It is no accident, then, that psychologists influenced by modern information theory are beginning to think in similar terms, even when they are the "hard-headed" behaviorist variety of psychologist. Thus, Frick brings to our attention the suggestion of E. R. F. W. Crossman that "Instead of a *stimulus* causing a *reaction* when the *threshold* is exceeded, we now think rather in terms of a *signal* which may be obscured by *noise,* providing the *information* needed to *select* a response."[21] Frick goes on to insist that such rephrasing is not simply playful, but influences our choice of variables and design of experiments.

---

18 George H. Mead, *Mind, Self, and Society* (Chicago: University of Chicago Press, 1934), p. 6, ftn. 5.

19 *Ibid.,* p. 7.

20 *Ibid.,* p. 6.

21 Frick, "Information Theory," 630.

Crossman, for example, continues his discussion by pointing out that, unlike a stimulus, a signal . . . implies a set of alternatives and thus emphasizes the effect on behavior of what might have been as well as what is immediately present. Furthermore, a signal in this sense functions purely as the basis for response selection. It can, according to the theory, be coded into a variety of physical forms and embedded in a variety of signal sets, without effect on its selective function.[22]

We mentioned, in an earlier chapter, the equally relevant "mediation" theories of symbol-based behavior of Osgood and Mowrer, as well as the blossoming of "decision theory." We also noted, and here reinforce the suggestion, that the mutually supporting work of Mead and of modern communication theorists provide a more fundamental basis for the ideas more discursively suggested by Max Weber's *verstehen,* W. I. Thomas' "definition of the situation," or Robert MacIver's "dynamic assessment."

From his conception of the act, Mead went on to develop its implications for the concepts of mind and intelligence, meaning, self-consciousness, and the social process. As Herbert Blumer recently argued, only Mead "has sought to think through what the act of interpretation implies for an understanding of the human being, human action, and human association."[23] Mead did not attempt to counteract a mechanical, external determinism of behavior with a vague appeal to "free will" or "voluntarism" as others did, but focused relentlessly on the symbolic nature of the act until he had worked his way through. Let us look at some of his insights, and in particular note the fully cybernetic nature of his analysis of human action as a feedback communication and control system. The central core of his interpretation is what he calls the *reflexiveness* of symbolically mediated behavior—"the turning back of the experience of the individual upon himself." This is made possible by the use of the symbol, and in turn makes possible the peculiarly human mental process or mind—the self, self-consciousness, self-control, and hence social control.

The "vocal gesture" or *significant symbol* makes it possible for the organism using it to evoke in himself the same response it evokes in the other to whom it is addressed. Since the meaning of a symbol is the tendency to respond to it in a particular way, we have here the basis for a common ensemble of meanings and responses in a group of individuals and hence a basis for common action and interaction. Thus, in illustrating his point by way of the songs and calls of birds, Mead says:

Where there is a specific sound that calls out a specific response, then if this sound is made by other forms it calls out this response in the form in question. If the sparrow makes use of this particular sound then the response to that sound will be one which will be heard more frequently than

---

22 *Ibid.*

23 Herbert Blumer, "Society as Symbolic Interaction," in *Human Behavior and Social Processes,* ed. Arnold M. Rose (Boston: Houghton Mifflin Company, 1962), pp. 180–81.

another response. In that way there will be selected out of the sparrow's repertoire those elements which are found in the song of the canary, and gradually such selection would build up in the song of the sparrow those elements which are common to both, without assuming a particular tendency of imitation. There is here a selective process by which is picked out what is common.[24]

Mead goes on to suggest that in symbolic communication, the individual must be continually responding to his own vocal symbols if he is to carry on a successful conversation.

The meaning of what we are saying is the tendency to respond to it. You ask somebody to bring a visitor a chair. You arouse the tendency to get the chair in the other, but if he is slow to act you get the chair yourself. The response to the vocal gesture is the doing of a certain thing, and you arouse that same tendency in yourself . . . You assume that in some degree there must be identity in the reply. It is action on a common basis.[25]

Generalizing from this, Mead tells us that he wants to isolate the mechanism involved in the fact that we unconsciously put ourselves in the place of others and act as others act "because it is of very fundamental importance in the development of what we call self-consciousness and the appearance of the self." Through the use of the vocal gesture we continually arouse in ourselves those responses we evoke in others such that "we are taking the attitudes of the other persons into our own conduct." That is:

The critical importance of language in the development of human experience lies in this fact that the stimulus is one that can react upon the speaking individual as it reacts upon the other.[26]

Being a behaviorist who is not afraid to look inside the "black box," Mead occasionally provides us with remarkably modern insights into the feedback control processes of the central nervous system. Thus, he suggests that if we try to find in the central nervous system something corresponding to the word "chair" what we should presumably find would be "an organization of a whole group of possible reactions so connected that if one starts in one direction one will carry out one process, if in another direction one will carry out another process." Thus the chair is a physical object on which one sits, such that one may move toward it and then enter upon the process of sitting down when it is reached.

There is a stimulus which excites certain paths which cause the individual to go toward that object and to sit down. Those centers are in some degree physical. There is, it is to be noted, *an influence of the later act on the*

24 Mead, *Mind, Self, and Society*, p. 65.
25 *Ibid.*, p. 67.
26 *Ibid.*, p. 69.

earlier act. The later process which is to go on has already been initiated and that later process has its influence on the earlier process . . . Now, such an organization of a great group of nervous elements as will lead to conduct with reference to the objects about us is what one would find in the central nervous system answering to what we call an object. The complications are very great, but the central nervous system has an almost infinite number of elements in it, and they can be organized not only in spatial connection with each other, but also from a temporal standpoint. In virtue of this last fact, our conduct is made up of a series of steps which follow each other, and the later steps may be already started and influence the earlier ones. The thing we are going to do *is playing back on* what we are doing now.[27]

And this feedback process underlying purposive human behavior is made possible by the fact, as such psychologists as Osgood and Mowrer are rediscovering, that the symbol can mediate by acting both as an evoked response and as a stimulus to further action. For Mead it is the relationship of the symbol "to such a set of responses in the individual himself as well as in the other that makes of that vocal gesture what I call a significant symbol." But there is something further involved in its acting as a significant symbol:

> . . . this response within one's self to such a word as "chair," or "dog," is one which is a stimulus to the individual as well as a response. This is what, of course, is involved in what we term the meaning of a thing, or its significance . . .
>
> When we speak of the meaning of what we are doing we are making the response itself that we are on the point of carrying out a stimulus to our action. It becomes a stimulus to a later stage of action which is to take place from the point of view of this particular response.[28]

On this basis, an organized "self" arises in the human individual and becomes the reflexive seat of decision-making and control of behavior. This *organized self* "is simply the organization, by the individual organism, of the set of attitudes toward its social environment—and toward itself from the standpoint of that environment . . ." That is:

> Reflection or reflective behavior arises only under the conditions of self-consciousness, and makes possible the purposive control and organization by the individual organism of its conduct with reference to its social and physical environment . . .
>
> Human intelligence, by means of the physiological mechanism of the human central nervous system, deliberately selects one from among the several alternative responses which are possible in the given problematic environmental situation . . .
>
> It is the entrance of the alternative possibilities of future response

27 *Ibid.,* pp. 70–71. Emphasis supplied.
28 *Ibid.,* pp. 71–72.

into the determination of present conduct in any given environmental situation, and their operation . . . as part of the factors or conditions determining present behavior, which decisively contrasts intelligent conduct or behavior with reflex, instinctive, and habitual conduct or behavior—delayed reaction with immediate reaction.[29]

And it is because present behavior is always both emergent from the past and conditioned by possible future results that it is never precisely predictable and always involves an element of spontaneity.

This is the sense, then, in which the human individual not only controls, but creates and recreates much of his effective environment. His ensemble of symbols represents mappings of possible behavioral relations with his environment, relations which are otherwise not given in nature but which may be continually created by the mutual stimulations and responses of gesturing individuals interacting in an environment.

The social process relates the responses of one individual to the gestures of another, as the meanings of the latter, and is thus responsible for the rise and existence of new objects in the social situation, objects dependent upon or constituted by these meanings . . . We pick out an organized environment in relationship to our response, so that these attitudes, as such, not only represent our organized responses but they also represent what exists for us in the world . . . Our world is definitely mapped out for us by the responses which are going to take place . . . The structure of the environment is a mapping out of organic responses to nature; any environment, whether social or individual, is a mapping out of the logical structure of the act to which it answers, an act seeking overt expression.[30]

In addition, Mead clearly recognized a point we made earlier stemming from information theory, that meaning or meaningful information is not a thing but a relation subsisting within a field of experience. This insight can be seen as a fundamental support of what came to be called "field theory":

Meaning is thus not to be conceived, fundamentally, as a state of consciousness, or as a set of organized relations existing or subsisting mentally outside the field of experience into which they enter; on the contrary, it should be conceived objectively, as having its existence entirely within this field itself . . .

What we need to recognize is that we are dealing with the relationship of the organism to the environment selected by its own sensitivity . . . The mental processes do not . . . lie in words any more than the intelligence of the organism lies in the elements of the central nervous system. Both are part of a process that is going on between organism and environment. The

29 *Ibid.,* pp. 91, 98.

30 *Ibid.,* pp. 78, 128–29.

symbols serve their part in this process, and it is that which makes communication so important. Out of language emerges the field of mind.[31]

And this brings us once again to "the essential condition, within the social process, for the development of mind," namely, reflexiveness— "The turning-back of the experience of the individual upon himself," so that he can take himself as an object in a wider field of experience.[32] In the language of cybernetics, such self-consciousness is a mechanism of internal feedback of the system's own states which may be mapped or compared with other information from the situation and from memory, permitting a selection from a repertoire of actions in a goal-directed manner that takes one's own self and behavior explicitly into account.[33]

The Interactional Field: A Dynamic System

Though it is part of conventional wisdom to start with the "individual" and his act, yet as Mead and many others have insisted, we cannot get to the social by way of the "individual" by simple addition or aggregation. Rather must we begin with an interactional field of interdependent organisms in an environment, and trace from *it* what we mean by the human "individual" and the social organization of such "individuals." Our basic model must, at a bare minimum, be based on a coupling of two organisms in some systemic manner. This perennial "locus" problem in social psychology[34] is particularly manifest in the confusion over what is meant when the term "individual" is used—confusion over whether we mean the skin-bound organism, or the "self" or "personality." In contrasting individual and social theories of the self and mind, Mead clearly chose a social, or field, view, which, as we shall see, is currently gaining strength.

> In defending a social theory of mind we are defending a functional, as opposed to any form of substantive or entitive, view as to its nature. And in particular, we are opposing all intracranial or intra-epidermal views as to its character and locus. For it follows from our social theory of mind that the field of mind must be co-extensive with, and include all the

31 *Ibid.*, pp. 78, 132–33. See James G. Taylor, *The Behavioral Basis of Perception* (New Haven, Conn.: Yale University Press, 1962) for a modern theory of perception as a total transaction of organism and environment that is strikingly parallel to the Dewey-Mead perspective, though applied to a different level of conscious activity. See also *Explorations in Transactional Psychology*, ed. Franklin P. Kilpatrick (New York: New York University Press, 1961) .

32 Mead, *Mind, Self, and Society*, p. 134.

33 See, for example, Karl Deutsch, *Nerves of Government* (New York: The Free Press of Glencoe, 1963) , Chap. 6; Donald M. MacKay, "Towards an Information-Flow Model of Human Behavior," *British Journal of Psychology*, 47 (1956) , 30–43; and George A. Miller *et al.*, *Plans and the Structure of Behavior* (New York: Holt, Rinehart & Winston, Inc., 1960) .

34 Cf. Abraham Edel, "The Concept of Levels in Social Theory," in *Symposium on Sociological Theory*, ed. Llewellyn Gross (New York: Harper & Row, Publisher, 1959) , Chap. 6.

components of, the field of the social process of experience and behavior, i.e., the matrix of social relations and interactions among individuals, which is presupposed by it, and out of which it arises or comes into being. If mind is socially constituted, then the field or locus of any given individual mind must extend as far as the social activity or apparatus of social relations which constitutes it extends; and hence that field cannot be bounded by the skin of the individual organism to which it belongs.[35]

By way of contrast, we note the tendency in much of sociology to insist on what is called an "analytical distinction" between "personality" (presumably intracranial), symbol systems (culture), and matrices of social relations (social systems), though the actual work of the proponents of the distinction shows it to be misleading or often untenable in practice.

Robert R. Sears is one of several psychologists who, in the last decade or so, have suggested a "dyadic" or interactional model as a basis for personality theory.[36] He argues for a combining of "individual and social behavior" (what an innocent distinction!) into a single theoretical framework, with a focus on "action" rather than on internal structures or processes. He points out, however, that this does not mean that such internal structures as needs or traits are irrelevant, since they may play an important theoretical role as intervening variables; but they may do so only if they help the theory to predict actions. Attribution of internal traits to a person is theoretically acceptable only if we add other variables that, together with the former, will "specify what kind of behavior can be expected from him under some specific circumstances."[37] And the particular circumstance of grave importance is the interpersonal milieu. Personality traits and interpersonal relationships are mutually determinative, and whether we take the group situation as antecedent and the individual as consequent, or vice versa, "the two kinds of event are so commonly mixed in causal relationships that it is impractical to conceptualize them separately." Thus, despite the fact that "psychologists think monadically," a dyadic unit—"one that describes the combined actions of two or more persons"—is essential. This is especially so when we consider that a great proportion of one's personality is formed originally in dyadic situations and can be measured only in reference to such situations.

On this basis, Sears sketches a model of the "dyadic sequence," hinging on the condition that the actions of one person "produce the environmental events for" the other, and vice versa (This is G. H. Mead's condition, also). When expectancies, or anticipatory reactions to the environmental events arise, stability in the dyadic unit has developed, and the behavior of the two persons have become truly interdependent.

---

35 *Mind, Self, and Society*, p. 223, ftn. 25.
36 Robert R. Sears, "A Theoretical Framework for Personality and Social Behavior," *American Psychologist*, 6 (1959), 476–84.
37 *Ibid.*, 478.

Thus the case is well made for the logical priority of interaction over action. We shall be concerned below to examine a little more closely such dyadic models underlying current social theory, particularly as they underpin the consensus or conflict models of society now so much in debate. But first we wish to bring out more vividly the implications of the dyadic or interactionist point of view, and in particular, the full sense in which the dyadic constitutes an emergent system with properties not found in, and not analyzable in terms of, its elements. The research study we shall review by way of illustration is not in the sphere of human symbolic behavior, but rather concerns the dyadic transactions of mating ring doves. On this level we get a clear-cut picture of the truly systemic interrelations of behavior, environmental or "situational" stimuli, and intraorganismic changes—a picture that unequivocally portrays the difference between the Dewey-Mead concept of the "act," and the mechanical S–R or "reflex arc" view of behavior.

Daniel S. Lehrman, a psychologist, undertook to study the reproductive behavior of the ring dove in order to discover the psychological and biological events giving rise to that behavior.[38] The normal cycle lasts about six or seven weeks and begins, in the laboratory setup, when a male and female with previous breeding experience are placed in a cage containing an empty nesting bowl and nesting material. Courtship occurs during the first day—with the male strutting, bowing, and cooing at the female—and culminates after a few hours with their selection of a nesting site by crouching in the bowl and uttering a distinctive "coo." For a week or so thereafter, nest building is carried on by both birds, and copulation occurs. Then the female becomes more and more attached to the nest, indicating she is about to lay her eggs. When they are laid, the male and female alternate sitting on them; in about two weeks the young are hatched and the parents begin feeding them "crop-milk" secreted at this stage of the cycle in the adult dove's crop located in the gullet. After about two weeks of such feeding, the young become able to peck from the floor and the parents begin to lose interest in them. In a short time the parents are ready to begin the cycle again.

Lehrman points out that the variations in behavior throughout the cycle are not casual, but rather are distinct phases representing "striking changes in the overall pattern of activity and in the atmosphere of the breeding cage." And these behavioral changes are not simply responses to changes in the external situation in some kind of S–R chain, but rather a complex interplay of environmenal events, behavioral interstimulations, and physiological changes (for example, hormone secretions). Thus, the birds do not build a nest simply because nesting material is there, but will do so if they have associated a while first. They will not sit on eggs simply

---

38 Daniel S. Lehrman, "The Reproductive Behavior of Ring Doves," *Scientific American,* 211 (1964) , 48–54.

if they find them there in the cage, but will do so if they were able to do some nest-building together. Development of the female's ovaries is not induced merely by seeing another bird, but by seeing or hearing it act like a male—which is a result of the male's hormones acting on his own nervous system. And the sight of the incubating female induces prolactin secretion in the male, but only if he is in the physiological state brought about by his earlier participation in nest-building. To put the matter more positively, Lehrman finds it apparent from his experiments that two major kinds of changes are induced in the birds: first, they are changed from birds "primarily interested in courtship to birds primarily interested in nest-building, and this change is brought about by stimulation arising from association with a mate." Secondly, when this latter phase has been obtained, there is a further change to birds primarily interested in incubating eggs, which is encouraged by participation in nest-building; stimuli provided by the male and aided by the presence of nest and nesting material induce secretion of gonad-stimulating hormones by the female's pituitary, and the readiness to incubate results from this process. And stimuli arising from participation in incubation, including the visual stimuli of seeing the mate sitting on the eggs, "cause the doves' pituitary glands to secrete prolactin."

The author concludes from these experiments that changes in endocrine activity are facilitated by stimuli from various aspects of the environment occurring at different stages of the cycle, and these hormone changes induce changes in behavior that are themselves sources of further stimulation. Thus we have here an example of a dyadic, "self-regulating" adaptive system complete with feedback loops—the type discussed by modern systems theorists. (See Figure 4–2)

The regulation of the cycle, Lehrman believes, depends at least

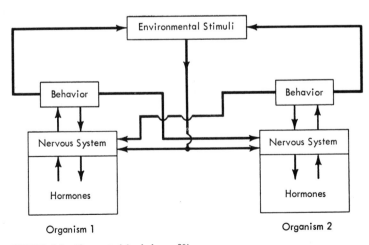

FIGURE 4-2 (*Suggested by Lehrman*[39])

partly on "a double set of reciprocal interrelations." First, there is the reciprocal relation between the effects of the hormones on behavior and the effects of the behavior and other external stimuli on the secretion of hormones. Secondly, there is "a complicated reciprocal relation between the effects of the presence and behavior of one mate on the endocrine system of the other and the effects of the presence and behavior of the second bird (including those aspects of its behavior induced by these endocrine effects) back on the endocrine system of the first." In sum, we have an emergent phenomenon: the "occurrence in each member of the pair of a cycle found in neither bird in isolation . . ." We should not have to elucidate the close structural similarity or methodological parallel to the Dewey-Mead concept of the act; nor need we remark on the important substantive differences, other than to note the vastly increased complexity and concomitant capabilities introduced into the system via the significant symbol and enlarged cortex.

We turn now to the conception of the basic social interaction process underlying the "consensus" model in current sociology. We saw, in dealing with this model, that in its view an established social system is characterized in terms of the complementary interaction of two or more individual actors in which "each conforms with the expectations of the other ('s) in such a way that alter's reactions to ego's actions are positive sanctions which serve to reinforce his given need-dispositions and thus to fulfill his given expectations."[40] This view of the whole social system stems from the underlying dyadic model that is used. One ideal type of stable dyadic relation is selected—the cooperative type; other types—competition, accommodation, conflict, and the like—are not developed, in spite of the fact that earlier sociologists dealt at great length with them. It is not that the consensus theorist does not recognize that they exist, but rather that he does not deal with them systematically, as he does with conformity, with the consequence that they find no comfortable place in his theoretical framework.

Thus, the basic dyadic interaction model in question focuses on the "complementarity of expectations" of two interacting individuals, each acting in terms of expectations about the probable reactions of the other, which thus operate as rewards or punishments for him. So far, there is no problem: we have a simplified form of Mead's scheme of symbolic interaction. But the consensus theorist concludes from this paradigm: "Hence the system of interaction may be analyzed in terms of the extent of *conformity* of ego's action with alter's expectations and vice versa."[41] Though

39 Lehrman, "The Reproductive Behavior of Ring Doves," p. 54.

40 Talcott Parsons, *The Social System* (New York: Free Press of Glencoe, 1951), pp. 204–5.

41 Talcott Parsons and Edward A. Shils, eds., *Toward a General Theory of Action* (Cambridge, Mass.: Harvard University Press, 1951), p. 15.

the possibility is left open, there is in fact no mention that such a system may *also* be analyzed in terms of a stabilized pattern of competition, accommodation, or conflict—wherein quite different kinds of complementarity of expectations obtain. *All* these models require systematic treatment, since all such patterns of interaction go to make up the "established state" of most real social systems. But Parsons makes the jump from the dyadic model to the characterization of the social system as a whole only in terms of a "mutuality of normative orientation," rather than, also, for example, in terms of a mutuality of competitive, accommodative, or conflicting expectations and orientations. The necessity of a significant degree of such conforming complementarity in any social system is, of course, not at issue here, only the wisdom of *defining* a social system in only these terms. The wonder is that the recent rash of counter proposals for a conflict model of society, or at least a more balanced answer to the "Hobbesian problem of disorder" did not come sooner. In fact, we may agree with Ralph Turner that this imbalance need not have arisen at all if closer attention had been paid to the Meadian interaction model.

> Role theory, originally depicting a tentative and creative interaction process, has come increasingly to be employed as a refinement of conformity theory. In consequence, the theory has become relatively sterile except with respect to the consequences of role conflict and other forms of deviation from the conventional model of role behavior. Role taking, however, suggests a process whereby actors attempt to organize their interaction so that the behavior of each can be viewed as the expression of a consistent orientation which takes its meaning or consistency from its character as a way of coping with one or more other actors enacting similarly consistent orientations. Conformity to perceived expectations is but one special way in which an actor's role-playing may be related to the role of relevant others.[42]

Exchange Theory

We turn now to a recent development that represents perhaps the most significant general theoretical reorientation of sociology in recent decades, variously referred to as theories of "exchange," "bargaining," "negotiation," and "games." These may be seen to represent an attempt at a rather complete overhaul of contemporary consensus theory by a return to social psychological basics and a rebuilding, from the ground up, of a balanced and dynamic conception of complex social organization. This overhaul promises to resolve at least the following central conflicts at issue today:

Sociologistic vs. psychologistic explanation. Social structure and culture *are* determinants of action and interaction, but jointly, by way of

---

42 Ralph H. Turner, "Role-Taking: Process Versus Conformity," in Rose, *Human Behavior and Social Processes*, pp. 37–38.

the situational framework of such action *and,* more directly, by way of
the interaction of mind on mind. Individuals do have an elaborate cortex
and use it, no matter how imperfectly, to make decisions effecting their
own and others' behaviors; but the human "mind" involves not only the
cortex, which can be conditioned, but also the "self," which implies much
more—being, as Mead and others have shown, an emergent social product.
Homans' recent exchange theory[43] (and to a certain extent the very
similar exposition of Thibaut and Kelley) [44] constitutes a direct and
dramatic challenge to normative determinism, though it is itself subject
to criticism as an overreaction of extreme psychologism. Put in another
way, the problem of "voluntarism" that played a part in Parsons' earlier
work is being reopened, and significantly, by Parsons' own recent brand
of exchange theory as it develops in the interchange with James S. Coleman and Raymond Bauer over the concept of "influence."[45]

   Structural vs. process model. Albion Small's prognosis of a shift from
analogical representation of social structure to real analysis of social process is only now being systematically implemented in current exchange
theory and recent extensions of social interactionism.[46] The emphasis on
process in earlier sociology, appears to be regaining ground and a major
goal is to understand institutional structure in its terms.

   Consensus and conformity vs. conflict and deviance. Exchange theory explicitly and systematically embraces the extremes, as well as the
intermediate grades of associative and dissociative interaction processes
and patterns found in most complex groups and societies. The "Hobbesian problem" of disorder and the Marxian dialectic are in the process
of rethinking and restatement.[47]

   Persistence vs. change. The newly developing model does not seem
to have any basic conceptual difficulty in embracing the processes of persistence of patterns, and their change, within the same framework. Since
social structure is not seen as particularly similar to a fixed organismic
structure embedded in homeostatic processes that are overwhelmingly
aimed at preserving that particular structure, it can now be seen more
clearly as a complex adaptive organization that may remain viable by re-
adjusting to external conditions and to its normal internal conflicts and
deviations.

---

43 George C. Homans, *Social Behavior: Its Elementary Forms* (New York: Harcourt, Brace & World, Inc., 1961).

44 John W. Thibaut and H. H. Kelley, *The Social Psychology of Groups* (New
York: John Wiley & Sons, Inc., 1959).

45 *Public Opinion Quarterly,* 27 (Spring, 1963), 37–92.

46 Most recently, in Rose, ed., *Human Behavior and Social Processes;* and Peter
M. Blau, *Exchange and Power in Social Life* (New York: John Wiley & Sons, Inc.,
1964).

47 See Blau, *Ibid.*

Categorical framework vs. deductive theory. Finally, the methodological implications of the new approaches are also profound. We only mention here the rather crucial distinction, raised also by Homans in his disengagingly direct manner, between the construction of an elaborate edifice of conceptual categories, classificatory pigeonholes, and *x*-fold tables, as against a logically systematic, empirically well-linked, deductive explanatory scheme. It is true that sociology is still very much in the categorizing phase of development, but this must not be mistaken or substituted for explanatory theory. It has been suggested that an emphasis on structure invites categorizing, whereas an emphasis on process invites causal explanation. In any case, the current theories of exchange seem capable of handling a balanced mixture of both.

Let us begin our discussion of exchange theory by way of Homans' treatment. He takes off from two postulates, drawn from elementary economics and from Skinner's brand of behavioral psychology. When pigeons, and presumably men, engage in behavior that is rewarded or "reinforced," they become conditioned to engage in that behavior at other appropriate times. Behavior is then viewed as a function of its payoff in terms of the rewards and punishments it fetches. Social behavior becomes an exchange of activity between two or more individuals that is more or less rewarding or costly. In *interaction,* each emits *activities* that entail the greatest *profits—rewards,* or units of *value,* less *costs* or punishments—measured against some standard of distributive *justice.* The rewards are not always or primarily material, but may involve psychic *profits,* activities called *"sentiments,"* of which *social approval* is especially important. The major operational variables are the *value* of a unit of activity, and the *quantity* of such units in a given period of time. The basic propositions built on this conceptual base are of the following form: "1) If in the past the occurrence of a particular stimulus-situation has been the occasion on which a man's activity has been rewarded, then the more similar the present stimulus-situation is to the past one, the more likely he is to emit the activity, or some similar activity, now." Or, "2) The more often within a given period of time a man's activity rewards the activity of another, the more often the other will emit the activity."[48]

Homans then goes on to illustrate such propositions and their corollaries with field and experimental research and much insightful discussion. What he does, in effect, is to build up (though surely not by sheer logical deduction alone) a number of the fundamental sociological constructs that underlie the analysis of complex sociocultural systems. These include: "influence," "norms," "conformity," "status," "esteem," "justice," "authority," and "equality." Thus, by way of illustration, the

---

[48] Homans, *Social Behavior,* pp. 53–54.

concept of "influence," defined as attempts to change behavior, is seen to follow from the basic propositions as follows: The more valuable to Person the activity (or sentiment) he gets or expects to get from Other, the more valuable and often the activity (or sentiment) Person gives to Other. But if the expectation goes unrealized, unrewarded by Other, Person emits the activity less and less often.

> Since the cost of Person's activity is the value of the reward that he would have gotten by another activity, forgone in emitting the first, the presence of alternative activities open to Person tends to increase the cost to him of any one of them. The less his current profit from his behavior—the less, that is the excess of value over cost—the more apt he is to change his behavior; and he changes it so as to increase his profit.[49]

Likewise with "esteem," "status," "justice," and "authority."

> We define *esteem* as follows: the greater the total reward in expressed social approval a man receives from other members of his group, the higher is the esteem in which they hold him . . . Social approval is an actual reward, but any activity (or sentiment) may be a stimulus as well as a reward, and we shall use *status* to refer to the stimuli a man presents to other men (and to himself) . . . what men perceive about one of their fellows . . .[50]
>
> Fair exchange, or distributive justice in the relations among men, is realized when the profit, or reward less cost, of each man is directly proportional to his investments: such things as age, sex, seniority, or acquired skill. As a practical matter, distributive justice is realized when each of the various features of his investments and his activities, put into rank-order in comparison with those of other men, fall in the same place in all the different rank-orders . . .[51]
>
> We say that a man who regularly influences more members than another does holds higher authority than the other; and the man who holds highest authority we call the leader of the group. A man earns authority by acquiring esteem, and he acquires esteem by rewarding others . . . Accordingly they come to recognize him as a man compliance with whose instructions is apt to be rewarding, and they get to be all the more prepared to comply with his instructions on some new occasion.[52]

This should suffice to give the flavor of Homans' exchange theory. Let us note that, on the basis of this apparently successful attempt, Homans went on, in later writings, to attempt to stand Durkheim on his head, so to speak: contrary to Durkheim, sociology *is* a corollary of psychology, and not Mead's behavioral psychology either, but Skinner's.[53] For these psy-

---

49 *Ibid.*, pp. 110–11.

50 *Ibid.*, p. 149.

51 *Ibid.*, p. 264.

52 *Ibid.*, p. 314. For a critique of Homans' use of Skinner's framework see Morton Deutsch, "Homans in the Skinner Box," *Sociological Inquiry*, 34 (1964), 156–65.

53 George C. Homans, "Bringing Men Back In," *American Sociological Review*, 29 (1964), 809–18.

chological propositions are *more general,* he argues, than those of functional theory, and if we turn from final causes to efficient ones, such functional theory can be reduced to individual psychology. His more general
psychological theory is to be built on propositions applying to all "men as
men," or "the behavior of men as members of a species."[54] And since this
is the only main type of alternative to what we agree is a defective general
structural-functional theory, we must deny that sociology "possesses any
theory distinctively its own."[55]

There is little doubt that such a position will provoke many counter-
attacks, and a good number of these will be made in an atmosphere of
ambivalence, if not cognitive dissonance, since so much of what Homans
has to say in this work is well-said good sense and of great value to the
development of sociological theory. We confine our own critical remarks
to a few brief points that bear directly on our own present thesis.

What Homans means in arguing for a "reduction" of sociological
to psychological theory is not that *all* sociological propositions contain
only psychological terms, but that *some* of them contain *some* such concepts. His general theory is "psychological" only "in the sense that the deductive systems by which we explain social behavior would, if completed,
contain among their highest-order propositions one or more of those
I call psychological."[56] He believes that structural explanations containing, for example, propositions about the relations between institutions
are not general explanations in sociology because "some, though certainly
not all, of the structural propositions can themselves be explained psychologically."[57] If Homans argues for no more than this, however, he really
has no grounds left for denying that sociology "possesses any theory distinctively its own." Let us grant that, depending on the explanatory goal
of the scientist, a sociological theory may contain few or many psychological concepts: if he is attempting to explain the specific occurrence, for
example, of suicide or delinquency in a particular person, many psychological variables might be needed if only as "intervening" variables;[58]
but if *rates* are at issue, he may not feel the need of any psychological
variables at all *for his particular purposes.* At what level one is willing to accept an explanation as "satisfactory" is not a scientifically
decidable question. And Homans is not questioning the validity of

---

[54] George C. Homans, "Contemporary Theory in Sociology," in *Handbook of Modern Sociology,* ed. Robert E. L. Faris (Chicago: Rand McNally & Co., 1964), p. 967.

[55] *Ibid.,* p. 970.

[56] *Ibid.,* p. 968.

[57] *Ibid.,* p. 969.

[58] Cf. Alex Inkeles, "Sociology and Psychology," in *Psychology: A Study of a Science,* 6, ed. Sigmund Koch (New York: McGraw-Hill Book Company, 1963), 317–87.

sociological level theory as such. In sum, if *any* particular science possesses a theory distinctively its own, then it cannot be denied any of those on a different level of reality. The only logical alternative would be to insist on a reduction all the way down to physics.

Homans believes that his psychological theory is "wholly compatible with the doctrine that human behavior is and has always been social," and simply assumes that the general propositions of psychology, for instance the "law of effect," "do not change when the source of reward for an action changes from being, say, the physical environment to being another human."[59] Now, we can all agree that the laws of psychology, and those of physics for that matter, do not cease to operate for social behavior. But this is not to say that they are *sufficient* for a theory of social behavior. Homans states that "to call an explanation psychological does not entail the adoption of any particular one of the many systems of psychological theory."[60] However, there is a wealth of difference between the laws of effect or of "operant conditioning," on the one hand, and, for example, Mead's social behavioristic theory of the human mind, self, and society, on the other. Homans suggests that a list of essential psychological propositions for social behavior would include those concerning "how values themselves are acquired," "how men perceive the circumstances in which they act," and the "kinds of circumstances that are apt to release emotional behavior."[61] But, we must argue, these cannot be derived, at least at present, from Skinner's laws of "operant conditioning," whereas our chances are much better if we start from Mead's theory. But Mead's theory does not meet Homans' requirements for psychological reductionism. For the group and its characteristics must be taken as logically and empirically prior to, or at least simultaneous with, the acquisition of social values, perceptual tendencies, and emotional reactions. No appeal to the common nature of "men as men" is sufficient to derive Homans' list of essential psychological propositions.

The psychologist Richard Littman has argued that psychology is the "socially indifferent science,"[62] concerned only with the mechanisms and processes of the individual and his nervous system, regardless of the nature or content of the external events that they do, of course, interact with. These latter events are assumed, but play no systematic part in psychological theory. The latter, presumably, aims at laws by which internal psychological events are related to broad classes of external events taken as separate, unrelated categories: visual or tactile stimuli, goal-blockages,

59 Homans, "Contemporary Theory in Sociology," in *Handbook of Modern Sociology*, pp. 969–70.

60 *Ibid.*, p. 967.

61 *Ibid.*

62 Richard Littman, "Psychology: The Socially Indifferent Science," *American Psychologist*, 16 (1961) , 232–36.

learning of skill, problem solving under varied conditions, and the like. However, when we leave the laboratory, where alone such isolated relationships can be studied, and try to understand an individual's behavior, we find that we must organize and systematize the external events that do interact with, and have interacted with, the individual. Only then can the psychological laws predict, out of the welter of specifiable combinations of external events, the conditions that may be relevant to behavior. In other words, the external classes of events must be *brought into the system* along with the "purely individual" events. Put in another way, a viable theory must incorporate not only the separate laboratory laws, but the "composition effects"—the complex interactions of a number of internal processes interdependent with a complex of interrelated external events, both together making up a systemic field. If psychology is socially indifferent, then it is *environmentally* indifferent in general—a view which, when so stated, brings us face to face with grave difficulties. Even our discussion of ring-dove behavior makes clear the sense in which the nature of pigeons as pigeons and the laboratory laws of operant conditioning are insufficient for a theory of uncontrived social behavior, and its emergent features.

Homans recognizes the principle of emergence but cannot take seriously its full implications:

> The composition effects, the ways in which the propositions work out to produce a concrete result, are much more complicated when the actions of each of two or more men reward the actions of the others, but the propositions themselves do not change. When we say that the whole of social life is more than the sum of its parts, the actions of individuals, all we are referring to is the complexity of the composition effects.[63]

But it is just these "composition effects," and only these, that make all the difference there is to be made between levels of reality. And it is not that some propositions *change* because of this difference, but that some have to be *added. All* the difference there is between a behaving human individual and a month-old corpse is the complexity and dynamics of the "composition effects." Let us simply note that, if we look at the various levels of science—atomic physics, chemistry, physiology, psychology, sociology—we can say that each is a science of the "composition effects" of the elements of the next lower level interacting among themselves and with their "environment." Thus, the interaction of a number of atoms in an environment of a certain pressure and temperature might organize them to the "chemical" level; a number of molecules in a particular biological environment might organize to the "physiological" level; a number of physiological (for example, neural) processes interacting in an external

---

[63] "Contemporary Theory in Sociology," in *Handbook of Modern Sociology*, p. 970.

environment might organize into "psychological" events; and a number of psyches interacting in a social environment might organize to the "sociocultural," or group, level. Before the systems perspective developed, we might have been willing to argue that, in principle, each science might eventually be reduced to the next lowest. Now, however, this seems rather meaningless, since to reduce it is to lose the composition, or the systemic organizational effects we are after.

When we look closely at Homans' development of exchange theory we see that, quite early in the game, he leaves far behind the kinds of laws that explain pigeon behavior. Otherwise he could never have arrived at such concepts as social approval, norms of justice, esteem, and so forth. He agrees that pigeons do not use symbols and men do, but he seems not to want to go the rest of the way to agree that men, and not pigeons, have selves and self-awareness, and will thereby suffer for long periods all kinds of deprivation, negative reinforcements, and even death for mere symbols and self-esteem. Perhaps we can discuss such behavior in terms of "conditioning" and profit-seeking. We cannot object to the usefulness of such concepts *per se,* under certain conditions. But to make them applicable to all and any kind of behavior whatsoever, no matter how "altruistic" or "egoistic," is to engage in tautology or truism. This is certainly one main reason why eighteenth century egoistic hedonism and its logical derivative, Bentham's Utilitarianism, have not survived rigorous analysis.[64] Homans' refurbishing of Bentham's famous "felicific calculus" cannot quite escape its errors. Just as the dissatisfied eighteenth century social thinker might have turned for balance to Hume's theory of sympathy and Adam Smith's *Theory of Moral Sentiments* (the latter being mainly responsible, we recall, for the pioneer American sociologist Franklin Giddings' famous "consciousness of kind") , the contemporary disaffected can turn to Mead's social interactionism and its solid theoretical underpinnings.[65]

When we look at the most recent exchange theories, particularly those of Peter Blau, James S. Coleman, and some current excursions of Talcott Parsons,[66] Homans' view appears as a glaring contrast—in spite of some close similarities. In the newer work, we find explicit notions of investment of *self* in others, exchanges of *self-identities, self*-rewards (for example, self-respect, enhancement of self) based on the concepts of social approval, interpersonal attraction, social influence, and the like, which

---

[64] For a recent pertinent discussion see John Plamenatz, *Man and Society,* 2 (New York: McGraw-Hill Book Company, 1963) , 1–15.

[65] Cf. Howard Becker and Harry E. Barnes, *Social Thought from Lore to Science,* 2 (New York: Dover Publications, Inc., 1961) , 529–38.

[66] Blau, *Exchange and Power in Social Life*; James S. Coleman, "Comment on 'On the Concept of Influence,' " *Public Opinion Quarterly,* 27 (1963) , 63–82; Talcott Parsons, "On the Concept of Influence," *Public Opinion Quarterly,* 27 (1963) , 37–62.

also underlie Homans' scheme. Individuals do not assess rewards and costs, and make decisions or choices, as independent monads in a Hobbesian situation, but rather as "selves" in an interpersonal matrix or field of at least partly matched or common symbols and intimate interchanges of information—making for a more than superficial bonding of the elements (originally only biological organisms) into social minds, personalities, and groups sharing a common fate. Here the close relation with G. H. Mead's behaviorism rather than with Skinner's variety is obvious. And the convergence becomes even more obvious when we consider current interactionist discussions of social organization as a transactional process of bargaining and negotiation. We shall discuss all of these at greater length in the next chapter.

Several other models of the basic interaction process must now be examined particularly with an eye to the different facets that are emphasized, and to the manner in which they tend to drive toward the modern systems conception.

Newcomb's A–B–X Model

In the last few decades, there have been a substantial number of other attempts to develop a fairly precise field theory or interpersonal model of behavior. These include Kurt Lewin's topological model, Walter Coutu's "tinsit" (tendency in situation) theory, Leonard S. Cottrell's "situational field" model, and Theodore Newcomb's *A–B–X* model.[67] Although all of these are well worth a closer look, we shall examine the Newcomb model particularly for its contrasting emphases as compared to other models. Whereas exchange theory focuses on the economic metaphor, game theory uses the gambling or game metaphor and "dramaturgical" models use the role-playing metaphor, Newcomb's *A–B–X* model, like Mead's, focuses on social interaction specifically as a process of communicative acts.

Because Newcomb defines interaction or exchange in terms of communicative acts, we are led to examine the central social-psychological mechanisms underlying the organization of behavior, particularly those involving the cognitive and affective *selection processes* made possible only by symbolic communication. We are led to study how communicative relations with others works by way of selective information exchange to build up a common definition of environmental objects, including their

67 Kurt Lewin, *Field Theory in Social Science* (New York: Harper and Row, Publishers, 1951) ; Leonard S. Cottrell, "The Analysis of Situational Fields in Social Psychology," *American Sociological Review,* 7 (1942) , 370–82; Walter Coutu, *Emergent Human Nature* (New York: Alfred A. Knopf, Inc., 1949) ; Theodore M. Newcomb, "An Approach to the Study of Communicative Acts," *Psychological Review,* 60 (1953), 393–404.

reward value. This feature of the model hinges, in turn, on the more equal weight given to the three corners of the triangular transaction involving Person *A*, Person *B*, and Object *X*. Whereas S–R exchange theory tends to assume one of these corners, and to bypass the problem of meaning (for example, assuming the value to *A* or *B* of object *X* as a given medium of exchange), the *A–B–X* model leads us to ask how Object *X* (for example, a Cadillac car, a particular woman, a certain style of music, or a particular social response) comes to be socially discriminated, defined, and validated and thus something to be symbolically oriented toward or to which to respond.

Thus, Newcomb's starting assumption is that "communication among humans performs the essential function of enabling two or more individuals to maintain simultaneous orientation toward one another as communicators *and* toward objects of communication."[68] A communicative act is seen as a "transmission of information, consisting of discriminative stimuli, from a source to a recipient."[69] In its simplest form, Person *A* transmits information to Person *B* about something *X*. A central concept is that of *co-orientation*, the simultaneous orientation (both cognitive and cathectic) of *A* toward *B* and toward *X* in an interdependent manner. Thus, the *A–B–X* transaction is to be regarded as a *system*, with certain definable relationships between each of the elements, and all viewed as interdependent. A given state of the system is assumed to exist when any such *A–B–X* communicative act occurs, and the act changes the system state (if only by reinforcing it).

The basic schematic is given in Figure 4–3. Four orientations are possible, and to be noted is the distinctive dynamic feature of the *A–B* interrelation as compared to the person-to-object relation: in the *A–B* relationship there is a generative reciprocal process, or feedback, that lies at the heart of human behavior.

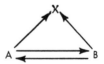

FIGURE 4-3   A-B-X System (After Newcomb)

Thus, the assumption is made that "co-orientation" is essential to human life in view of the complementary facts that person-to-person orientations are virtually never made and sustained in an environmental vacuum, and that person-to-object orientations are seldom, if ever, made in a social vacuum of communicating others. *A–B* relations are almost always con-

68 Newcomb, "An Approach," 393.
69 *Ibid.*

tingent on the development of common interests in the environment, and
A–X orientations come to be defined and confirmed in a social reality of
communicating others. Hence, "To the degree that A's orientation either
toward X or toward B is contingent upon B's orientation toward X, A is
motivated to influence and/or to inform himself about B's orientation
toward X."[70] Communication is the most common and effective means of
doing so, and therefore must play a central role in any interaction model
in addition to any consideration of the rewards and punishments that
accrue in the process.

On the basis of this model, and the additional assumption that there
are persistent forces or "strains" on the A–B–X system toward preferred
states of "equilibrium," further postulates and propositions are derived
concerning the conditions of "symmetry" of orientations of A and B
(either sameness or complementarity of orientations of A and B toward
X). It is argued that advantages are seen to accrue from such symmetry
—for example, the predictability of others' behavior and validation of
one's own orientation—such that communicative acts leading to symmetry
are likely to be rewarded, thus acquiring secondary reward value. The
basic postulate, then, is: "The stronger the forces toward A's co-orientation in respect to B and X, 1) the greater A's strain toward symmetry with
B in respect to X; and 2) the greater the likelihood of increased symmetry as a consequence of one or more communicative acts."[71] We shall
not go into the several testable propositions and hypotheses that Newcomb derives, but simply reiterate the point that the explicit introduction of the concept of symbolic communication into our model or deductive system, and hence the introduction of the apparatus of symbolic
interactionist theory, permits us to get at finer and subtler details of social
behavior and social organization than does any scheme utilizing only fre-
quencies, rewards, and conditioning. One example will suffice: Under
certain situational conditions, one of the parties of an A–B–X system may
perceive asymmetry of orientation toward X, such that any of a number
of dynamic changes in the system may occur. Thus, A is confronted with
a problem:

> . . . which he can attempt to solve behaviorally (i.e., by communicative
> acts) and/or cognitively (i.e., by changing either his own orientations or
> his perception of B's orientations) . . . If A is free either to continue or
> not to continue his association with B, one or the other of two eventual
> outcomes is likely: (a) he achieves an equilibrium characterized by rela-
> tively great attraction toward B and by relatively high perceived symmetry,
> and the association is continued; or (b) he achieves an equilibrium charac-
> terized by relatively little attraction toward B and by relatively low per-
> ceived symmetry, and the association is discontinued.[72]

---

70 *Ibid.*, 395.

71 *Ibid.*, 396.

72 *Ibid.*, 401.

However, when *A* is constrained to continue the association, this constraint also dictates the requirements for co-orientation, which are now independent of attraction. "The empirical data suggest that the degree to which attraction is independent of symmetry varies with the degree of *perceived* (rather than the degree of objectively observed) constraint."[73]

Secord and Backman's Interpersonal Theory of Personality

Dyadic models of the basic interaction process have been utilized as a foundation for the sociological study of social organization, for the social psychological study of social behavior, and for the study of personality. Secord and Backman focus on personality, taking what many see as a radical position on the still thorny issue that G. H. Mead opened up some decades ago—namely, the *locus* of the personality. Thus, contrary to the view that personality is not to be conceived as intracranial, Gordon Allport believes that most Western theorists—including himself—adhere to the "integumented view" (though he recognizes that this may well represent a deep-rooted Western bias) .[74] His conservative position, he states, is justified on two grounds:

> . . . (a) there is a persistent though changing person-system in time, clearly delimited by birth and death; (b) we are immediately aware of the functioning of this system; our knowledge of it, though imperfect, is direct, whereas our knowledge of all other outside systems, including social systems, is deflected and often distorted by their necessary incorporation into our own apperceptions.[75]

He grants that the personality theorist must be well versed in all the social situational contexts the individual's behavior may fit but, at the same time:

> . . . he should not lose sight—as some theorists do—of the fact that there is an internal and subjective patterning of all these contextual acts. A traveler who moves from culture to culture, from situation to situation, is none the less a single person; and within him one will find the nexus, the patterning, of the diverse experiences and memberships that constitute his personality.[76]

We believe there are great difficulties in this argument. We are not too sure whether the "clear delimitation," by birth and death or by way

---

73 *Ibid.* Newcomb has gone on from these beginnings to develop and utilize this model in illuminating detail. See "The Prediction of Interpersonal Attraction," *American Psychologist*, 11 (1956) , 575–86; and *The Acquaintance Process* (New York: Holt, Rinehart, & Winston, Inc., 1961) .

74 Gordon W. Allport, "The Open System in Personality Theory," *Journal of Abnormal and Social Psychology*, 61 (1960) , 301–311.

75 *Ibid.*, 308.

76 *Ibid.*

of the single traveler, does not beg the question by confusing the skin-bound organism and the person-system; and we are more sure that the rest of the statement opens up a Pandora's box of rather well-worn philosophical issues that we shall close without further ado. The question still remains whether the "internal and subjective patterning" (which must be physiological) can be completely equated with personality (which is behavioral).

J. Milton Yinger has recently pointed out, in a well-argued paper, that the radical field view of personality does not eliminate or minimize the principle of continuity of personality.[77] If we recognize that the various facets of the person-system are to be interpreted as a readiness to act, rather than as behavior, there is no conflict. There is clearly much continuity in a complex of tendencies to act: but *behavior* is a function of the tendency-system and situational field, not of the tendency-system alone. In a word, it cannot be supposed that ready-made behavior is carried around in the head. Yinger's position implies that the extent of personality continuity is an empirical question, and that such continuity can be expected to vary with individuals and with learning or socializing conditions. Furthermore, Yinger points out, personality is not so homogeneous that it continues as a unitary whole:

> Some aspects of personality are more malleable than others; judgments may change more readily than opinions, opinions more readily that attitudes, attitudes than values, and values than self-image—to put the issue in overly simple terms. Personality changes are least likely to occur when the group structures with which the individual is involved remain stable.[78]

This last point brings us to the dyadic model we wish to look at, that of Paul F. Secord and Carl W. Backman.[79] Attacking the assumption that behavioral stability is a function only, or primarily, of an assumed stability of personality structure, they build a truly interpersonal model which places the locus of behavioral stability and change squarely in the interaction process rather than in either the individual or the normative culture. The core of the model is the set of functional relationships between three components making up an interpersonal matrix: 1) an aspect of the self-concept of a person S; 2) his interpretation of those elements of his behavior related to that aspect; and 3) his perception of related aspects of the other person O with whom he is interacting. The behavior of any person is seen in terms of his participation in a number of such shifting matrices over varying periods of time. The dynamic component

---

77 J. Milton Yinger, "Research Implications of a Field View of Personality," *American Journal of Sociology,* 68 (1963), 580–92.

78 *Ibid.,* 589.

79 Paul F. Secord and Carl W. Backman, "Personality Theory and the Problem of Stability and Change in Individual Behavior: An Interpersonal Approach," *Psychological Review,* 68 (1961), 21–33.

of the model is provided by the assumption that a person strives to shape the interaction process so as to achieve "congruency" among the components of the matrix, "congruency" being seen as a cognitive phenomenon involving the perceptual experience of the individuals. A state of complete congruency among the components is defined "when the behaviors of S and O imply definitions of self congruent with relevant aspects of the self-concept."[80]

Thus, there are important similarities and differences between the emphases of this model and those of Newcomb's. First, we note the explicit incorporation of the self or self-concept into the model, and even more important, the inclusion of Mead's central dynamic mechanism of "reflexivity" based on one's taking oneself as object and thereby being able to interpret one's own behavior from that perspective. The explicit inclusion of this feature in Newcomb's A–B–X model would complicate but enrich the structure and dynamics of that system, though a close look at Newcomb's use of the model shows that "reflexivity" is implicit and indeed essential to his analysis. Secondly, the Secord and Backman model does not, on the other hand, explicitly incorporate environmental objects and actors' orientations to them; furthermore, it assumes the selective function of communication *per se*. The A–B–X model, by explicitly including environmental objects—material objects and interests—makes room for consideration of the important role of nonnormative elements, or the *"material base"* of social action, thus breaking down the presumption that social patterns are arbitrary self–other products generated in an environment devoid of material interests.[81] The concept of "cognitive congruency" used in both these models (and in others) can be seen, however, as a subjectivistic restatement of the pragmatist's view that men have cortexes and use them to solve problems—social, psychological, and material—which are subjectively felt as "incongruencies" or "dissonances." These "problems" involve the orientations of the individual toward himself, toward others, and toward environmental objects. An important contribution of the recent work on cognitive congruence or dissonance is the notion that the cognitive element, acting either independently or in very close relation to "nonrational" elements, is itself a source of tension or strain that affects behavior. Simplistic notions of "rationality" and "nonrationality" are thus being fruitfully challenged.

On the basis of their model, Secord and Backman advance a view of the dynamics of personality and behavioral stability and change. A number of their principles concern the processes of achieving and maintain-

---

80 *Ibid.*, 23.

81 Cf. David Lockwood, "Some Remarks on 'The Social System'," *British Journal of Sociology*, 7 (1956) , 134–46; Reinhard Bendix, *Max Weber: An Intellectual Portrait* (New York: Doubleday & Company, Inc., 1962) , especially pp. 41–48 and Chap. 15; and, of course, Karl Marx's discussions of the problem.

ing "congruent" states in the individual. Several of these are similar to those derived from quite different models, for example, exchange theory. Thus: 1) a person tends to repeat those interpersonal encounters that were previously congruent; 2) a person involved in a non-congruent matrix will tend to modify it in a more congruent direction; 3) two persons in "congruent" interaction with one another tend to develop mutual affect and to perpetuate the interaction. If we substitute "rewarding" for "congruent," we have Homans' typical propositions of exchange, and the question becomes one of the theoretical advantages of one of these concepts over the other. Our discussion suggests that the concept of reward easily leads one to rest on a simple "law of effect" and thus to bypass the essential explanatory richness of the self–other communicative dynamics to which the concept of "congruency" leads.

In dealing with the problem of the stability of interpersonal relations, Secord and Backman suggest a number of processes that tend to counter the ever-present tendencies toward change arising from the normal unfolding of role careers, fortuitous shifts of situation, or social pressures. Some of these stabilizing processes operate through some transformation of O, the other, in the interpersonal matrix: by, for example, selective interaction with others, selective evaluation of others, selective comparison with aspects of others, or misperception of others. Other stabilizing processes operate in terms of a transformation of S, the person's self, or behavior, by selective presentation of self to match one's perception of others, or misinterpretation of one's own behavior to achieve "congruency." We direct attention here, if such is needed, to the extent to which these conceptions implicitly lean on the concept of the "selective function" of communication and meaning discussed earlier and which is, to some extent, incorporated in Newcomb's model.

Finally, the Secord and Backman model explains change in self or personality in terms of a three-step process: 1) the existence of an "incongruency" in the interpersonal matrix; 2) the formation of a new "congruent" matrix involving a changed component of self; and 3) the adjustment of other relevant social relations affected by the changes. Thus, the same set of interpersonal processes involved in stabilizing an interpersonal matrix is involved in the explanation of change in one's self. This must be so, if the locus of personality is in the interpersonal process. Personality remains stable only when it is consistent with an ongoing "congruent" process of interaction, it is argued, and the fact that most individuals maintain a stable personality "is a function of the fact that the behavior of others toward the individuals in question is normally overwhelmingly consistent with such maintenance."[82] In sum, what a person normally strives to maintain is not some set of traits or habits, but "con-

---

82 Secord and Backman, "Personality Theory," p. 29.

gruent" interpersonal matrices. Under conditions of a marked shift in such matrices, as when a person moves from one social class to a very different one, intrapersonal structure and behavior may be expected to change significantly. If such a conception seems too radical, it can be tempered by considerations such as Yinger's, namely, that the various levels of functioning of personality manifest differential degrees of resistance to change. The general idea, however, appears to be in accord both with sound theory and substantial data, and must await further empirical testing before it can be dismissed. For the present, purposes we view it as an important contribution toward the systematization of social interactionist theory.[83]

Ackoff's Behavioral Theory of Communication

Let us, finally, turn to one more explicit model—Russell Ackoff's behavioral theory of communication.[84] While it is not specifically a model of social interaction *per se,* it is of particular interest as a concise articulation of many of the factors going into the other models we have discussed, with special attention to the general mechanisms whereby communication mediates "the effect of one mind on another." Ackoff attempts to operationalize this notion by way of a formal definition of the behavioral elements in an individual's "purposive state." Without attempting to adhere to his degree of formality, we can state these behavioral elements to include: 1) the existence of at least two alternative *courses of action* available to the individual in his given environment; 2) at least two of the objectively available courses of action are subjectively *potential choices* of the individual (to which probabilities are theoretically assignable); 3) these potential courses of action have *some effectiveness* ("efficiency") in bringing about an *outcome or objective* of the individual (also definable in terms of probabilities; and 4) the outcome has some *value* to the individual (negative or positive). Ackoff then defines the nature of communication. A *message* is defined as a set of "signs" (or symbols) that signify something to somebody, i.e., that *produce responses* to things other than themselves. *Communication* exists between *A* and *B* if *B* responds to a set of symbols selected by *A,* who is in a "purposive state." The definition is intended to imply that *A* may communicate to himself; and that, as sender, he may not intend or desire to communicate to a receiver in order to do so in fact. (It is to be noted that these definitions are very close to those of MacKay and others discussed earlier.)

---

[83] Especially pertinent here, also, is Anselm Strauss, *Mirrors and Masks* (New York: Free Press of Glencoe, Inc., 1959) .

[84] Russell L. Ackoff, "Towards a Behavioral Theory of Communication," *Management Science,* 4 (1957–1958) , 218–34. Also see Donald M. MacKay, "Towards an Information-Flow Model of Human Behavior," *British Journal of Psychology,* 47 (1956) , 30–43; and "Operational Aspects of Some Fundamental Concepts of Human Communication," *Synthese,* 9 (1954) , 182–98.

All these definitions are then organized into a conceptualization of the communicative act. In general, the receipt of a communication involves a change in some aspect of the receiver's "purposive state." The change (s) may be in one or more of the following: 1) the probabilities of choice associated with the possible courses of action; 2) the efficiencies of the courses of action for the outcome (s) or objective (s) ; 3) the value (s) of the outcome (s) ; or 4) new courses of action that may become possible for the individual. On this basis, Ackoff analyzes communication into three components: the transmission of *information,* of *instruction,* and of *motivation.* Thus, a communication or message which changes the number of, or the probabilities of choice of, potential courses of action thereby *informs;* one which changes the efficiencies of the choices relative to desired outcomes thereby *instructs;* and one that changes the values of outcome (s) and thereby the basis for selecting among them, thereby *motivates.*

Ackoff goes on to suggest measures of these in terms of information theory, which we shall not discuss here. Of particular interest to us is the extent to which he has defined, in behavioral terms, the *selective function* of communication and tied it to the notions of purpose, value, perception of alternative actions, choice or decision making, and the influence of another. What is brought out once again is the dynamic, systemic nature of communicative interaction, and the nature of the mechanisms by which the system's changes of state are specifiable functions of the selective nature of information. And the inherently probabilistic nature of the model provides an especially suggestive starting point for those who would follow up Max Weber's insight that social relationships can be given meaning only in terms of the *probability* that meaningfully oriented social action of a particular kind will take place.

Game Theory

Before concluding this section, some mention must be made of "game theory" as an approach that would seem to bear closely on the kinds of models we have been discussing. In a restricted sense, game theory can be seen as an attempt to develop models of the basic interaction process, an attempt that is of particular interest to us because it focuses on the neglected end of the social relations continuum, namely, conflict. But game theory, strictly speaking, is a branch of mathematics that deals only with the logical structure of games or conflict situations in which certain parameters can be clearly defined and quantified. As Anatol Rapoport has recently argued,[85] game theory cannot be construed as a descriptive theory —a branch of behavioral science, nor is it more than partially a norma-

---

[85] Anatol Rapoport, "Game Theory and Human Conflict," in *The Nature of Human Conflict,* ed. Elton B. McNeil (Englewood Cliffs, N.J.: Prentice-Hall, Inc. 1965) , Chap. 10.

tive theory of rational conflict. Rather, it abstracts the structure of events entirely from their content and describes this structure in mathematical terms. The success of game theory as a normative theory rests mainly on its success in specifying and providing solutions to the "two-person, zero-sum" game. But the range of application of this model is restricted to situations where: 1) two parties are in conflict over completely opposed interests, such that any coincidence of interests and, hence, coalitions are excluded; 2) the rationality of the players can be assumed and unambiguously defined; and 3) the situation is indeed a "game," defined such that *a*) two or more "players" *b*) have a set of choices of "strategies," *c*) with knowledge of all possible outcomes of all possible combinations of strategy choices and *d*) a preference among the outcomes that can be ordered on an interval scale. We may note, on the one hand, the fairly close correspondence between these and Ackoff's concepts, or those of exchange theory, but the static nature of the game model, on the other hand, is clearly revealed in such a comparison. The dynamics of communication among the "players"—which ties the "game" into a system of interdependent and shifting variables and gives it the real quality of social behavior—is absent.

As game theory extends beyond the two-person, "zero-sum" model to involve questions of coalition formation, communication among players, cooperation as well as conflict, and such concepts as bargaining, mutual trust, and fair collective payoffs, we leave the realm where the mathematics are clean, solutions are unique, and rationality is clearly definable. For the game theorist starts his work only after the rules of the game, and the utilities or value hierarchies defining the payoffs, have been specified. The genesis of the conflict, its social-psychological features, and its sociocultural setting are beyond the scope of analysis. It is easy to accept Rapoport's suggestion that the value of game theory to behavioral science has been just its weaknesses: in uncovering the basic structure of conflict situations, it has forced attention to the unspecified assumptions and "givens" of the model—the social psychology, the problem of communication, and the question of values.

Such considerations as these have no doubt contributed to the enthusiastic welcome accorded Thomas C. Schelling's study of the strategy of conflict—a study often couched in game-theoretic terms, but which, in fact, as Jessie Bernard recently suggested, is essentially an interactionist social psychology.[86] Rather than focusing solely on the logical structure of the game, Schelling analyzes the "strategy" of conflict—focusing on the *interdependence* of the adversaries' decisions or choices of action, and thus getting at the social-psychological content of the conflict process. Thus, *A*'s

---

[86] Thomas C. Schelling, *The Strategy of Conflict* (Cambridge, Mass.: Harvard University Press, 1960); Jessie Bernard, "Some Current Conceptualizations in the Field of Conflict," *American Journal of Sociology*, 70 (1965), 442–54.

best course of action depends on his *expectations* of *B*'s behavior, and on *A*'s ability to *influence B*'s choice of actions by influencing *B*'s expectations as to how *A* will act or react. Clearly, this brings us back to the same problematics found in the other models of interaction, with the dynamics of intercommunication at the center of things. Part of the analysis is, in fact, a theory of bargaining or exchange that recognizes the intricate mixture of common and conflicting interests in the great bulk of social behavior, whether it is personal friendship or political cold war. Perhaps one of the more important of the many insights in Schelling's study is this suggestion that the theory of strategy does not discriminate conflict from common interest or cooperation; thus, it can embrace the gamut of normal social relations. The theory degenerates, he argues, at the two extremes—complete absence of common interests or possible accommodations, and no conflict at all and no problem of identifying and reaching common goals.

One other important contribution we should mention here is Schelling's discussion of the difficult concept of "rationality," a concept that is problematic not only in advanced game theory, but in most other behavioral theories.[87] Schelling accepts the assumption of rationality as a first approximation to theory—as a bench mark against which to assess alternative courses of behavior. But he points out that such a usage can elucidate the *multidimensional* nature of "irrationality" (and hence of "rationality"). Thus, irrationality may mean a disorderly or inconsistent value or utility scale, or a faulty calculation of alternatives or of outcomes, or an inability to receive messages or to communicate efficiently, or the presence of random influences in decision making or of "noise" in the transmission of information. Or it may simply reflect the collective nature of the decision-making process among varying individuals and subgroups, their organizations, values, and communication systems. In terms of a system model, if rationality is a characteristic of behavior, and behavior is an emergent function of a number of components in a system, then rationality or irrationality can be a function of any one or more of these components: calculation of alternatives and outcomes; preference scales; communication links and symbolic systems; conceptions of self and of others; and the like. This is the sort of thing implied in Peter Blau's pregnant statement that "To administer a social organization according to purely technical criteria of rationality is irrational, because it ignores the nonrational aspects of social conduct."[88]

By way of recapitulation, the following basic features of the interaction process may be reemphasized:

---

87 See also the relevant discussion by Herbert A. Simon, "Economics and Psychology," in *Psychology: Study of a Science*, 6, ed. Sigmund Koch (New York: McGraw-Hill Book Company, 1959), especially pp. 709–18.

88 Peter M. Blau, *Bureaucracy in Modern Society* (New York: Random House, Inc., 1956), p. 58.

1. The basic interaction model should include at least the following components: a. the biological individual, his inherent impulses to action, and his self-conception and self-consciousness; b. environmental objects of potential relevance or interest to him; and c. another individual similarly endowed. These components are intimately linked together by d. communication and information interchanges to constitute a complex adaptive system—not simply an equilibrium or homeostatic system—operating as an ongoing process or transaction which is continuously generating, maintaining, or altering meanings and patterns of behavior to which we attach various labels (for example, cooperation, conflict, and competition) .

2. Orientation to environmental objects is contingent on and contributes to the individual's cortical "mapping" of the environment into an ensemble of alternative "readinesses-to-act"—a process referred to as learning. But such orientation seldom takes place in a social vacuum.

3. Orientation to other individuals (and groups) is contingent on and contributes to, a similar mapping of such others and their gestures and characteristic actions, and consequently a mapping of one's own feelings and action, and one's self, into an ensemble of alternative attitudes and sentiments—a process referred to as socialization, which though involving learning, depends on a higher level of dynamics sufficient to produce a qualitative difference between animal and human behavior. These differences involve self-consciousness, symbolic representation and communication, and past and future orientation.

4. This system of components is mediated in terms of a more or less common ensemble of symbols at least partly mapped against the individuals' potential alternatives of action, such that communication acts as a selective device calling forth cognition, emotion, value, and thus behavioral responses which may relate to environmental objects, to one self, or to others or any combination. Symbolic communication occurs within any one individual's mental processes as well as between individuals. The selective function of communication is demonstrated in the important concepts of selective perception, selective definition, and selective interaction and behavior. Communication between individuals, as well as orientation toward information from the physical environment, can only be as effective or meaningful as the degree of common mappings of the relevant ensembles of variety. Processes of decision-making, reference group orientation, role-taking and role-playing, and the like, rest on the above considerations.

5. Communicative interaction between individuals, together with their self-conceptions and the environmental situation, constitutes a *system* the driving forces of which are variously analyzed and described. Theorists speak in terms of: bargaining and the exchange of rewarding things and events (exchange theory) ; normative cooperation or compliance with stabilized expectations (consensus theory) ; maintenance of congruency of relations under conditions of changing interpersonal matrices (Newcomb's, and Secord and Backman's models) ; communication of information, instruction, or motivation in a meeting of purposive minds (Ackoff's) ; maximizing of payoffs or playing strategies (game and strategy theory) ; or enhancement of self in presenting oneself before audiences on the stage of life (dramaturgical models) . Each of these gets at one or more important aspects of the system's dynamics; some metaphors are looser, or less comprehensive, or more static than others.

To reiterate, no matter what metaphor or conceptualization is used, we are dealing with a system of interlinked components that can only be defined in terms of the interrelations of each of them in an ongoing developmental process that generates emergent phenomena—including those we refer to as institutional structure. We turn next to consider conceptualizations of this morphogenic process beyond the dyadic level.

Making the jump from microprocesses of dyadic interpersonal relations to larger scale social organization or "institutional" structure leads us into a central problem of sociological theory. Discussions of microprocesses typically, and often of necessity, are made under the assumption of a surrounding social structural vacuum. Once the structural surround is introduced, the central question arises as to how, and to what extent, it engulfs and "determines" the interpersonal processes, and, indeed, what it means to say this. Much of sociological theory makes a rather abrupt leap from dyadic and small group processes to "institutions," along with an assumption of non-problematic structural maintenance and stability founded on normative consensus, legitimate authority, common values, internalization of roles via socialization, and the like. As we have seen, the dynamics of interpersonal and intergroup processes have thereby tended to become lost in a welter of structural terminology and static categorization. Growing reactions against this tendency, however, have recently led to a rather complete overhaul of the methodological approach and conceptualization of social organization. The recent exchange theories of Homans and Blau, for example, are to be seen in this light. It is no accident that they have gone back to basics, starting from scratch with the basic interaction process, the Hobbesian problem of order and disorder, the Machiavellian problem of faith and morality, Bentham's "felicific calculus," and Adam Smith's laws of private profit and loss. It appears that Parsons' attempt to lay these ghosts with the "theory of social action" was not entirely successful.

It has become apparent that we must question both the view that institutional structure is "only" personal association writ large, and on the other hand, that institutional structure "molds" the situation of action as well as personality to the extent of determining behavior beyond a minimal residue of choice and decision-making that is unique and innovative. The issue seems primarily one of conceptualization, and the use (and misuse) of terminology. We do

organization 5
and its genesis:
2–roles and institutions

not leave the realm of action and interaction—of processes of association and dissociation—when we enter the "institutional" sphere, though the relationships and intercommunications become more drawn out, more indirect, more complex and differentiated. Nor do we leave the institutional sphere when we focus on even the most superficial forms of sociability—as Simmel and many social interactionists have so well shown. The present problem is to specify and conceptualize the processes and mechanisms by which the more complex and indirect sociative structures or communication matrices are generated out of less complex, less indirect and patterned sociative processes—on how the former feed back to help structure the latter; and on how each may continually interact to help maintain or to change the other.

THE MORPHOGENIC PROCESS: GENERAL CONSIDERATIONS

We are arguing that the abstract model of the morphogenic process in complex adaptive systems (described earlier) constitutes a very general framework within which many current conceptualizations of the genesis, maintenance, or change of social structure may be organized. Whether we are trying to understand the process by which modern Western institutions developed out of the decay of the *ancien régime,* or the more recent institutionalization of labor–management relations, this model appears to embrace the common underlying dynamics. We recall that the model assumes an ongoing system of interacting components with an internal source of tension, the whole engaged in continuous transaction with its varying external and internal environment, such that the latter tend to become selectively "mapped" into its structure in some way (e.g., as coded information, meanings, and tendencies to act in certain ways) . This adaptive process thus involves a *source of variety* against which to draw, a number of *selective mechanisms* which sift and test this environmental variety against some *criteria* of viability, and processes which tend to *bind and perpetuate* the selected variety for some length of time. The continual shifting of the environment and internal milieu guarantees a continual "cycling" of this process, leading very often to an accumulation of structural and processual complexity. The *structure* of such a system is thus viewed in terms of *sets of alternative actions,* or tendencies to act in certain ways, associated with the components, and the *constraints* that specify or limit these alternative actions. The genesis of organization is thus the generation of these sets of alternatives and the constraints defining them.

The sociocultural system is to be seen as such a complex, adaptive organization of components. It continually attempts to "map" the variety of its external environment through science, technology, magic, and religion, and its internal milieu through common understanding, symbols, expectations, norms, and values. A constant flow of potentially usable variety is provided by social differentiation, individual and subgroup differences, experience, exploration, turnover of components, and cultural diffusion. The internal source of dynamics for the ongoing process is the continuous generation of varying degrees of tension, "stress" or "strain," within and between the interacting components; such tension is now being recognized as an inherent and essential characteristic of such systems. A number of psychological and social selective mechanisms are now being conceptualized and studied, especially under the headings of individual and group decision making, selective interaction, selective perception and evaluation, and selective orientations to norms, values, audiences, and reference groups.

The analysis of interacting individuals striving to maintain "congruency," balance, symmetry, or "consonance" are essentially studies of the psychological and social psychological factors underlying such selective mechanisms. Esteem and prestige, authority and power, expertise and leadership are also being viewed as mechanisms of social selection, underlying as they do intergroup decision-making; that is, they underlie the selection of communication content and interaction networks, of the rulemaking apparatus, of ecological settings and physical layouts, and so forth, all of which work to channel actions, attitudes, collective behavior, and decisions.

On such a basis, the genesis and crystallization of new social and psychological structures occurs, sometimes crescively and sometimes fairly abruptly, with greater or with lesser conscious and deliberate purpose, sometimes taking place within the existing institutional organization and sometimes starting from relatively unstructured collective processes outside the institutional spheres. The institutionalization of labor unions or of the modern corporation are examples. Social role structures of interactive matrices come to be built up or reorganized differentially and tend to reinforce and perpetuate the selective perceptions, interpretations, and decisions emerging out of the transactions. The institutional paraphernalia—symbols, communication networks, ecological arrangements, and material props—are gradually or rapidly, but always selectively, built up to help channel certain perceptions, actions, and interactions, and to exclude others. Instruments of direct coercion, of course, often play a central role, at least until the slower processes of persuasion, socialization, and member turnover become effective. In this manner, complex organizations and institutions are generated—including those that have a solid and undistorted basis of legitimacy, those that are largely unlegitimized, and even those that may be, to a significant extent, illegitimate.

A principle we shall find important in studying the morphogenic social process is that the amount of information available as the basis for the selective actions or decisions of the individuals in a complex system is never sufficient to specify more than the general rules or broader outlines of the total structure. The total structure must thus be seen as generated both by the limited rules and decisions channeling the various actors taken separately, and also by the ongoing interactions and accommodations of these components as they come into conjuncture. This principle is partially recognized in sociology when we say that the norms and roles of a group can specify, at best, only a *range* of expected or acceptable behaviors, and it is within this range that much of the essential dynamics of society occur. It was also recognized in MacIver's concept of "social conjuncture": institutional patterns are the resultant of a large number of individual or group lines of actions directed at various ends or purposes that are crossing, running parallel, converging and diverging, such that the total product only partially matches any original plans or purposes. That many of us tend to equate the end product with the initial intentions is probably largely due to our limited and selective observation and to our tendency to confuse idealized verbalization and symbolic representation with socio-cultural reality. Many institutionalized structures such as racial oppression, institutionalized crime, or social classes, are to be seen, not as inevitable consequences of the operation of a social system as such, but of the particular selective and perpetuating mechanisms that have characterized its past operation.

Structure is never self-maintaining; a constant expenditure of energy of some kind is required to maintain any open system's "steady state." Discrepancies or exigencies of one kind or another lead to continual re-mapping and reorganization. This means, not only that any given social structure must always fail, to some degree, to define, specify, or provide adequately for some exigencies or unstructured events, but that it will itself positively generate such exigencies: conflicts of interest, ambiguous standards, role discrepancies, and failure to achieve goals.

In an open system, then, the "normal operation" of its institutions constantly generates an input of variety and strains thereby contributing to a continuous process of "structure—elaboration" and reorganization. Not only are such inputs normal to such a system, they are inherent features contributing to, though not guaranteeing, its viability.

INSTITUTIONALIZATION

A general conception such as this can only provide a guide for the more difficult job of conceptualizing and systematizing the more detailed mechanisms and processes underlying the social order. In what follows we shall discuss a number of recent contributions to this task and try to show that, despite their differences, there is a substantial convergence in the direction of the adaptive system model that we have been outlining. These contributions work toward a more dynamic conception of the process of institutionalization and institutional maintenance by way of new developments in the areas of collective decision processes, role theory, exchange and bargaining models, and theories of tension and conflict.

Partial approaches to a theory of institutionalization may be roughly divided into the structural and categorical, largely sociologistic, approach; the "collective behavior" approach; and the primarily social psychological, for example, the social interactionist, approach. We are interested in the possibility of developing a satisfactory theory that incorporates the essential contributions of each of these approaches. Though we shall not attempt to review the three orientations, we may briefly recall the more important features as a point of departure.

Much of the earlier work on the theory of institutionalization was an attempt to characterize, categorize, and account for the development of Western civilization. The broadest views recognized that in the simpler of the preliterate societies the social complexes we refer to today as "institutions" are not empirically separable. The development of civilization, then, could be treated in terms of the increasing differentiation and developing autonomy of the various institutional spheres. The causes and consequences of this elaboration were related to changes in the quality and quantity of certain types of social relationships, shifts in the interrelationships between subgroups or subcultures, the kind of social control operating, and the nature of the social cohesion. Thus arose the long progression of analytical classifications: militarist-industrial society, mechanical-organic solidarity, Gemeinschaft-Gesellschaft (or status-contract) social organization, folk-urban, sacred-secular, universalistic-particularistic, and the like. Ties between this structural level of analysis and the social psychological process level have been made by way of such concepts as primary and secondary social relationships, and their more recent elaboration in terms of the "pattern variable" schema and role and reference-group theory. But despite the large amount of work on social-psychological dynamics, it has not been systematized and articulated with the broader study of institutionalization, and the latter has thus continued largely in terms of structural categorization and classification (though with some notable exceptions).

The work of Max Weber, and its continual dialogue with Marxian dynamics, for example, has been especially durable because, in spite of its structural and typological emphasis, it not only provided continuous concrete historical reference, but—perhaps most importantly—it constantly flirted with (we cannot really say, systematically treated) the underlying psychological and interactional dynamics. We refer, of course, to Weber's concern with "ideas," material and ideal "interests," the role of "under-standing" and "subjective meaning," and consequently, with the endemic role of opposition among "ultimate" values. Conflicts of power and ideological struggles for "legitimacy" among competing status groups were taken as basic to the genesis and dominance of one institutional and cul-tural system rather than another. It is noteworthy that contemporary consensus theory has borrowed heavily, but very selectively, from Weber; the concerns of Weber just mentioned are precisely the ones selected for almost systematic exclusion from that theory's more formal framework. As Bendix has pointed out, Weber conceived of "meaningful action" as ranging on a continuum from innovation to conformity, and consequently tended to avoid the use of structural or collective concepts except as con-venient labels for "tendencies of action."[1] Thus, he uses *Vergesellschaf-tung*, instead of "society," to refer to societal tendencies of action based on considerations of material advantages or utility, and *Vergemeinschaf-tung* to refer to tendencies of action stemming from a sense of solidarity or social affinity with others. Such structural or collective entities as "society" or the "state" do not "act" or "maintain themselves" or "func-tion."

From this perspective Weber pursued his central theme of account-ing for the genesis of the types of institutional arrangements characteristic of Western civilization. His studies of the great classical religions were prolegomena to this, and tried to show that the dominant institutions of the day "are the relics of past struggles among 'suffering, striving, doing' men."[2] An initial interplay of material interests and "charismatic inspira-tions" of the few becomes the "life-style" of a distinct status group, which in turn—after conflicts occurred among a composite of such status groups whose ideas and interests at least partially diverged—eventually becomes the dominant orientation, the "common value system" of a whole nation or civilization. This image of society, Bendix suggests, shows up in Weber's conception of political action, "which seeks to encompass both the very great limitations that every social situation imposes upon the individual and the great opportunities for action that are inherent in the instability of social structures."[3] In a word, Weber conceived social structure as—to use newer terminology—an inherent polarity between a variety of alterna-tives of action, on the one hand, and the structural constraints that never-theless limit this variety, on the other. A point he emphasized was the openness and fluidity of the "structure," despite the constraints, within which the adaptive social process or dynamics occurs. Much of our current

---

[1] Reinhard Bendix, *Max Weber: An Intellectual Portrait* (New York: Double-day & Co., Inc., 1962) , pp. 262, 473–78.

[2] *Ibid.*, p. 266.

[3] *Ibid.*, p. 261.

theoretical dialogue centers here: functional, consensus, and equilibrium theories emphasize the structural constraints and minimize the play in the range of alternatives that are continually shifting the limits of those constraints, whereas their critics emphasize (and perhaps sometimes over-emphasize) the openness and fluidity.

On the other side, however, Weber's use of the typological method of simplifying his structural entities had the unfortunate effect of elimi-nating ambiguity and inconsistency from the ideological orientations of his historical status groups, thereby obscuring the social-psychological processes by which these orientations worked their imperfect effects on the everyday practical life of these groups. In Bendix's words:

> . . . he neglected the modifications by which practical men as well as in-tellectuals develop even their most sacred beliefs in relation to the exigen-cies of circumstance and of historical change.[4]

In other words, Weber did not carry out consistently and in sufficient depth his insight into the role of "subjective interpretation" of the situa-tion of action, and thus he missed the opportunity to confront the role of what we now call cognitive dissonance, incongruency of interpersonal matrices, or asymmetry of object orientations, on the generation of "sub-jective meaning" and consequent actions and interactions. Today we can appreciate more fully and systematically Weber's insights on this score. Such psycho-social dynamics, acting as intervening variables between "structural" forces and behaviors, are beginning to provide the basis for the deeper explanation of organizational dynamics that cannot be pro-vided by structural categorizations and correlational analysis between such categories.

Before discussing other approaches, we should mention the recent revival of social evolutionary theory and the promising efforts of struc-turalists to build on work such as Weber's. We shall confine our com-ments to papers of Talcott Parsons and Neil J. Smelser.

In his recent paper on the "evolutionary universals" necessary for the development of societies from the "primitive condition" to that of the "archaic civilizations,"[5] Parsons makes explicit reference to the analogy between society and—not the organism, now—but rather the *species*, and the selective process *vis à vis* the environment that leads to adaptive *change* of the system structure as an inherent capability. Like vision, or the hand and brain in organic evolution, a societal evolutionary universal is seen as "a complex of structures and associated processes the develop-ment of which so increases the long-run adaptive capacity of living systems

---

[4] *Ibid.,* p. 275.

[5] Talcott Parsons, "Evolutionary Universals in Society," *American Sociological Review,* 29 (1964) , 339–57.

in a given class" that only they can attain a higher level. Furthermore, such "universals are apt to generate major changes of their own, generally by developing more complex structures."[6] In other words, the sociocultural system is a complex adaptive system, as we have developed that notion, not basically an equilibrial or homeostatic system.

Two of the evolutionary universals that Parsons suggests may underlie the "breaking out" of the primitive stage of evolution are 1) "the development of a well-marked system of social stratification," and 2) "a system of explicit cultural legitimation" of a differentiated "political function, independent of kinship," which becomes necessary as the first universal develops. "Stratification" is defined here with unusual clarity as "the differentiation of the population on a prestige scale of kinship units such that the distinctions among such units, or classes of them, become hereditary to an important degree."[7] Thus groups become differentiated "relative to an advantage-disadvantage axis"—that is, an upper class develops with higher degrees of prestige or community status, wealth, and power relative to a lower class. This differentiation "tends to converge with the functional 'need' for centralization of responsibility"—that is, a necessary condition for the development of "archaic civilization" out of the primitive state is the breaking down of the rigidly conservative "seamless web" of kinship ascription and diffuse reciprocal obligations, and the establishment of centralized leadership focusing on political and religious control. The need for centralized control is stimulated by the increased complexity of the society due to population, and possibly territorial, growth, which raise problems of "internal order" such as the control of violence, defence of property and other rules, external defence, and the like.

Thus, power and prestige stratification, and the consequent concentration and generalization of control, mean a tendency toward the exclusive assumption of prerogatives and functions of higher status. These include claims on the services and resources of lower groups and the use of these to pursue narrower advantages or to coordinate wider collective goals. But the use of advantaged position to innovate at the risk of the resources of others adds to the strains already inherent in the differentiation and stratification that has been occurring. Hence, the upper class leadership finds it necessary to legitimate its positions and actions, to justify its advantages and prerogatives as against the burdens and deprivations suffered by others. Cultural legitimation means "the emergence of an institutionalized cultural definition of the society of reference, namely a referent of 'we' (for example, 'We, the Tikopia' in Firth's study) which is differentiated, historically or comparatively or both, from other societies,

---

6 *Ibid.*, 340–41.

7 *Ibid.*, 344.

while the merit of we-ness is asserted in a normative context."[8] Along with this goes the institutionalization of structures with explicit, culture oriented, legitimizing functions.

Without going into the other universals suggested by Parsons, we may outline the general model as follows. Population growth and territorial expansion, presumably aided by improved technology, create unspecified social–psychological pressures on the minds and decision-processes of group members; the result is the differentiation and specialization of functions previously embraced in a more homogeneous sociocultural web of interrelationships; this, in turn, exacerbates the pressures and tensions due to increasing complexity, resulting—again presumably by way of unspecified social-psychological processes—in decisions giving rise to further cultural and structural differentiation, such as an ideological superstructure that is presumed to integrate or support the earlier differentiation. We underscore here the gaps created by the lack of specification of the social–psychological processes involved in the institutionalization process, because other recent studies that we focus on below are notable for the fact that they highlight them.

As an aside, we should note how transparent is the function of functionalism as a methodological tool in the above framework: it serves as a substitute for these very social–psychological processes at issue. Differentiation, specialization, centralization, and the like occur—not because of the social-psychological forces operating in a particular ecological situation, but because of the "needs" of an evolving social system. Not that Parsons does not invoke an intuitive appeal to social psychology:

> Stratification, therefore, is an essential condition of major advances in political effectiveness, because, as just noted, it gives the advantaged elements a secure enough position that they can accept certain risks in undertaking collective leadership.[9]

But the main argument is functionalistic:

> The functional argument here is essentially the same as that for stratification . . . political leaders *must* on the long run have not only sufficient power, but also legitimation for it. Particularly when bigger implementive 'steps are to be legitimized, legitimation *must* become a relatively explicit and, in many cases, a socially differentiated function. (Emphasis added) [10]

A related differentiation model of institutionalization is Smelser's framework for analysis of economic development in underdeveloped coun-

---

8 *Ibid.*, 345.
9 *Ibid.*
10 *Ibid.*, 346.

tries, but without the functionalism. Whereas Parsons speaks in terms of functional "musts," Smelser *describes* the process, in ideal-typical terms, as it seems to be occurring historically. Economic development, seen in terms of increasing technology, commercial agriculture, industrialization and urbanization, are all postulated to give rise to structural differentiation and specialization, integration, and the tensions or disturbances that arise from the unequal progress of these latter. Structural differentiation represents the break with traditional institutions and is defined as "the evolution from a multi-functional role structure to several more specialized structures."[11] The main case is, again, the breakdown of the "seamless web of kinship" with its multi-functional organization and the genesis of new structures specializing in these lost functions. But a concomitant of the growing division of labor is the development of institutional arrangements that tend to coordinate the increasingly diverse, and potentially conflicting, organizations. This in turn, however, tends to produce even further differentiation—the development of such institutions as unions, political parties, voluntary associations, and state administrative bodies. Finally, such structural changes are disruptive and tension producing because they conflict with traditional ways, progress unevenly through the culture and through time, and thus generate *anomie* and give rise to integrative structures which may themselves, however, contribute to the conflict.

The modern systems theorist recognizes here all the makings of a fully systemic morphogenic process, with rather good possibilities of an explosive positive feedback situation. Thus, it represents a step in the direction in which we are going, but further advance requires a more detailed knowledge of the social-psychological mechanisms involved if we are to understand the varying concrete outcomes occurring in actual societies. Just as the exciting advances in developmental biology are occurring in terms of the chemical microprocesses of information processing by genetic molecules, so will advances in the sociology of institutional development and change require more attention to microprocesses of group decision-making and group generation of meanings and norms, and the like, that underlie the process of institutionalization.

COLLECTIVE BEHAVIOR AND INSTITUTIONALIZATION

The "collective behavior" approach to the problem of institutionalization has recognized that many of the characteristic features of the major

---

[11] Neil J. Smelser, "Mechanisms of Change and Adjustment to Change," in *Industrialization and Society*, ed. Bert F. Hoselitz *et al.* (The Hague; Unesco— Mouton and Company, 1963), p. 35.

institutions of modern Western society—economic, political, religious—
have their origins in, and are partly maintained and rejuvenated by,
relatively unstructured collective processes. This perspective views the
generation of institutional structure in terms of a natural history, which
starts from a situation of "social unrest" and a tendency toward breakdown or rejection of existing tradition and institutional controls, and proceeds through various forms of spontaneous collective behaviors (crowd
or mob actions, public discussion, and opinion formation) to more
organized forms of collective decision-making and action (social movements, political party formation, or revolution), culminating in some
cases in the institutionalization of a new order. There is no implication,
however, of unilateral sequences or necessary stages.

Such an orientation, developed particularly by social interactionists,
complements the structuralist approach particularly by attempting to fill
in the social-psychological dynamics. Central concern is given to the
processes whereby, in minimally structured—usually stressful—situations,
new perspectives, definitions, symbols, norms and values are collectively
generated in a more or less spontaneous, though not random, manner. On
the other hand, as a theory of institutionalization, it does not deal with
the more deliberate, "rational," socially structured, and less directly disruptive processes of institutional elaboration. Consider for example, the
qualitative changes in modern economic and political institutions which
are the cumulative results of the largely uncoordinated, often unlegitimized, plans of action of the constituent organizations. An integration of
both structural and collective decision analysis, such as that found in some
of the recent work in complex organization theory, is needed to tap this
area.

What is required, in particular, is to make more explicit the recognition that institutionalization is an ongoing, circular, systemic process,
and not an open-ended chain of events with clear-cut antecedents and
consequences. From a systems view, we might see it as a feedback, or
pseudo-feedback, process that contains both negative (stabilizing or rigidi-
fying) elements and positive (structure-elaborating, or increasingly disorganizing) features. (See Figure 5-1) As some of the newer views are
beginning to suggest, such closure is essential for a fully dynamic model
of the sociocultural system. In one way or another, the point is being
made that institutional structures help to create and recreate themselves
in an ongoing developmental process. The modern systems perspective is
providing conceptual tools that are taking the mysticism out of the notions of "immanent change" and the harboring of "seeds" of an institution's own destruction—or construction. Whether directly inspired by the
modern perspective or not, current theory is moving in similar or compatible directions.

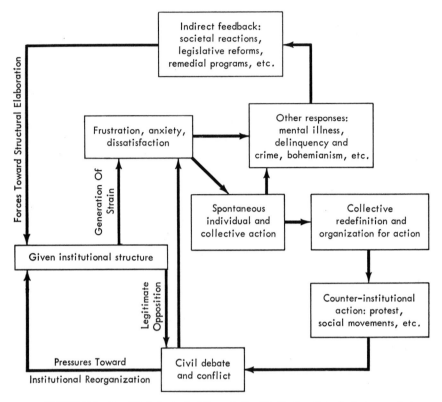

*FIGURE 5-1   Simplified Systemic View of the "Collective Behavior" Approach to a
Theory of Institutionalization*

EXCHANGE AND NEGOTIATION
MODELS OF INSTITUTIONALIZATION

A third distinguishable approach to institutionalization has started
its theory at the level of elementary interaction (such as discussed in the
last chapter). We refer particularly to exchange and bargaining theories
and interactionist role theory. As suggested earlier, much of this work
represents attempts at a general conceptual reorientation that is reopening
some of the fundamental classical issues of social theory in its rejection
of the more static consensus model. The reopening of the "Hobbesian
problem of order" in the context of a rejuvenated utilitarian (that is,
exchange) theory, for example, can only be fully understood in terms of
the current crisis in sociological thinking.

These points were brought out in some recent statements by James
S. Coleman, who also provided an introduction to the application of
exchange theory to the problem of institutionalization. In a discussion of

"Collective Decisions," Coleman argues against the characteristic strategy of sociologists which "views norms as the governors of social behavior and thus neatly bypasses the difficult problem that Hobbes posed."[12] Thus, such theorists are unable to deal, except in *ad hoc* fashion, with the problem of collective decisions about matters for which no norms exist. To correct this, Coleman adopts the strategy of the "opposite error." He begins with an image of man as:

> unsocialized, entirely self-interested, not constrained by norms of a system, but only rationally calculating to further his own self-interest . . . here we are concerned with the primitive state of a set of actors engaged in decisions in which power and interests are distributed among them . . .[13]

He goes on to develop a number of postulates and deductions specifying the conditions under which a war of each against all can be avoided and under which collective decisions can occur without the use of external power. On the other hand, he clearly recognizes what is being sacrificed in this strategy of excluding norms and socialization, namely, the richness of actions due to the "investment of the actors in one another and in the collectivity itself." He suggests, nevertheless, that a major aspect of socialization is not so much the "internalization of norms" but the learning of long-term consequences to oneself of one's strategies of action, and that, though norms do develop in social systems:

> it is not norms, and individuals socialized to them, which are the starting points of a fruitful theory of social systems, but instead, collective actions and rational actors, each with interests and power relative to these actions.[14]

In a paper written shortly before, however, Coleman argued that:

> the essence of a social system is interdependence, and the essence of interdependence is men's investment of themselves in other men and in collectivities that exist within the system. It is these investments that tie the system together, and give it strength . . .[15]

Such a confrontation rather clearly begs for a *rapprochement,* and a reassessment of the conceptual foundations of such abstract sociological concepts as trust, justice, status, legitimate authority, and consensus. First, an appeal mainly to norms and socialization is certainly insufficient. Second, there is the recognition of the large element of calculative and manipula-

---

[12] James S. Coleman, "Collective Decisions," *Sociological Inquiry,* 34 (1964), 166–81. Quote is on p. 167.

[13] *Ibid.,* 167, 170.

[14] *Ibid.,* 180.

[15] James S. Coleman, "Comment on 'On the Concept of Influence,'" *Public Opinion Quarterly,* 27 (1963), 63–82.

tive behavior characteristic of secular, industrial, civilization—showing up, for example, in Etzioni's recent suggestion of a middle category of "utilitarian" compliance lying between the traditional sociological dichotomy of "coercive" compliance and "normative" compliance[16] (to say nothing of the large welcome accorded game theory) . Third, an issue is raised that becomes a point of contention between the exchange theories of Homans and of Peter Blau, concerning the qualitatively different, emergent nature of "institutional" phenomena relative to the Hobbesian "pre-social" level of human interchange. The methodological position taken here can be crucial, determining whether we try to analyze complex institutional phenomena by some kind of aggregation of lower-level elements and processes, or whether we treat them as developmental, systemic resultants demanding reconceptualization on a higher level and requiring explanation in terms of more complex interlinkages and feedbacks than an aggregative approach allows.

For example, to appeal only to the Hobbesian or classical economic sense of "self-interest" is to miss G. H. Mead's interpretation of this concept, and thus to ignore the all-important distinction between an exchange in which the "self" is not directly involved and that in which it is. In fact, this distinction may itself be normatively defined for a group or organization, as recognized, for example, in the conceptual distinction we make between "primary" and "secondary" relations, or between "universalism and specificity," on the one hand, and "particularism and diffuseness," on the other. Or consider Coleman's discussion of the notions of "reputation" and "status," in which he suggests that

> . . . persons often invest much of their identity in others with high status, not because of what they can get out of the interaction but because, thus identified with the other, they vicariously share in the other's glory.[17]

To argue, as Homans might, that such persons are nevertheless simply making an exchange for vicarious glory is to move scientifically downhill in the direction of conceptual grossness and *ad hoc* explanation.

HOMANS' THEORY OF INSTITUTIONALIZATION

Despite Homans' reductionistic position,[18] his attempt to bridge the gap between the elementary forms of social behavior and the institutional level—a task undertaken somewhat apologetically in the spirit of an "orgy"

---

[16] Amitai Etzioni, *A Comparative Analysis of Complex Organizations* (New York Free Press of Glencoe, Inc., 1961) , pp. 14 ff.

[17] James S. Coleman, "Comment," 70.

[18] Cf. his earlier "emergence" view, discussed above in Chap. 2.

—constitutes a valuable contribution to a theory of institutionalization. He begins by recognizing that, though the two levels have points in common, they are not alike:

> . . . if only because in an informal group a man wins status through his direct exchanges with the other members, while he gets status in the larger society by inheritance, wealth, occupation, office, legal authority—in every case by his position in some institutional scheme, often one with a long history behind it.[19]

Two basic principles are seen to be at work here: 1) in complex organizations, activities come to be maintained not by their "natural or primary rewards" but also by "contrived rewards" such as money and social approval; 2) the process of exchange of rewarding activities comes to be more and more indirect as the network of obligations and interactional ties becomes stretched out. And these two processes are seen to be based on an increasing reliance on explicitly stated norms and orders. Institutions—"explicit rules governing the behavior of many people"—are thus seen to be continuous with elementary social behavior, in that they continually grow out of the latter; and the fundamental processes of behavior, "governed by its pay-offs and its stimuli," Homans argues, are "identical" in the two cases, the difference lying in the fact that at the institutional level "the relations between the fundamental processes are more complex."[20]

Homans furnishes an illustration of how some institutions might have thus arisen. Restriction of output by an industrial group might have originated because some members found its results rewarding, but these results depend on a large number of others also conforming to the output norm. Nonconformists, who would deprive others of the reward, are nevertheless induced to conform—not because of the primary reward for doing so, but for fear of losing the esteem of the others. The norm of output restriction is thus "well on its way to becoming an institution, taught to new members and even to new generations as one of the laws of life in the factory. Such combinatory processes can snowball into immense institutional piles."[21]

Recognition of the possibility that such "secondary sanctions" may come to replace the more primary rewards for large numbers of people, often without their awareness, leads Homans to a new way of stating an important hypothesis from his earlier work: institutions cannot be maintained by sheer force of norms and secondary rewards alone; sooner or later, either the primary rewards must be forthcoming, alternative be-

---

[19] George C. Homans, *Social Behavior: Its Elementary Forms* (New York: Harcourt, Brace & World, Inc., 1961) , p. 379.

[20] *Ibid.*, p. 380.

[21] *Ibid.*, p. 382.

haviors with new primary rewards will be presented by innovators, or institutional decay will set in. "Institutions do not keep on going forever of their own momentum."[22]

Delving more deeply into the mechanics of his second principle of institutionalization—the increasing indirectness of the exchange of reward, or division of labor—Homans offers, in the remainder of his book, the kernel of a theory of social evolution. Given some "capital"—material surplus and, especially, a moral code supporting trust and confidence between men—a society is apt to "invest" it in innovative behavior that leads to a more complex intermeshing of behaviors of larger numbers of persons in more complex and indirect ways, requiring the spelling out of more explicit sets of norms. For example, the development of the feudal system or the rise of industrialism might be cited. These longer, indirect chains of transactions mean that the innovations link larger numbers of people together, lead to greater specialization, and thereby decrease the richness of particular ties. And the larger the number of persons involved and the more complex their interdependence, the more their mutual adjustments must "go by the rule" rather than be left to "the rough and tumble of face-to-face contact." This means greater impersonality, and the eventual development of an organization specializing in the sanctioning of norms, that is, a legal system. But all this institutional elaboration and innovation may not "pay off" and hence may not persist; it is always problematical. The institutional arrangements must ultimately be satisfying to individuals, not simply because they share a particular culture, but "because they are men." Furthermore, the more elementary forms of behavior will continue to proliferate, not only in areas of life not covered by institutions, but deeply within institutions themselves. This is so because norms cannot prescribe behavior in detail, and individuals conform only within a range—that is, there is much greater play within institutional role structures than most structural theory would suggest.

Sometimes these subinstitutional growths provide solid support for institutional aims, but often the two are in conflict. The result of such conflict is not necessarily the collapse of the institutional and a return to the elementary forms: Homans offers, rather, the rudiments of a typology of possible system responses.

1. Adaptive evolution: there may be the emergence (Homans prefers the "founding") of a new institution designed to maintain subinstitutional values or primary rewards—for example, the development of labor unions out of industrial conflict.
2. Adaptive adjustment: "good administration" within the given institutional framework may compensate for many of the latter's deficiencies by judicious use of various mechanisms of control, for example, the "successful" persistence of so many autocracies of the past.

---

22 *Ibid.*, p. 383.

3. Disintegration: "the society may tear itself apart in conflict."
4. Malintegrative persistence: institutional deficiencies and chronic problems "may simply persist without issuing in overt conflict but without resolution either." Potential adjustive innovations remain too risky or are not invented, people are largely apathetic, and institutions remain " 'frozen' in an unnatural equilibrium," for example, the current state of American industry, including the unions.

Aside from Homans' many debatable points and unanswered questions, his work is a contribution to the critique of consensus theory, and its perspective and major thrust are well taken. Society, whatever else it might be, is recognized as a complex adaptive system with great flexibility and room for action and internal dynamics despite—or even because of—its complex institutional structure. Oversimplified as it may be, Homans' discussion tells us that when we do build a theoretical structure of complexly interrelated analytical categories and concepts, we must allow plenty of room for dynamic processes at the social-psychological level of interpersonal transaction, as well as for a wide range of levels of "integration" within which the "normative order" may "function" and persist.

BLAU'S MODEL OF INSTITUTIONALIZATION

Peter M. Blau has very recently offered a further development of the exchange theoretic perspective, but on the basis of sharp methodological differences with Homans.[23] In particular, Blau rejects psychological reductionism in favor of an explicit emergence view of institutionalization. In practice, this means a serious attempt to derive a set of intermediate concepts from elementary phenomena (for example, differentiation of status and power, authority, legitimacy, substructures) and to use these intermediate concepts in their own right as a basis for an understanding of the complex processes and structures of associations which are too far removed from the "ultimate psychological base of all social life"[24] to permit direct translation. Such sociological concepts point to emergent properties of collectivities, properties that have no counterpart in corresponding attributes of individuals and that cannot be adequately explained in terms of individual motives—especially since motives derive much of their character from these very collective properties. On the other hand, Blau also attempts to avoid using the typological or categorical abstractions that are too remote from psychological reality to yield testable hypotheses and too impersonal to involve the inter-human processes in which they are rooted.

---

23 Peter M. Blau, *Exchange and Power in Social Life* (New York: John Wiley & Sons, Inc., 1964).
24 *Ibid.*, p. 20.

A second important departure from Homans' position is a clear recognition of the problem of rationality embedded in the economic exchange metaphor. Thus Blau expresses awareness of the tautological nature of a principle that is extended to apply to all behavior, and restricts his use of "social exchange" to action that is oriented toward ends only achievable through interaction with others, and which seeks to adapt means to achieve those ends. Excluded is behavior based on the "irrational push" of emotional forces, that based on coercion, and "expressive" behavior oriented toward more ultimate values or questions of conscience rather than toward immediate rewards. And social exchange is further distinguished from economic exchange "by the unspecified obligations incurred in it and the trust both required for and promoted by it."[25] It is explicitly *not* assumed by Blau that men have complete information, have no restricting social commitments, have a consistent or constant preference scale, or pursue one ultimate goal to the exclusion of all others.

In sum, Blau presents a "prolegomenon of a theory of social structure" which joins the current critique of consensus theory and its "preoccupation with value orientations which has diverted theoretical attention from the study of the actual associations between people and the structures of their associations."[26] But at the same time, he attempts to moderate any overreactions and to sustain a sociological perspective which nevertheless maintains intimate relations with fundamental human social processes.

Blau accepts Homans' general characterization of institutional level phenomena in terms of the secondary nature of the rewards exchanged, the indirect network of interrelations among people, and the importance of more explicit norms. A major effort is made, however, to conceptualize these emergent processes more fully and systematically by way of an intermediate conceptual apparatus. The latter includes: the differentiation of status and power out of the exchange process, the emergence of consensual authority out of legitimizing processes, the contrast of institutional values and opposition values, and the principles of inherent imbalance and dialectic change. Thus, after a relative lull in general sociological theory represented by the dominance of consensus theory,[27] we find ourselves back picking up the threads of Weber's and Marx's theories of institutionalization. We shall return to Blau's model later on.

When we conceive of institutionalization in terms of power, authority, and legitimacy, it is clear that we are focusing on the problem of social "order" or "social control" from a perspective that must include,

---

25 *Ibid.*, p. 8.

26 *Ibid.*, p. 13.

27 An important exception here is the neglected work of Hans Gerth and C. Wright Mills, *Character and Social Structure: The Psychology of Social Institutions* (New York: Harcourt, Brace & World, Inc., 1953).

not only the normative, but also the non-normative elements of social action and interaction. In fact, the normative is specifically taken to be problematic, and not just assumed or given. We are forced to allow for at least the possibility that some institutional arrangements in some societies, some of the time, do not have an ascertainable basis of "legitimacy" in any underlying "social consensus"—whether we are looking at political structures, economic organization, or even "legal" structures. As we suggested before, if our conceptual apparatus is to reflect reality, it must not try to settle empirical questions by definitional fiat. We can, of course, define institutionalized structures as thereby "legitimized," but then we must be prepared to distinguish them from otherwise similar structures embedded in social life, and especially must we avoid identifying *the* social system only with those structures assumed to be legitimized.

MODELS OF INSTITUTIONAL PROCESS

We have examined several approaches to a conceptualization of the origins and development of institutional structures, and have noted the constant attempts to get underneath the broad structural categorizations by bringing in the underlying social psychological dynamics. We turn now to a number of recent conceptualizations and empirical studies of the on-going institutional process occurring within relatively stabilized "structures," noting in particular the attempts to build social psychological dynamics into our often static structural concepts.

As we have seen, the process view of symbolic interactionist theory has developed in constant opposition to the conventional, structural conception. As Blumer has recently put it, interactionism recognizes the fact of organization in society but treats it differently along two major lines. First, the organization of society is the "framework inside of which social action takes place and is not the determinant of that action"; secondly, this organization and changes in it "are the product of the activity of acting units and not of 'forces' which leave such acting units out of account."[28] Structural features—"culture," "roles," "statuses," and the like —set the conditions of action by shaping situations of action and providing a common coinage of symbols. But it is *people* who act toward and interpret their situations, whether in formal or informal associations, such that "streams of new situations arise and old situations become unstable," and organizational behavior takes on a processual character of creation and re-creation of meanings and expectations in a succession of

---

[28] Herbert Blumer, "Society as Symbolic Interaction," in *Human Behavior and Social Processes,* ed. Arnold M. Rose (Boston: Houghton Mifflin Company, 1962) , p. 189.

situations that are only partially or not at all regularized and standardized. Norms indeed are to be found in operation, but, as Shibutani observes, they are "creatively reaffirmed from day to day in the social interaction of the participants."[29]

Turner's Conception of Role-Making

Ralph Turner has elaborated on this perspective in a conceptual area fundamental to the analysis of institutions, namely, roles and role-taking.[30] The many valid criticisms of the more static and over-determining conception of roles are due, he believes, to the dominance of Ralph Linton's view of role and the use of an oversimplified model of role functioning.[31] Viewing role-playing and role-taking, however, as a *process,* Turner shows that there is more to it than just "an extension of normative or cultural deterministic theory," and that a dynamic view of role adds novel elements to the notion of social interaction.

The morphogenic nature of role behavior is emphasized from the start in Turner's concept of *"role-making."* Instead of postulating the initial existence of distinct, identifiable roles, he posits a tendency to create and modify conceptions of self- and other-roles as an interactive orienting process. Since actors behave *as if* there were roles—although roles actually exist only in varying degrees of definitiveness and consistency—the actors attempt to define them and make them explicit, thereby, in effect, creating and modifying them as they proceed. The key to role-taking, then, is the morphogenic propensity "to shape the phenomenal world into roles." Formal organizational regulation that restricts this process is not to be taken as the prototype, but rather, a "distorted instance" of the wider class of role-taking phenomena. To the extent that the bureaucratic setting blocks the role-making process, to that extent is organization maximal, "variety" or alternatives of action minimal, actors cogs in a rigid machine, and the morphogenic process frustrated.

Role interaction is a tentative process of reciprocal responding of self and other, challenging or reinforcing one's conception of the role of the other, and consequently stabilizing or modifying one's own role as a product of this essentially feedback testing transaction. The conventional view of roles, which emphasizes a prescribed complementarity of expectations, thus gives way to a view of role-taking as a process of "devising a

---

29 Tamotsu Shibutani, "Reference Groups and Social Control," in Rose, *Human Behavior and Social Processes,* p. 143; see also Edward Sapir, "Social Communication," *Encyclopedia of the Social Sciences,* IV (New York: The Macmillan Company, 1935), 78.

30 Ralph H. Turner, "Role-Taking: Process Versus Conformity," in Rose, *Human Behavior and Social Processes,* Chap. 2.

31 Ralph Linton, *The Study of Man* (New York: Appleton-Century-Crofts, Inc., 1936).

performance on the basis of an imputed other-role," with an important part being played by cognitive processes of inference testing. In a manner consistent with models of the basic interaction process reviewed in the previous chapter (especially those of Newcomb, and Secord and Backman), Turner views as a central feature of role-taking "the process of discovering and creating 'consistent' wholes out of behavior," of "devising a pattern" that will both cope effectively with various types of relevant others and meet some recognizable criteria of consistency. Such a conception generates an empirically testable hypothesis of relevance to our concern here with institutional morphogenesis: "Whenever the social structure is such that many individuals characteristically act from the perspective of two given roles simultaneously, there tends to emerge a single role which encompasses the action."[32]

Turning directly to the implications for formal, institutional role-playing, Turner argues that the formal role is primarily a "skeleton" of rules which evoke and set into motion the fuller roles built-up and more or less consensually validated in the above ways. Role behavior becomes relatively fixed only while it provides a perceived consistency and stable framework for interaction, but undergoes cumulative revision in the role-taking process of accommodation to and compromise with the simple conformity demanded by formal prescriptions.

The purposes and sentiments of actors constitute a unifying element in role genesis and maintenance, and hence role-taking must be seen to involve a great deal of selective perception of other-behavior and differential emphasis in the elaboration of the role pattern. This selection process operates on the great variety of elements in the situation of relevant objects and other-behaviors which could become recognized components in a consistent role pattern. Not all combinations of behavior and object relations can be classed into a single role, so that there must be criteria by which actors come to "verify" or "validate" the construction of a number of elements into a consistent role. This verification stems from two sources: "internal validation" of the interaction itself, and "external validation" deriving from "the generalized other" of Mead. The former hinges on successful prediction or anticipation of relevant other-behavior in the total role-set, and hence on the existence of role patterns whereby coherent selection of behaviors judged to constitute a consistent role can be made. But the notion of fixed role prescription is not thereby implied, since, first, roles—like norms—often or usually provide a *range of alternative* ways of dealing with any other-role, or, as is most common, the small segment of it activated at any one time; and secondly, the coherence and predictability of a role must be assessed and seen as "validated," not in terms of any one other-role, but in terms of the Gestalt of all the accom-

---

32 Turner, *loc. cit.*, p. 26.

modative and adjusted requirements set by other-roles in the actor's role-set and generated in the ongoing role-making process.

An example is provided by the study by Gross *et al.*, of the school superintendent role.[33] It is found that encumbency in this role: 1) actually involved a great deal of choice behavior in selecting among the alternative interpretations and behaviors deemed possible and appropriate, and that 2) the consistency and coherence of an incumbent's behavior could be seen only in terms of the total role as an accommodation to the correlative other-roles of school board member, teacher, and parent, with which the superintendent was required to interact simultaneously. As they put it, a "system model," as against a "position-centric" model, involves the important inclusion of the *interrelations among the counter positions.*

> A position can be completely described only by describing the total system of positions and relationships of which it is a part. In other words, in a system of interdependent parts, a change in any relationship will have an effect on all other relationships, and the positions can be described only by the relationships.[34]

Thus Turner sees the internal validation criterion as insuring a constant modification, creation, or rejection of the content of specific roles that occurs in the interplay between the actor's ideal role conceptions and his experience of their concrete implications.

The basis of "external validation" of a role is the judgment that the behavior constitutes a role by others who are assumed to have a claim to correctness or legitimacy. The criteria here include: discovery of a name in common use for the role: support of major norms or values, anchorage in the membership of recognized groups, occupancy of formalized positions, and the experiencing of key individuals as role models acting out customary attitudes, goals, and specific actions.

Under the "normal loose operation of society," Turner argues, these various internal and external criteria of validation are at best only partially conveyant and consistent in identifying the same units and content as roles. The resulting inevitable discrepancies between formal, institutional rules and roles, and the goals, sentiments and selective interpretations arising from the experience of those actually trying to play them out, makes role conceptions "creative compromises," and insures "that the framework of roles will operate as hazily conceived ideal frameworks for behavior rather than as an unequivocal set of formulas."[35]

In sum, institutions may provide a normative framework prescribing

---

33 Neal Gross *et al.*, *Explorations in Role Analysis* (New York: John Wiley & Sons, Inc., 1958) .

34 *Ibid.*, p. 53.

35 Turner, *loc. cit.*, p. 32.

roles to be played, thus assuring the required division of labor and mini-
mizing the costs of exploratory role-setting behavior. The actual role
transactions that occur, however, generate a more or less coherent and
stable working compromise between ideal prescriptions and a flexible role-
making process—between the structured demands of others and the requirements of one's own purposes and sentiments. This conception of role
relations as "fully interactive" rather than merely conforming, contributes
to the recent trends "to subordinate normative to functional processes in
accounting for societal integration"[36] by emphasizing the complex adaptive interdependence of actors and actions in what we see as an essentially
morphogenic process—again, in comparison to a merely equilibrial or
homeostatic process.

Institutional Process as a "Negotiated Order"

A recent empirical study of a formal organization admirably illustrates many facets of Turner's conception and contributes further to our
thesis. In their study of the hospital and its interactive order, Anselm
Strauss and his colleagues developed a model of organizational process
that bears directly on the basic sociological problem of "how a measure
of order is maintained in the face of inevitable changes (derivable from
sources both external and internal to the organization) ."[37] Rejecting an
overly structural view, they assumed that social order is not simply normatively specified and automatically maintained but is something that must
be "worked at" and continually reconstituted. Shared agreements that
underlie orderliness are not binding and shared indefinitely, but involve
a temporal dimension implying an eventual review, and consequent re-
newal or rejection. On the basis of such considerations, Strauss and his
colleagues developed their conception of organizational order as a "negotiated order."

The hospital, like any organization, can be visualized as a hierarchy
of status and power, of rules, roles, and organizational goals. But it is also
a locale for an ongoing complex of transactions among differentiated
types of actors: professionals, such as physicians, psychiatrists, residents,
nurses and nursing students, psychologists, occupational therapists, and
social workers; and nonprofessionals, such as various levels of staff, the
patients themselves, and their families. The individuals involved are at
various stages in their careers, have their own particular goals, sentiments,
reference groups, and ideologies, command various degrees of prestige,
esteem, and power, and invest the hospital situation with differential sig-

---

36 *Ibid.*, p. 38.

37 Anselm Strauss *et al.*, "The Hospital and Its Negotiated Order," in *The Hospital in Modern Society*, Eliot Freidson (New York: Free Press of Glencoe, Inc.,
1963) , p. 148.

nificance. The rules supposed to govern the actions of the professionals were found to be far from extensive, clearly stated, or binding; hardly anyone knew all the extant rules or the applicable situations and sanctions. Some rules previously administered would fall into disuse, receive administrative reiteration, or be created anew in a crisis situation. As in any organization, rules were selectively evoked, broken, or ignored to suit the defined needs of personnel. Higher administrative levels, especially, avoided periodic attempts to have the rules codified and formalized, for fear of restricting the innovation and improvisation believed necessary to the care of patients. Also, the multiplicity of professional ideologies, theories, and purposes would never tolerate such rigidification.

In sum, the area of action covered by clearly defined rules was very small, constituting a few general "house rules" based on long-standing shared understandings. The basis of organizational order was the generalized mandate, the single ambiguous goal, of returning patients to the outside world in better condition. Beyond this, the rules ordering actions to this end were the subject of continual negotiations—being argued, stretched, ignored or lowered as the occasion seemed to demand. As elsewhere, rules failed to act as universal prescriptions, requiring judgment as to their applicability to the specific case.

The ambiguities and disagreements necessitating negotiation are seen by the researchers to be patterned. The various grounds leading to negotiation include: disagreement and tension over the proper ward placement of a patient to maximize his chances of improvement; the mode of treatment selected by the physician (which is closely related to his own psychiatric ideology and training) ; the multiplicity of purposes and temporal ends of each of the professional groups as they maneuver to elicit the required cooperation of their fellow workers; the element of medical uncertainty involved in treating the patient as a unique, "individual case," and the consequent large area of contingency lying of necessity beyond specific role prescription; and finally, the inevitable changes forced upon the hospital and its staff by external forces, by the unforeseen consequences of internal policies, and the round of negotiations themselves. What is concretely observed, then, in researching the organizational order of the hospital, is negotiation between the neurologically trained and the psychotherapeutically oriented physician, between the nurses and the administrative staff, between the nonprofessional floor staff and the physician, and between the patient and each of the others.

The negotiation process itself was found to have patterned and temporal features. Thus, different physicians institute their own particular programs of treatment and patient care, and in the process develop fairly stable understandings with certain nurses or other institutional gate-keepers such as to effectuate an efficient order of behaviors with a minimum of communication and special instructions. Such arrangements

are not called for by any organizational role prescriptions, but nevertheless represent part of the actual organization generated in the morphogenic process of negotiation (or role-making and -taking, in Turner's
terms). Thus, agreements do not occur by chance but are patterned in
terms of "who contracts with whom, about what, as well as when . . ."[38]
There is an important temporal aspect, also, such as the specification of a
termination period often written into an agreement—as when a physician
bargains with a head nurse to leave his patient in a specific ward for "two
more days" to see if things will work themselves out satisfactorily.

In a final section of their paper, Strauss and his colleagues bring out
the full implications of their negotiation model for genuine organizational
change. The model presents a picture of the hospital—and perhaps most
other institutionalized spheres of social life—as a transactional milieu in
which numerous agreements are "continually being established, renewed,
reviewed, revoked, revised." But this raises the question of the relation
between this process and the more stable structure of norms, statuses, and
the like. The authors see a close systemic relation between the two. The
daily negotiations periodically call for a reappraisal and reconstitution of
the organizational order into a "new order, not the reestablishment of an
old, as reinstituting of a previous equilibrium." And, we would add, it
contributes nothing to refer to this as a "moving equilibrium" in the
scientifically established sense of the term. The daily negotiative process
not only allows the day-by-day work to get done, but feeds back upon the
more formalized, stable structure of rules and policies by way of "a
periodic appraisal process"—modifying it, sometimes slowly and crescively,
sometimes rapidly and convulsively. And, it can be argued, virtually every
formal structure extant can be traced from its beginnings to its present
apparently timeless state through just such a morphogenic process—a
process characteristic of what we have called the complex adaptive system.

Institutional Process as Resolution of Role Strain

Views such as those of Turner and of Strauss *et al.*, are not simply
two new ways of looking at social organization, but represent part of the
recent convergence of views which, by the force of its logic and its empirical relevance, is seriously challenging the normative–structural point of
view. Another important exemplar, a more general theoretical statement
applicable on the societal level, is William J. Goode's "Theory of Role
Strain."[39] His central argument is that social order or stability is to be
explained, not by either the "normative consensual commitment" of the
individuals of the group or by integration of the norms themselves, but

---

[38] *Ibid.*, p. 162.

[39] William J. Goode, "A Theory of Role Strain," *American Sociological Review*,
25 (1960), 483–96.

as a result of a cumulative process characterized by dissensus, role strain stemming from the normal felt difficulty of fulfilling role demands, and the consequent role bargaining that serves to organize actors' total role systems and their performance. "Institutions" are the current cumulative state of this ongoing, essentially morphogenic process.

In developing this theme, Goode weaves a conceptual web that contributes further to the interlinking of "social structure," decision-making processes, and the emergent products of social interaction. Social structures are seen as made up of role relationships, which themselves consist of role transactions or sequences of "role bargains" which in turn involve interacting individuals who are attempting to resolve the more or less normal strains of typically over-demanding roles. The resolution of role strain occurs in a process characteristic of the complex adaptive system as outlined in our modern systems model.

It is argued by Goode that the widely accepted Lintonian role-model of society—based on the assumption that role-continuity and hence societal maintenance are due mainly to consensual commitment and normative integration—fails to explain the facts of complex modern society. For example, that some individuals do not accept even "central" values; emotional commitment varies significantly among individuals, by social class, age and sex, region, and the like; people often accept contradictory values; their values and commitments often change significantly with changes in social position, and so forth. Furthermore, it is recognized once again that norms and role definitions specify only a range of behaviors and hence are not adequate guides for action even when accepted.

An individual's total role obligations, Goode argues, are idealized and over-demanding. In reality, they are not always intrinsically pleasurable, and are often ambivalent, contradictory, inconsistent, or conflicting. Hence, the assumptions of institutional integration and norm–commitment cannot account for either the actual working integration of one individual's total role system or the integration among the role systems of groups of individuals. As we have seen, it is precisely by assuming normative integration, and by oversimplifying or reifying social structure that traditional consensus theory has often lost sight of the dynamics of social process. Goode's perspective, like that of Turner, Strauss, and others, forces us to "de-reify" the notion of social structure, and to explicate it in terms of the inter-individual transactions and accommodations that lead to the emergence of relative stabilities of expectations and patterns of actual behavior that we find when we study concrete organizational phenomena.

Far from finding any "law of social inertia," Goode sees a constant push behind this activity which he conceptualizes in terms of normal psychic tension or "role strain"—"the felt difficulty in fulfilling role obligations"—that accompanies individuals' daily rounds of activities and interactions. Individuals continually, and only more or less systematically, allocate their time, energies and skills among the various formal and informal demands of role partners and of their own self-conceptions. The existing "institutional structure"—the previously stabilized and formalized accommodations—limits and patterns this interplay of decisions and interactions, but the structure itself undergoes continuous modification as a result.

Goode shows how such a model can generate intermediate categories of structuring of social action and interaction, and in a way that articulates, we believe, with some of the more fruitful categories of consensus theory, for example, the "pattern variables." Thus, it is suggested that the individual may utilize two sets of techniques in attempting to reduce his role strain. One set concerns the decision as to whether or when he will enter or leave a role relationship, and includes: "compartmentalization" of various role demands; "delegation"; "elimination" of role relations; "extension" of some role obligations to justify the ignoring of others; and the setting up of "barriers to intrusion," such as a secretary or other gatekeeper. The effective use of such techniques—which, we note, become institutionalized as important facets of organizational structures and processes—provides some leeway whereby the individual may select a set of roles that are reasonably congenial, mutually supporting, and not too conflicting. We recognize this conception as complementary to Turner's analysis of the "role-making and -taking" process, and to the interaction models outlined in the last chapter.

The other set of techniques focuses on the actual role transactions with others once a relationship is permitted or required. This leads to the consideration of role bargaining, which we have already met in the theories of exchange, negotiation, games, and the like.

The given institutional structure is seen once more, then, as a framework or setting that limits and helps shape the decision-making role transactions by helping to determine, for example, the techniques used to reduce role strain. What is meant is that previous role transactions and expectations have become stabilized long enough to be supported by a cultural growth of more or less internalized ideals, values, and ideologies, as well as by external symbols, material props, and especially, organized sanctioning instrumentalities upholding social positions of power and authority. But, as we argue in more detail in the next chapter, even when dealing with the basic phenomena of power, authority, and legitimacy, we are still looking at the day-to-day accommodations of partly spontaneous and creative role transactions which underlie the presumed social order and bar us from the too easy assumption of a normative consensus and integration. As Goode argues, the sum total of role decisions of the many individuals and groups attempting to resolve role strain establishes the flow of role performances that constitute the working institutions, and thus determines the prevailing degree of integration among the various aspects of institutional structure. And though this complex of performances ordinarily maintains a society, it may also change it significantly, or even fail to maintain it, despite all the institutional trappings. There are no automatic guarantees, though this type of system—as our model argues—contains the *potential* for adaptation. Likewise with the individual: his total role pattern may or may not turn out to support him; the conflicts and internal pressures generated may lead to adaptive personality changes or to maladaptation and destruction.

Two Illustrative Studies

We shall conclude this chapter on institutional "structure" as a morphogenic process by looking briefly at two supporting empirical studies that will lead us to a recapitulation of our general systems model of society as a non-equilibrial, complex adaptive system. The first is the above-mentioned study by Gross *et al.*, of the role system of the school superintendent and his counter-role partners, the school board member, the teacher, and the parent. A major burden of their empirical study is to demonstrate, once again, the research sterility of the Lintonian conception of role, and structural theories built on it, due principally to the postulate of consensus on role definition. Their study showed a majority of significant differences in the definitions of their roles by a sample of incumbents of the same social position and by incumbents of different but interrelated counterpositions. This fact led them to the demonstration of a number of important theoretical consequences derived from their rejection of the postulate of role consensus. It is often assumed that the socialization process, by which roles are "acquired," provides a set of clearly defined and agreed upon expectations associated with any particular position. But the discovery of differential *degrees of consensus* seriously challenged this assumption. In terms of our systems model the recognition of degrees of consensus is tantamount to the recognition of a continuous source of "variety" in the role system. This leads us to seek the various *selective* processes occurring in the role transactions. At least for the occupational positions studied, it was found that the assumption that socialization occurs on the basis of prior consensus on role definitions was untenable, and deserved "to be challenged in most formulations of role acquisition, including even those concerned with the socialization of the child."[40]

Second, the research showed that, instead of assuming role consensus and explaining variations of behavior of incumbents of the same position

---

[40] Neal Gross *et al.*, *Explorations in Role Analysis*, p. 321. Also see Robert L. Kahn *et al.*, *Organizational Stress: Studies in Role Conflict and Ambiguity* (New York: John Wiley & Sons, Inc., 1964).

in terms of personality variables, one could better explain them in terms of the varying role expectations and definitions—which may be unrelated to psychological differences.

The implications are also of importance for a theory of social control. Instead of a model assuming that the application or threat of negative sanctions leads to conformity to agreed upon norms, Gross *et al.* found numerous situations in which, due to variant or ambiguous role definitions, the same behavior resulted in negative sanctions imposed by some role partners and positive sanctions by others. Sometimes there was even a failure to apply sanctions because of perceived ambiguity; and sometimes nonconformity to perceived expectations of another occurred, despite negative sanctions, because other expectations were defined as more legitimate.

Another Lintonian postulate challenged by this research is that, though an actor may occupy many positions, even simultaneously, he activates each role singly while the others remain "latent." It is found, however, that individuals often perceive and act toward role partners as if simultaneous multiple roles were being activated. For example, one may hold different expectations regarding a teacher who is male, young, and unmarried as compared to one who is female, older, and married. In other words, standards and expectations are applied to the whole person—as a result, in part, of the complex of positions the person is perceived as occupying at that time. A related consideration involves the time over which two or more individuals interact: other positions they occupy enter progressively into their perception of each other and consequently modify their evaluations and expectations. Thus the authors generalize their point into a broader theory of social interaction by suggesting that evaluative standards shift over time from those applied as appropriate to the incumbent of a *particular* position, to those applied to a *total person* with particular personality features and capacities stemming from the multiple positions.

Finally, their rejection of the consensus model led these researchers to find a process of role strain or role conflict generation and resolution similar in principle to that conceptualized by others discussed above. Having defined the role set they were studying as a true *complex system* of interrelated components, and having then uncovered and analyzed the *variety* continuously introduced into the system by way of variant, ambiguous or changing role definitions, they then focused on the *selection process* whereby this variety was sifted and sorted in the give and take of role transactions. Thus, given a situation in which a role incumbent was faced with the incompatible expectations of two of his counter-role partners, a theory was constructed to answer the question of how the actor may choose from among four alternatives in resolving the conflict. From our present perspective, their theoretical scheme constitutes another important contribution to the forging of a conceptual link between the dynamics of the role transaction and the more stable surrounding social structure—a link that is too often missed by the consensus theorist's identification of social structure with consensual role playing. This linkage is made in terms of the concepts of perceived *legitimacy* of the conflicting expectations, an assessment of the *sanctions* that might be applied, and a predisposition to give primacy to a *moral* orientation, an *expedient* orientation, or a balance of the two. We are thus dealing with questions of power, authority, internalized values, and material interests, which we have already seen to be central to the analysis of institutional processes. We face once again the dual question of how role transactions are conditioned by the surrounding social structure and how that structure is generated and regenerated as a product of the complex of role transactions.

The four alternatives that Gross and his colleagues see as open to an actor who is attempting to resolve a role conflict between incompatible expectations A and B are: 1) conformity to expectation A, 2) conformity to expectation B, 3) a compromise, an attempt to conform in part to both expectations, or 4) an attempt to avoid conforming to either expectation. The first criterion that the theory postulates to underlie the choice of alternatives chosen is the actor's definition of the *legitimacy* of the expectations. Thus the predictions of behavior using this criterion are that, when only one expectation is perceived as legitimate, the actor will conform to that one; when both are defined as legitimate, he will compromise; and when neither is seen as legitimate, he will engage in avoidance behavior of some kind. The second criterion is the actor's perception of the *sanctions* that would be applied for nonconformity. This could create pressures to conform if strong negative sanctions are foreseen. However, the criterion does not predict for the case in which both expectations A and B are perceived to lead to few, if any, negative sanctions.

It is assumed that for any role conflict situation an actor would use both of these criteria and make his decision accordingly. At this point, predictions on the basis of the theory lead to determinate resolutions of conflict in seven of the sixteen combinations derived from the four types of legitimacy and the four types of sanctioning situations, but the other nine combinations are left indeterminate. This is because the two criteria predispose the actor in different directions at the same time, and at least a third criterion is needed to determine the net outcome. The authors thus appeal to the actor's predisposition to give primacy to either the legitimacy criterion or to the sanctions dimension, or else to balance the two. This leads to the postulation of three types of predisposing orientations to expectations, as listed above—the *moral,* the *expedient,* and the balanced *moral-expedient*. All the combinations of situations now become predictable.

The accuracy of the predictions was tested empirically with the data from the study of the superintendent role for four "incompatible expectation situations." The evidence supported the theory, though there were some incorrect predictions.

The implications of this conceptualization and empirical analysis are far-reaching, as already suggested, for general sociological theory. The study is concerned with what must be considered "institutional" organization and process, and it supports a model of that structure and process that is quite different from the more traditional models. As the authors point out, one strong advantage of the theory is its conceptualization of institutional role behavior in terms of "expectations," whether legitimate or illegitimate, rather than in terms of "obligations" (legitimate expectations) as is assumed in consensus theory. It thus allows for the possibility that illegitimate expectations constitute a significant part of institutional role behavior, and underlie much of the conflict that occurs—as we know very well to be the case—within the institutional process. It follows, further, that deviance—nonconformity to expectations—is a more intimate and normal element of institutional behavior than consensus theory would permit. And it also permits theoretical recognition of the possibility that a great deal of organizational behavior is based, not on internalized norms and values, but on an *expedient* calculation of self-interests and of possible rewards and punishments. This, in turn, leaves open the theoretical possibility that power, as well as legitimized authority, may often be a controlling factor in institutional behavior.

The second empirical study we shall sketch is more explicitly based on an understanding of the modern systems approach, focusing as it does on a theory of "self-generating internal change." Ronald Cohen, an anthropologist, reports a theoretically well-organized analysis of his field study of role conflict and change among the Kanuri of Nigeria.[41] The study focuses on "goal ambiguity" and "conflicting standards" within a facet of the joint native-colonial political administrative hierarchy, and particularly on the pivotal position of native "district head," which had come to combine the quite diverse cultural orientations of the colonial British and the Kanuri. This diversity between, as well as within, the two cultures made for inconsistencies, ambiguity, and conflict in political goals as well as in role standards and performances, and these problems were continuously exacerbated by the variety of pressures put on district

---

41 Ronald Cohen, "Conflict and Change in a Northern Nigerian Emirate," in *Explorations in Social Change*, ed. George K. Zollschan and Walter Hirsch (Boston: Houghton Mifflin Company, 1964), Chap. 19.

heads by the central native administration, the colonial administration, and the colonial technical departments.

Cohen analyzes the consequences of this situation for the political system in terms of A. G. Frank's theory of organizational process and change.[42] Given the conditions of ambiguity and conflict of standards and goals, it is postulated that a process of *selective performance* and *selective enforcement* of standards will occur. Subordinates will be forced to decide on which expectations to meet, and superiors will be required to evaluate these performances and, hence, to selectively enforce some standards over others. This postulate leads to a number of predictions that Cohen proceeded to test. In essence, he predicted that a continuous process is set up, one that appears, though in exaggerated form, much like the "role strain," "role-making," "negotiated order" situations we met earlier. Role players fail to meet, or feign meeting some standards, and differentially select those they will meet. As a result, the role system is postulated to exhibit a strain toward substantive rationality (in Weber's sense), shifting standards for members, widespread role innovation or "deviance," ready adaptation to environmental changes, and an active and widespread circulation of information about standards and goals by "intermediary dealers in information" and by members seeking to reduce the ambiguity and conflict embodied in these standards and goals. The process is thus a feedback circuit wherein superiors continuously modify their standards or expectations as the definitions of political objectives change, and subordinates adapt their decisions and performances to these changing expectations and surrounding circumstances; and this, in turn, changes the state of the total situation toward which the superiors are acting. The role system, then, is seen as continuously receptive and responsive to external and internal pressures which demand some kind of workable "mapping" of the abundantly available situational "variety," which in turn makes possible—though not guaranteeing—the evolution of more or less adaptive, institutionalized, organizational procedures.

Applying this theory to the Kanuri, Cohen found the predictions to be borne out to a substantial degree. We leave the detailed description of these phenomena to the original study, which drew the general practical conclusion that—in spite of its apparently conservative anti-progressive traditionalism—the Kanuri political role system showed greater compliance toward the varied pressures of superiors and situational exigencies than toward the tenets of tradition. It thereby proved to be a self-generating system containing the mechanisms for its own transformation. The implications of this for policy relating to "developing countries" are of obvious importance.

---

[42] A. G. Frank, "Goal Ambiguity and Conflicting Standards: An Approach to the Study of Organization," *Human Organization,* 17 (1959), 8–13.

On the theoretical side, Cohen clearly recognizes the implications of his mode of analysis for a model of sociocultural evolution:

> This model depends basically on two conditions. First, the evolving phenomenon must be shown to be *variable* in terms of its constituent units, and second, there must be analytically distinct *selective factors* which operate on the variation within the phenomenon to produce a constantly adapting and thus an evolving history of development. Although there are more or less stable orientations of tradition present in Bornu, conflicts in the political organization produce a variability of response by the actors upon which selective pressures exerted by superiors in the political hierarchy may operate to bring about innovations and changes that are incremental in their nature, i.e., evolutionary rather than revolutionary.[43]

Conclusions

In the last two chapters we have tried to develop a conception of the processes whereby sociocultural structures, or institutions, are developed, maintained, elaborated, and changed. In doing so we have argued for the complex adaptive system model, in contrast to an equilibrium or homeostatic system model, and have tried to show that it organizes more adequately what we believe we know from empirical observation of the dynamic nature of societies. We believe that modern theory and research are, in fact, moving toward such a model, whose beginnings had been quite prominent in the earlier sociology of this century before the rise of structuralist "consensus theory."

Questioning the main assumptions of consensus theory, it was argued that the degree of commonness and specificity of norms and values in a society is empirically problematic, and in any case such theory cannot account for the working structures and processes found in reality. Norms and values, and hence roles and institutional structures in general, do not specify concrete behaviors; they are more or less general rules or guides, and do not contain enough "information" to specify the detailed operation of the system or to "map" more than a small part of the "variety" of the environment or the internal system. The dynamic–system model denies that the sociocultural system can be adequately characterized as a pre-programmed machine; the notion of complex adaptive organization suggests rather the generation of alternatives which are continually being selected during the process of operation by decision-making units. In this process, sociocultural structures of all levels of complexity may be generated, maintained, elaborated, or changed.

Given this more fluid and tentative nature of the sociocultural structure, the newer model suggests that we focus on the following features. First is the nature and sources of the *variety* in the system, including

---

[43] "Conflict and Change," p. 519. Emphasis supplied.

that actively generated by the given structure itself. Thus, in addition to the unmapped "exigencies" of the external and internal environment, the normative ambiguity, and the range of permissive alternatives, we also have planned and unplanned innovation, random and structured deviance, and social and cultural differentiation of many kinds. Second, we must view *tension* as a normal, ever-present dynamic agent which, far from being "reduced" by automatic system processes, must—like the level of variety—be kept at an optimal level if the system is to remain viable. "Tension-*reduction*" theories must not lose sight of the positive contributions of tension-*production* in complex systems. Third, there are the *selection processes* whereby the perceived variety, showing up as uncertainty, ambiguity, or conflict, is sorted and sifted in intra-individual and interpersonal interchanges. Communication networks and information flows can be seen as vehicles whereby tensions, intentions, and expectations are communicated as social pressures or interpersonal influences, and whereby selective responses are made whose sum total at any period contributes to the "institutional" order (or disorder) at that time. This *transactional process* of exchange, negotiation, or bargaining is thus inherently a morphogenic process out of which emerge relatively stable social and cultural structures; that is, definitions, expectations, motives, and purposes developing within (and outside) a given institutional framework act to reconstitute, elaborate, and change it by a complex of various levels of feedbacks. Fourth, there are the processes of *perpetuation and transmission* of some of these stabilities. Out of the continuous transactions emerge some relatively stable accommodations and adjustments. The mechanisms underlying these may be divided, very generally, into two main types: There are the sometimes consciously negotiated, sometimes fortuitously found, *congruencies* or *symmetries of coorientations* within interpersonal role matrices—as suggested by the interaction models of Newcomb, Secord and Backman, and others, and by the role theories of Turner, Goode, and Strauss *et al.* Such "congruencies" or "symmetries" constitute the foundations of a legitimate order and its normative system of authority and control. On the other hand, the primary stabilizing mechanism may be a *differential power distribution* within "role matrices," such that patterns of compliance are institutionalized on the basis, ultimately, of coercive sanctions—despite the persistence of "incongruencies and asymmetries of coorientation" within "role matrices." This lies at the basis of what we may refer to as a non-legitimized order of institutionalized power. These two general types of mechanism embrace, of course, a continuum of varying subtypes that concretely merge into one another.

The selection processes continue such that some of the role matrices come to be established as more enduring organizations or institutions, the new frameworks within which the dynamic social process occurs. But they themselves, in turn, generate their own brand of variety and tension, carrying on this series of system processes as long as some minimal level of viability is maintained.

One thing that becomes painfully apparent from our discussion is the profound inadequacy of the concept of "institution" as it has come to be used in sociology. While one of the most heavily utilized terms in the field, it has only the vaguest of referents. Just what is the basis of these "stable sets of expectations" that we so often assume to exist, when we in fact find a great deal of dissensus, ambiguity, conflict, and change in the actual operating rules lying at the core of social structures? And how much of the social stability we find is the result of mere formality or legality, or of physical and ecological arrangements, which have been in existence for some time and are only more or less tacitly acquiesced in by participants? The problem of defining an "institution" often comes to a head when we are confronted with the concept of "legitimacy." The two terms are often taken to mean pretty much the same thing, or to imply one another, thus begging the central problems of social power, disorganization, malintegration, and deviance. It is often assumed that whatever is "institutionalized" is thereby founded on internalized, consensual norms and values, and is consequently "legitimized." The study of social disorganization, deviance, and "social problems," as well as of social change, has foundered for some time on such an assumption. But a great deal of research suggests that organized crime, political corruption, economic fraud and exploitation, and other "social problems" are so pervasive, stable, and difficult to root out precisely because they are "institutionalized." That is, they involve complex interpersonal, and often highly organized, networks of expectations, communications, normative interpretations, interests, and beliefs, embedded in the same sociocultural matrix as are "legitimized" structures. Hence, if we are going to use the term "institution," it appears that we must be prepared to distinguish: "legalized" from "legitimized" institutions, and "legitimized" from "nonlegitimized" institutions; social power from legitimized authority; and utilitarian or coercive compliance from normative conformity and value consensus.

We turn, in the final chapter, to central aspects of this large problem area—those concerned with power, authority, legitimacy, and "social control."

In this final chapter we shall discuss, though all too generally and briefly, some ways in which the modern systems perspective relates to important problems in the traditional area of "social control," namely, conformity and deviance, power and authority, and processes of group goal-seeking.

On the face of it, the field of cybernetics, with its emphasis on self-regulation and control, should have a great deal to offer in this area. However, it should not be forgotten that many of the cybernetics engineer's principles derive from the observation of human behavior, and re-application of those principles to such behavior is not apt to be as simple as their application to target-seeking guns and other hardware. In particular, we must not let the notions of "automatic control" and "self-regulation" run away with us. Applied to machines, these terms are relative to a human reference point; that is, they refer to machines that control their own operations without human intervention. But when we are talking about human or social systems, where man himself is part of the system, the concept of "self-regulation" can be misleading unless it is carefully used. Any notion that a sociocultural system is self-regulating cannot mean a guarantee that—regardless of men's decisions and actions—stabilizing or adaptive control mechanisms will automatically come into play when "disturbances" occur in the system. We have to be prepared for the possibility that a social system may generate and maintain deviant and disorganizing forces in just as "automatic" a way as it generates mechanisms of conformity and organization. A self-regulating system can only refer to one which embodies certain parts and interrelations of parts that have the potential of responding in some adaptive or boundary-maintaining way to external and internal forces—within certain limits and with no guarantee.

Care must also be taken to distinguish (as we argued earlier) between self-regulation of a given system structure—which tends to maintain that structure in its essential form (as in homeostasis) — and self-direction (or control) of the system itself, which may imply

social control: 6
deviance, power,
and feedback processes

frequent change of its particular structure (as in biological and socio-cultural evolution). We have argued that the latter represents the more characteristic feature of sociocultural systems, whereas the former represents a highly selective and circumscribed perspective on that type of system, one closely associated with consensus theory.

In the first section of this Chapter we shall discuss briefly the general sociological conception of "social control" and a recent attempt to reformulate it in terms of the modern systems perspective. The second section continues with an important facet of this area, namely, social "deviance," and focuses on recent theories that emphasize deviance as a sociogenic phenomenon emerging out of the interplay of certain social and psychological forces. We see this new theory as illustrative of modern systems research, though it was not explicitly inspired by it. A final section investigates the possibilities of using the cybernetic feedback model of goal-seeking behavior to analyze a particular kind of social control, that involving the control or coordination of behaviors of members of a society or social organization specifically and consciously aimed at the attainment of group goals. The three sections attempt to deal in a more unified manner with a complex and conceptually confused area of social control, one overlapping with those discussed in previous sections, that is usually treated under the rubrics of "power", "authority", and "legitimacy". In these sections the reader should not look for more than a restatement of some of the many conceptual problems of traditional concern, along with a few indications of the large gains that might possibly be made by a serious use of the modern systems framework.

SOCIAL CONTROL

The notion of "social control" has not had a very successful career in sociology because of difficulties of conceptualization. It has perhaps most often been made virtually synonymous with sociology itself, concerned, for example, with the problem of social order in the broadest sense. Sometimes it has focused on the conditions for conformity and deviance-containment; sometimes on the authority and legitimacy maintaining a given institutional structure.[1] In any case, the consensus or equilibrium models of society have worked hand in hand with the "social control" concept to reinforce one another's weaknesses.

Our perspective embraces the view so well argued by Homans: "social control" is not a separate part of a system—something "set up" by

---

[1] For recent surveys of the "social control" concept see Kurt Wolff, "Social Control," in *Contemporary Sociology*, ed. Joseph Roucek, (New York: Philosophical Library, 1958), 110–31; Roger Nett, "Conformity-Deviation and the Social Control Concept," *Ethics*, 64 (1953), 38–45.

or imposed upon a system—but is inherent in the interrelations and inter-actions of elements that make up the system. In cybernetic terms, control is at best only partly pre-programmed in the system structure in anticipa-tion of particular disturbances or deviations; an important part is "error-regulated," in the sense that the system is continually processing feedback information about its own state and its goal deviations. The notion of built-in mechanisms of control, on the other hand, implies a pre-pro-gramming of constraints, designed to maintain a given structure despite the possibility that later challenges may demand changes of that struc-ture for adaptive flexibility. Much of our discussion in previous chapters has attempted to show this to be so.

To deny the existence of special mechanisms of control is not to say that we should not focus on special areas—such as the role of group pres-sures in promoting conformity, or of socialization in producing ordered behavior—as long as it is made clear that conformity and ordered be-havior do not exhaust the significance of group pressures and socializa-tion; that is, that the latter are, in fact, also responsible for just the op-posite.

We have appealed to the principle that norms and values alone do not specify action, that it is the norms and values, *plus* the interactions of those differentially interpreting them, that generate the social be-haviors we are trying to explain. To use a simile, social action is like a chess game: the rules and the goal constitute a framework of action, but the particular state or structure of the chessboard at any one time is a function of the particular interactions of the pieces up to that time. But in the case of society, some of the very rules and goals change as an emer-gent product of the ongoing interactions and the inevitable generation of "deviations."

In his paper on "Social Control and Self-Regulation," S. F. Nadel proposed a distinction between the more explicit, intended, or formalized social controls supported by rewards and punishments and the more basic self-regulating process inherent in social systems.[2] Customs, social habit, norms, or expectations are not themselves the basis for social order, but require two other conditions to operate reliably: either the normative behavior is in itself considered desirable and is valued apart from its also being expected or customary; or the behavior constitutes a routine affording maximum success with least risk. These Nadel finds to be "the true elements of self-regulation." Such conditions support the more fundamental structures and processes of society, and make for an "instrumental nexus" or complex of ramifying relations between the various means and goals of society. This means that adherence to socially

---

[2] S. F. Nadel, "Social Control and Self-Regulation," *Social Forces*, 31 (1953), 265–73.

channeled behavior leads, in the natural course of societal events, to "premiums" (not "rewards"), and deviation leads to "penalties" (not "punishments"). Thus, for example, a man in a certain folk society who does not marry finds that many of the valued things as defined in that group are just not available to him due to his bachelor status, though no punishments are consciously meted out to him. Thus, Nadel saw a circular feedback process underlying this self-regulation. It is the very following out of channeled behaviors that demonstrates in many ways their own validity; that is, the transactions involved generate "information sustaining further action of that character." We cannot appeal simply to the "social controls" of public criticism or institutionalized education, for these:

> not only safeguard but also presuppose values and hence represent, not so much controls acting from outside upon the desired conduct, as phases in a circular process whereby values engender conduct and conduct reinforces values.[3]

But this kind of self-regulation is most characteristic of primitive societies; complex, highly differentiated and heterogeneous societies do not as easily come by this kind of cohesion. If the network of social relations, information flows, and meanings structured in the society at a particular time do not in fact generate such premiums and penalties, then, regardless of an increased reliance on explicit controls, the system is in a condition under which the transition probabilities of other system states, so to speak, are increased, and we may find such phenomena as collective attempts to redefine or restructure the network of relations and meanings, diffuse manifestations of mental disturbance, deviance of both positive and negative kinds, and intergroup conflict.[4]

DEVIANCE

Both conformity and deviance, we are coming to fully appreciate, are understandable in terms of similar principles of the social process, specifically those discussed earlier in terms of "the act," the basic interaction or transaction process, and the elaboration of these into relatively stable structure. The traditional view sees structures of "social controls" which, when they break down, let loose a flood of deviance that is assumed to have mainly negative consequences for society. The newer view does not require structures to "break down," though this can be a factor; it

---

[3] *Ibid.*, p. 272.

[4] For a similar view, expressed in different terms, see George C. Homans, *Social Behavior* (New York: Harcourt, Brace & World, Inc., 1961), Chap. 18.

says that very hearty and tenacious structures, well supported from many sides, help to generate deviance in a continuous and ramifying stream, and that this deviance, as a "variety pool," contains essential positive elements for the group.[5] The morphogenic process discussed in the last chapter is applicable, it appears, to the generation of deviant mental and social structures as well as to conformity structures. The sociocultural system, as such, does not recognize any distinction between conformity and deviance—they are, equally, representations of the system in operation. The distinction is defined, rather, by certain individuals and subgroups, or "moral entrepreneurs," as Howard Becker calls them.[6]

A better perspective might be gained by an oversimplified sketch of the development of theories and methodological approaches to deviance. Early causal theories were of the "bad seed" type; the source of deviance was in the individual from the start, apparently inherited or due to a chance genetic combination. As theory developed, the causal forces expanded to include aspects of the environment or to embrace a more complex set of psychological forces. Thus, early social environment and acquired psychological traits become the antecedents, and the "bad seed," once planted, unfolded its consequences in later life almost regardless of the newer circumstances. After the nature–nurture battle subsided and the concept of the mutual interaction of social and psychological forces was established, the sociologist looked to the macro-structures and processes that might be at work: the structural means–cultural ends discrepancy, *anomie,* differential association in a subcultural or ecological matrix, or the like. Then, from antecedents and macro-structures, the focus shifts to the more immediate events at the micro-level of social transactions. Finally, concern is gradually being shown today to close the feedback loop from the transactionally generated deviance and its manifestations to the structural and normative background from which it emerged, the latter thereby undergoing modification.

These latter two stages of theory, representing the current dynamic trend, we see as lying squarely within the spirit of the modern systems view. Deviance is a systemic product generated out of a network of ongoing events or processes that involve: the historically generated institutional and cultural structure, with its vested interests and "moral entrepreneurs"; the matrix of interpersonal transactions within this structure whereby the strains of everyday role-playing generate adjustments, bargainings, and random or trial deviations which, in a context of "societal reactions," may lead to a "labeling" and consequent definition of the self as deviant; the resultant build-up of career deviants—whether aggregates of the mentally ill or the unusually creative, subcultures of the alienated

---

5 Cf. Nett, "Conformity–Deviation."

6 Howard Becker, *Outsiders* (New York: Free Press of Glencoe, Inc., 1963) .

or of political activists, or formal organizations of criminals; and finally, the feedback of the reactions of these groups, directly and indirectly, into the sociocultural structure, to contribute to its elaboration or disintegration.

Thus, Albert Cohen, in a recent article pulling together the highlights of recent deviance theory, cogently states:

> Until recently . . . the dominant bias in American sociology has been toward formulating theory in terms of variables that describe initial states, on the one hand, and outcomes, on the other, rather than in terms of processes whereby acts and complex structures of action are built, elaborated, and transformed.[7]

He points out the links between anomie theory, the "cultural transmission" and "differential association" theories, and the general theory of subcultures and the deviant opportunity structures they provide. The common core of such theories is their argument that deviance (and conformity as well) is not typically generated within the solitary individual but is rather "part of a collaborative *social* activity" within which meanings, values, and instrumentalities are generated. Thus, illegitimate opportunity structures already existing in some subcultures provide the individual in that milieu with the opportunity to learn and perform deviant acts and to receive the moral support of the subculture when the individual—under pressure from the conforming community—comes to define himself as deviant and to break with conventional norms and values. Or, in the absence of an established deviant subculture and social organization, a number of individuals with similar frustrations or deprivations who for one reason or another find themselves in effective communication may join together and generate within their congruent transactional matrix a subculture at variance with the conventional community.

Cohen sees that this is a kind of feedback mode in that the sort of deviant structure that emerges is a function of the nature and strength of the deviation-amplifying and deviation-reducing feedback processes operating in the system. The nature of the emerging deviance is a function of the opportunity structure in the effective milieu, and this in turn is a matter of the meanings and actions of other people. These actions of others, in their turn, are partly reactions to the potential deviant's behavior and may change in response to it.

> The development of ego's action can, therefore, be conceptualized as a series of responses, on the part of ego, to a series of changes in the opportunity structure resulting from ego's actions.[8]

---

[7] Albert K. Cohen, "The Sociology of the Deviant Act: Anomie Theory and Beyond," *American Sociological Review*, 30 (1965) , 9.

[8] *Ibid.*, p. 10.

On this basis Cohen develops a typology of responses of the opportunity structure to ego's tentative deviant act, focusing on whether legitimate or illegitimate opportunities are opened up or closed off.

Finally, Cohen recognizes the larger feedback loop stretching from the deviant structures and subcultures to their possible consequences for society's larger normative structure, suggesting that one aim of deviance theory "is to determine under what conditions feedback circuits promote change and under what conditions they inhibit change in the normative structures."[9] But this broad question leads us, among other things, to problems of power, authority, and legitimacy.

Thomas J. Scheff's recent sociological theory of mental illness represents a suggestive systematic and more detailed statement of this transactional generation of a different kind of deviance.[10] The accompanying flow-chart suggests the complex systemic nature of the process, including some of the deviation-amplifying feedbacks characteristic of the complex adaptive system we are studying. (See Figure 6–1) In outline, the theory is as follows. For diverse causes—biological, psychological, and/or social—most individuals at some time or other engage in *residual rule-breaking* or unusual behavior that is potentially definable by some members of society as abnormal or wrong. (These "diverse causes," of course, call for the plugging in of sociological and psychological theories of strain generation.) Most such residual rule-breaking is *denied,* not defined or reacted to as of consequence, and is thus not amplified; it is transitory and without issue. On the other hand, depending on the status of the individual, the visibility of his residual rule-breaking, community tolerance level, and so on, his behavior and its effects on family or friends may lead to a "public crisis" wherein it comes to be defined and "labeled" as "mental illness." These social responses of others significant to him, in conjunction with his own suggestibility at such a time of stress, and along with the stereotyped behaviors of the mentally disturbed he has learned during the normal socialization process, all contribute to his definition of himself as deviant. (This is very much the same process whereby *any* aspect of one's role and self-conception are socially elaborated, though without the stress and crisis.) Inasmuch as this is unsettling to an already disturbed person, his self-control is further impaired, making further episodes of "unusual" behavior likely. A deviation-amplifying feedback loop is thus set up as suggested in Figure 6–1, reverberating from "ego" and his behavior to significant others, to the public such as psychiatrist, court judge, family physician, or solicitous neighbor, and back to ego's self-conception. Ego's advance into overt deviant role-playing is furthered when the psy-

---

9 *Ibid.,* p. 12.

10 Thomas J. Scheff, "The Role of the Mentally Ill and the Dynamics of Mental Disorder: A Research Framework," *Sociometry,* 26 (1963), 436–53; *Being Mentally Ill* (Chicago: Aldine Publishing Company, 1966).

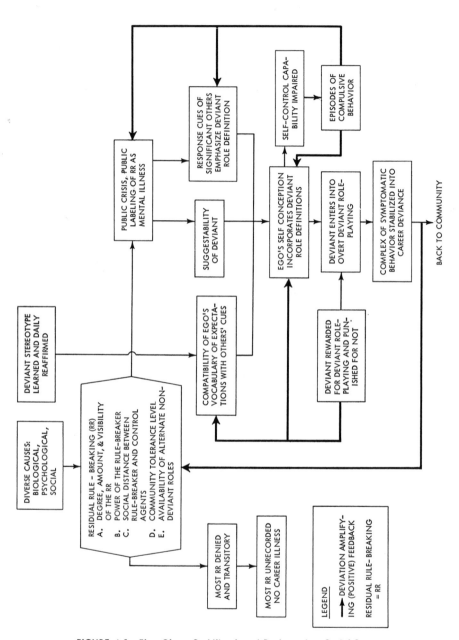

FIGURE 6-1   Flow Chart: Stabilization of Deviance in a Social System

chiatrist, for example, attempts to fit ego's presumed symptomatic behaviors into traditional clinical categories, and inadvertently rewards ego for the "correct" behavior symptoms and verbal responses and punishes him for attempting to deny his deviant role. This also constitutes a potential deviation-amplifying source, contributing to the final stabilization of ego into the career deviant role—the neurotic or psychotic. Finally, the aggregation of such deviant roles has its feedback effects on the community, its structure, its tolerance level, and the consequent nature of the "societal reaction" to further deviance.

One final example of current research on deviance, this one explicitly influenced by modern systems theory, is Leslie T. Wilkins' attempt at a general theory of deviance.[11] Wilkins views deviance as relative to cultural definitions constructed in a matrix of socially generated perceptions and "information sets" within a structural context of legitimate and illegitimate "opportunity structures." An important feature of the system is the degree to which there is an informational feedback loop into the system regarding its own functioning, such as to influence the "experience set" by which members act and which affects their definitions of deviance. Thus, some societies or groups treat deviance with great intolerance while others are able to accept a greater degree of deviance, "and, *as a result* of such tolerance, experience less serious deviance." As if in recognition of Nadel's theory of self-regulation, Wilkins goes on to say,

> It seems that it is possible for a society to operate in such a way that its social-sanctions systems become devalued. If such a feedback mechanism is in operation, the system within which it is applied tends towards instability. If a small initial stimulus generates a response, part of which response becomes a further stimulus, a highly critical and powerful servomechanism results.[12]

Applying the general deviation-amplifying model to the particular question of crime, he proposes the following principles and propositions:

1. In certain types of social systems, certain kinds of information lead to more acts being defined as deviant. (In our earlier terminology, information exercises its selective function to reduce, in some cases, the range of alternatives within the group's ensemble of acceptable behaviors.)

2. The individuals performing acts so defined as deviant are alienated from the larger community values by the very process of societal definition.

---

11 Leslie T. Wilkins, *Social Deviance* (Englewood Cliffs, N.J.: Prentice-Hall, Inc., 1965).
12 *Ibid.*, p. 87.

3. "The defining act provides an information set for the individuals concerned, and they begin to perceive themselves as deviant."

4. The societal reaction and self-definition lead to the isolation and alienation of the individuals from the group communication network.

5. These steps constitute the first part of a deviation-amplifying system (in our terms, a potentially morphogenic system).

6. This means that the deviant groups will tend to generate their own social organization and values, which may run counter to the institutionally dominant organization and values.

7. This structuring of deviant groups, and the increase in deviant acts, result in more forceful deviation-reducing pressures against them by conventional groups.

8. The selective information received about the behavior of the deviant groups by the conforming groups may lead to more acts being defined as deviant, or to more severe action against the deviants.

In this manner, the whole system "can itself continue round and round again in an amplifying circuit."[13]

To recapitulate this all too brief sketch of current deviance theory: the modern systems model is not simply seeking antecedents or prior "causes," nor is it appealing to consequences for, or "functional requisites" of, the system as such, nor is it looking at the mutual interaction of two or three elements of a system presumably "in equilibrium." Rather, the attempt is made to understand the total network of transactions of a complex adaptive system characterized by a psycho-social process moving through time and capable of generating a number of different possible states, often out of very similar earlier or "initial" conditions. Traditional social control theory, by focusing on how conformity is developed and maintained *vis à vis* dominant institutional sectors of society, has retarded recognition of the possibility that the same processes of "social control" may also be instrumental in generating and maintaining deviance.

FEEDBACK CONTROL OF SOCIAL GOAL-SEEKING

One of the more successful aspects of modern systems research is the field of cybernetics, and more specifically the concept of the feedback loop as a basic mechanism underlying system regulation and control. We wish to discuss briefly in this Section the possibilities of borrowing this latter principle as the basis of a model of societal or organizational goal-seeking, where the goals or purposes are explicit, conscious, and intentional.

---

13 *Ibid.*, p. 92. Wilkins offers some supporting empirical research, pp. 95 ff. See also Edwin M. Schur, *Crimes Without Victims* (Englewood Cliffs, N.J.: Prentice-Hall, Inc., 1965).

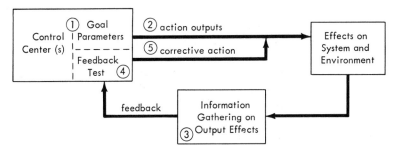

FIGURE 6-2

A social feedback model has been suggested occasionally since the mid-forties by a few social scientists, though it was not developed at any length until recently in the works, for example, of Geoffrey Vickers, Karl Deutsch, and David Easton.[14] Thus, Kurt Lewin, in a 1947 article, treats of "Feedback Problems of Social Diagnosis and Action."[15] Planned social action, he suggests, usually emerges from a more or less vague idea that develops into a "plan" when the objective has been clarified, the goal-path and available means have been determined, and a strategy of action worked out. Recognizing that this plan, or "blueprint for action," should be kept flexible and subject to modification as the action is carried out, he then makes reference to the self-steering missiles and other armaments developed during the war, and carries the underlying feedback principle over to the social sphere. After pointing out the important assumption underlying such steering, namely, that fact-finding methods have been found that permit a close enough determination of the nature and position of the social goal, as well as the direction and amount of "locomotion" brought about by a given action, he goes on to say:

> To be effective, this fact-finding has to be linked with the action organization itself: it has to be part of a feedback system which links a reconnaissance branch of the organization with the branches which do the action. The feedback has to be done so that a discrepancy between the desired and the actual direction leads "automatically" to a correction of actions or to a change of planning.

In the general cybernetic model of the error-regulating feedback system, we may distinguish—though more or less arbitrarily—five stages. (See Figure 6–2)

14 Geoffrey Vickers, *The Undirected Society* (Toronto: University of Toronto Press, 1959); Karl Deutsch, *The Nerves of Government* (New York: The Free Press, 1963); David Easton, *A Systems Analysis of Political Life* (New York: John Wiley and Sons, Inc., 1965).

15 Kurt Lewin, "Frontiers in Group Dynamics," Part II, B, *Human Relations*, I (1947), 147–53.

1) A control center establishes certain desired goal parameters and the means by which they may be attained; 2) these goal decisions are transformed by administrative bodies into action outputs, which result in certain effects on the state of the system and its environment; 3) information about these effects are recorded and fed back to the control center; 4) the latter tests this new state of the system against the desired goal parameters to measure the error or deviation of the initial output response; 5) if the error leaves the system outside the limits set by the goal parameters, corrective output action is taken by the control center.

This kind of model calls for a great deal of caution by the user, for while it may serve to illuminate the systemic nature and complexities of societal or organizational goal-seeking, any attempts at concrete application warn us against the hope of an easy breakthrough. Put in another way, such a model seems valid as a generalized picture of what *tends* to occur in group goal-seeking, or what *would* (or perhaps should) occur were it not for "complicating factors"; but these complicating factors are just what prevents the analyst from any easy use of the model. The following brief discussion expands on this point; though largely negative in tone, it is not intended to discourage further exploration of the feedback model in social analysis.

Starting with stage one of the feedback model as it might be applied to societal goal-seeking, we immediately run into some formidable problems. Is there *a* control center in the society that can validly be taken as a unified focus of societal goal decisions that alone have significant effects on the state of the system or its environment? If not, then we cannot hope to follow out the rest of the feedback cycle without determining the other important decision centers, assessing their systemic interrelations, and attempting the difficult task of tracing their joint effects throughout the cycle. If several feedback loops are circulating through the same system at the same time, with some running counter to others, the task may become unmanageable.

Assuming we know the control center (s), there are problems in interpreting the goals or goal parameters, the preference hierarchies required when there are several goals, and the possible consequences of the means that are chosen. Governments, for example, often set goals that are not much more than expressions of general societal values, making it difficult to specify the concrete criteria used to inform us of error or success; they avoid establishing preference scales for different goals or even questioning whether some are incompatible with others; and the means chosen often appear to have little relation to ends sought. And then there is the question of whether we dare assume that the main outputs into a social system always or even usually stem from central decision centers in the first place. Here we raise the problem of the role of planned, purposeful goal decisions relative to the aggregate of large numbers of individual and group goal decisions that may be more determinative of the state of the system at any time. Is the feedback model relevant only to societies or organizations with a high degree of centralized planning?

In the second stage of the model, goal decisions are translated by an administrative apparatus into concrete activities and rules of action to be applied by still another set of groups and individuals. Thus, the distance and number of linkages from the intended goal program—for example, a Poverty Program or a Farm Program—make possible a large amount of "slippage," reinterpretation of or selective attention to the original action outputs, or outright sabotage, such that it might not be at all clear whether subsequent goal deviation was due to the original outputs or to later administrative failures. The idealized model thus tends to assume not only a consensual, unified control center, but an automatic and unfailing transformation of decisions into final actions.

Consideration of the problems of the third stage—the gathering and feeding back of goal-deviation information—is bound to hit an especially sensitive spot for the social scientist, who must be acutely aware of the absence or inadequacy of scientific procedures and methodolgy necessary for such a task. We may be fairly well along with quantitative economic measures and a few others associated with census-taking, but a large-scale, and yet refined, assessment of most social, psychological, and cultural features of a society or complex organization has a long way to go. Given adequate techniques of data gathering and measurement, however, there is still the problem of following through with the full collection of what Paul Lazarsfeld has called "happiness data" from all the significant nooks and crannies of social life. Not only are we lacking the sociological theory or conceptual framework to direct us in tracing the important consequences of decisions and their reverberations throughout society, but there is the psychopolitical problem of full commitment of governing bodies to the task of ferreting out the *negative* consequences, the goal deviating results, of their decisions, wherever they may be found. And finally, the reader has probably already thought of the problem of the often long time lag between an action output and the concrete manifestations of its more important consequences. The system may not be able to wait until the full knowledge of results is in, or if it does wait, it may then be too late to take corrective action before disaster occurs. Furthermore, effects that show up some time after the action outputs may be hopelessly confounded with the consequences of subsequent outputs.

Ignoring the problem of relaying fully and rapidly the feedback information to the control center (s) , there are difficulties to be faced in the fourth stage, the testing of the feedback information for mismatch between output results and the established goal parameters. Can the various pieces of information be associated with the relevant goal outputs? Were the original goals specified in a sufficiently concrete and unambiguous way to permit a meaningful test of results? And considering the nature of most governing bodies today, what of the problem of selective attention to, and selective interpretation of, the feedback information, some of which may be too easily accepted as indicative of success and some hastily rejected as insufficient to establish failure?

Finally, the last stage—taking corrective output action—brings us back to problems of the first stage and adds others. The amount and timing of the corrective action, for example, may pose special difficulties, such as the avoidance of overcorrection, or of unnecessary interference with other goal activities. More serious, perhaps, is the introduction of "politics," and potential social upheaval, as complicating factors when the feedback information indicates that significant changes in the very structure of the socio-cultural system, hence in attitudes and behavior habits, are necessary for goal attainment to occur. And as a last difficulty we may mention the question of the conditions under which the most viable system response may be a change in the very goal parameters themselves—a response that has been seen as a kind of group or organizational learning. For societal goals and values do change, as well as the means for attaining them, and this opens up the large theoretical problem of the conditions under which this occurs and how it relates to the feedback model.

There is no doubt that we have barely touched on many of the difficulties to be faced in the use of such a model. It should be explored much more fully, but with caution and moderate expectations in the short run. It may not be especially applicable to society at present primarily because the controllers of contemporary societies have hardly discovered its applicability. In the next section we turn back to the more traditional conceptions of social goal-seeking.

POWER, AUTHORITY, AND LEGITIMACY

Whereas theories of social control have probably focused more intensively on the more implicit social processes at work, they have also been concerned with the more explicit and conscious attempts of some individuals and subgroups to channel the behaviors of others for the sake of goals or interests as the former, and sometimes the latter, define them. But this leads us to the subject of power, authority, legitimacy, and the process of institutionalization. To refer to these simply under the traditional heading of "social control," however, would be to beg the fundamental questions. For we must ask, "Control for what, or whose, ends?" The notion of "control" implies some end or goal, but the sociocultural system, as such, can only metaphorically be said to have a goal. True, its normal processes promote conformity to some set of norms or other, but they also promote deviance and dissensus. From this point of view, the more proper study of social control is the study of power, authority, and legitimacy and of the related purposeful forces that tend to maintain *or* to change the dominant institutional structure. For, to focus only on the forces of maintenance is to give some kind of priority to the given structure.

Another way of posing the issue is to ask: To what extent, and in what senses, are the existing social and cultural structures the results of the purposeful, goal-seeking actions of men, and to what extent are they the "blind" consequences of the confluence of sociocultural "forces?" When we look at our large urban centers and their over-all social, subcultural, and ecological configurations, the question seems to gather force. On second thought, however, the many pitfalls in the phrasing of the question itself appear. It would begin to appear obvious that the goal-seeking actions of men enter in at every point, except that: 1) these actions are not coherent or "congruent," but interact to produce the accommodations, compromises, and "side effects" producing the over-all "blind" configuration; and 2) the goal-seeking actions of some individuals and subgroups ramify but little into the social fabric, while those of others —whether playing official or nonofficial roles—account for important seams and patterns in that fabric. The first of these exceptions we have already discussed under the heading of the morphogenic process; the second is the problem of power, authority, and legitimacy.

Since this latter problem is so important for any theory of institutionalization, we shall devote some space to a discussion of various conceptualizations, from MacIver's suggestive treatment to Blau's quite similar views. As a focus to the discussion, we shall attempt to support the following points: First, there are at least two analytically distinguishable, though often phenomenally similar, patterns of social behavior that should be kept separate in our thinking. One such pattern is characterized by the control, direct or indirect, of behavior of numbers of people, against their "will" or without their informed commitment or understanding. The other pattern is characterized by such direction or control of behaviors, but with the informed and committed "consent" or consensus of those directed. Having made this oversimplified dichotomy, however, it should be recognized that a more adequate analysis would do well to treat it as a continuum, these two patterns being opposite poles. Second, these two patterns have usually been referred to as "power" and "authority," respectively, and the latter is said to be based on some principle of "legitimacy." But most often, the conceptual distinction has then been lost by the practice of defining authority in terms of power. This, we shall insist with MacIver, is inept, and has continually plagued conceptual and empirical analysis. Third, the mere fact that a majority of individuals and subgroups are overtly complying with a set of normatively defined role expectations in any organization or institutional setting is not to prejudice the separate question as to whether such norms and role-structure have a certain basis of legitimacy. A great deal of knowledge on the level of social-psychological dynamics would be essential to any answer. Fourth, power and authority have been found by many researchers to be significantly related to the primacy, in a group, of competitive goal orientations or of cooperative goal orientations, respectively. This central principle has been blurred in traditional consensus theory along with, and as a function of, the blurring of the distinction between power and authority. But its continual reappearance in important empirical research suggests its importance for understanding organizational dynamics.

These three distinctions—between power and authority, dissensus and consensus, and competitive or cooperative goal orientations, are closely interrelated. From the modern systems view, they are related in a complex systemic process, such that no one of them can be taken as *the* causal determinant, each being emergent, in its current social and personal manifestations, from the interplay of all of them. This is roughly suggested in the two diagrams of Figure 6.3. Out of the systemic process

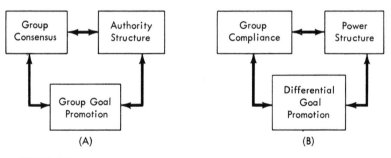

FIGURE 6-3

depicted in (A) is generated what we call "legitimacy"; it is a function, not simply of a structure of "official" positions, but of this structure in conjunction with individual and collective goal promotion and the related group consensus seen in terms of shared perspectives and emotive commitment. At the other ideal-typical extreme suggested in (B), the system process tends to generate group cleavage and dissensus, as well as coercive institutional control systems and ideologies that may succeed in maintaining a "social order" of overt compliance over fairly long periods.

To begin with a provocative reference, consider Walter Lippmann's comment on United States intervention in the Dominican Republic's civil war:

The predicament of the United States arises from the fact that it may take the Organization of American States and the United Nations years to overcome the political vacuum, to find, to promote, to defend and to finance a government which can be independent because it rests on popular consent . . .

It is as certain as anything can be in a situation of this kind that a workable policy must invoke the principle of legitimacy and must be directed to progressive reform. Legitimacy is important because only a government which derives from the only genuine election the Dominicans have ever known can hope to command the confidence and respect of the Dominican masses . . . The government which the OAS backs, and we along with it, should have as its cornerstone the Constitutionalist Party . . . For the decision to make the Constitutionalists the cornerstone will be the certain proof that President Johnson did not intervene in order to support a military dictatorship working for reactionary interests and that he is in fact genuinely committed to popular progressive reform.[16]

Here we find all the major ingredients of our subject. The distinction between power and legitimate authority, clearly implied here, was brought out by Robert MacIver in the following way:

By social power we mean the capacity to control the behavior of others either directly by fiat or indirectly by the manipulation of available means.[17]

By authority we mean the established *right*, within any social order, to determine policies, to pronounce judgments on relevant issues, and to settle controversies, or, more broadly, to act as leader or guide to other men. When we speak of *an* authority we mean a person or body of persons possessed of this right. The accent is primarily on right, not power. Power alone has no legitimacy, no mandate, no office. Even the most ruthless tyrant gets nowhere unless he can clothe himself with authority. . . .

The conclusion immediately follows that the authority of government does not create the order over which it presides and does not sustain that order solely by its own fiat or its accredited power. There is authority beyond the authority of government. There is a greater consensus without which the fundamental order of the community would fall apart. This consensus plays a different role under different forms of government . . . But always, whether mainly acquiescent or creatively active, it is the ultimate ground on which the unity and the order of the state repose.

We see, then, how inept is the identification of authority with power, and how superficial and misleading is the old-fashioned notion of sovereignty. . . .

Government, so understood, exercises authority for two main ends . . . One end is the maintenance of the established code . . . The other end of government is the readjustment of this order to new conditions and to emergent needs.[18]

---

[16] Walter Lippmann, column in the *Santa Barbara News-Press*, May 18, 1965.

[17] Robert M. MacIver, *The Web of Government* (New York: The Macmillan Company, 1947) , p. 87.

[18] *Ibid.*, pp. 83–87.

We should be careful to note that this is not a normative theory stating how government should be founded, but a sociological theory of societal stability and change: societies that are based on power will not persist, or will operate at a low level of efficiency and a high level of tension, malintegration, and/or conflict. Societies based on authority are more apt to persist, and at a higher level of personal satisfaction, group effectiveness, and cooperation. For, MacIver argued, force alone never holds a group together; in any constituted government, authority of some kind lies back of force, which is otherwise futile. "Authority is responsive to the underlying social structure," and the force of government is but the instrument of this authority which depends for its endurance "primarily on the prevailing myths," the ideologies, values, or knowledge systems, of those over whom it is exercised. "These myths, arising from and playing upon man's social nature, bring to government a ratification without which no prince or parliament, no tyrant or dictator, could ever rule a people."[19] MacIver went on to discuss this central "myth of authority" and its institutionalization in increasingly complex societies, its conformation "by institutional devices of increasing formality." These devices making for the "sanctification of authority" include the paraphernalia of office, investiture and insignia, ceremony, honorific titles, wealth, segregation of the person in authority from his fellow men, and so forth—aspects of institutionalization that have been almost totally neglected in contemporary sociology as if they were no longer relevant in the modern world.

Until recently, most other systematic attempts in this area have departed significantly from MacIver's valuable beginning, either confusing power and authority by definitional fusion, reversing the relative primacy of force and consensus in sustaining social order, or ignoring the power side of the continuum as if its empirical referent in society were not important or did not exist.

One of the more systematic and influential discussions has been that of Robert Bierstedt.[20] He defines "power" as "latent force," "force" as "manifest power," and "authority" as "institutionalized power." Of particular interest to us here is his attempt to equate authority and power by way of institutionalization. The locus of power he finds in three areas: in formal organization, in informal organization, and in the unorganized community. Let us consider the implications of his definition of power for the development and maintenance of organization and order in society. In the following quote, where Bierstedt uses the term "power" we shall substitute his definiens, "latent force."

---

19 *Ibid.*, 16–17, Chap. 3.
20 Robert Bierstedt, "An Analysis of Social Power," *American Sociological Review,* 15 (1950) , 730–38.

[Latent force] is required to inaugurate an association in the first place, to guarantee its continuance, and to enforce its norms. [Latent force] supports the fundamental order of society and the social organization within it, wherever there is order. [Latent force] stands behind every association and sustains its structure. Without [latent force] there is no organization and without [latent force] there is no order.[21]

We have here a theory of social order that is starkly opposite to that of MacIver, and typical of classical political science. But is it what Bierstedt really means? Further discussion shows that it is. The problem of the locus of power in formal organization is dismissed as "a fairly simple problem for analysis":

It is in the formal organization of associations that social power is transformed into authority. When social action and interaction proceed wholly in conformity to the norms of the formal organization, power is dissolved without residue into authority. The right to use force is then attached to certain statuses within the association, and this right is what we ordinarily mean by authority.[22]

This appears to be a neo-Hobbesian answer to the problem of order, but it is still not clear just what role the "norms" play here. Are they established and maintained by the "latent force" of the authority, or do they rather underlie the "right" of the authority? In a later paper, Bierstedt wrestles further with the problem.[23] As a tentative answer to the question of "whether authority is a phenomenon exercised by coercion or consent," he makes a distinction between voluntary and involuntary association, and argues that in voluntary associations authority is institutionalized leadership, and in involuntary associations it is institutionalized power. "In the former authority rests upon consent; in the latter, upon coercion." But he is not satisfied with this solution. Not only is it difficult to distinguish in some cases between these types of association, but, probably more important, he feels that:

There is something mandatory, not merely arbitrary, about the acceptance of authority . . . In order to retain the central connotation of the concept we are examining it seems desirable to assert that authority is always a power phenomenon. It is power which confers authority upon a command. But it is sanctioned power, institutionalized power. The power resides in the majority of the members.[24]

Here Bierstedt is up against the stubborn paradox once more. On the one hand, he is arguing that it is consensual authority that sanctions

---

21 *Ibid.*, 735.

22 *Ibid.*, 733.

23 Robert Bierstedt "The Problem of Authority," in Morroe Berger *et al.*, *Freedom and Control in Modern Society* (Princeton, N.J.: D. Van Nostrand Co., Inc., 1954) , Chap. 3.

24 *Ibid.*, p. 79.

power, but on the other, he states that it is power (albeit institutional-ized power) which confers authority. His argument amounts to the state-ment that the majority consents to being coerced. Now, there is an important sense in which this is true: although a majority may consent to a system of control, different individuals at different times will find themselves on the losing end of majority decisions and must therefore consent to accept the occasional defeat. This, perhaps, is the mandatory element that Bierstedt feels to be lacking in a definition of authority resting on consent. Nevertheless, we do not believe that this is sufficient warrant to base a general theoretical conception of authority on coercion rather than on its predominant characteristic, some kind of over-all con-sent. We must reaffirm MacIver's view that the identification of power and authority is inept,[25] and reject a neo-Durkheimian or Hobbesian theory of social constraint. And as in the case of Durkheim and Hobbes, the lacking ingredient involves a fuller appreciation of the internal, psy-chological dynamics of the group members and the inter-psychic network of relationships. Internal self-control may be as mandatory as external control, and social control may be seen at bottom as self-control. The sociocultural system is the only natural adaptive system in which the over-all direction and control become largely a function of the self-direction and control inherent in the individual (including subgroup) units that make it up. This is just another way of stating Lester Ward's distinction between the "telic" or conscious purposive nature of the social process and the "genetic" or blind evolutionary process of response to external environmental constraints on the sub-human level.

The issue is most concisely and explicitly brought out in the defi-nitions of Lasswell and Kaplan. After defining power as "simply the exercise of a high degree of coerciveness," involving either "severe depriva-tions or indulgences," they continue:

> . . . the conception of power here developed does not exclude or even minimize the element of consent in power relationships. "Coercion by consent," while verbally a paradox, has reference to a familiar and impor-tant aspect of the power process—specifically, to the perspectives of those over whom power is being exercised. Identification, expectations, and de-mands render power authoritative, and this constitutes consent to the power structure and practices. The fact that power, by definition, rests on coercion does not entail that the power situation itself cannot be the result, in part, of choice.[26]

We do not believe that elevating conceptual confusion into a paradox is very helpful, although their appeal to psychological mechanisms is a step in the right direction.

---

25 MacIver, *The Web of Government,* pp. 86–87.

26 Harold D. Lasswell and Abraham Kaplan, *Power and Society* (New Haven, Conn.: Yale University Press, 1950) , pp. 98–99.

Robin M. Williams, Jr., takes a step in MacIver's direction, but straddles the issue:

> Political authority, based upon a value consensus in the relevant social group, never lasts indefinitely without the backing of coercive power; but, on the other hand, political power without authority cannot maintain itself for long.[27]

Looking at the first half of the statement, at least three interpretations are possible: 1) there is always a minority of deviants who must be coerced for the greater good (but this is relatively trivial for his argument, and sidesteps the issue) ; 2) consensus erodes over time and coercion becomes necessary to maintain the existing structure (but this means that the original authority no longer exists, having passed over into power) ; and 3) majority consensus requires coercion for its maintenance (and this is precisely the paradox we met above).

Not too long ago, Talcott Parsons viewed the concept of power in terms fairly similar to those of most other sociologists. For example, in his *Social System* of 1951 he defined it in terms of "control over the actions of other." His view of "authority" and its relation to "power" was likewise similar:

> The problem of control of political power is above all the problem of *integration*, of building the power of individuals and sub-collectivities into a coherent system of legitimized authority where power is fused with collective responsibility.[28]

In his more recent essays, however, Parsons' conception of power leaves the mainstream, becomes a much more generalized notion elevated to the status of a "functional prerequisite" of society, and no longer has anything directly to do with the controlling actions of concrete individuals and groups and their more proximate ends. Power is now defined as the "generalized capacity of a social system to get things done in the interest of collective goals."[29] One main reason for this shift appears to be a heuristic one, based on his strong and long-standing attachment to, and attempt to follow out, an analogy between the economy and the "polity," both viewed as subsystems that "articulate" between the institutional and collectivity (specific organizational) levels of social action. Just as the economy produces wealth, so does the polity "produce" power. Just as the economy mobilizes and allocates the factors of production for

---

27 Robin M. Williams, Jr., *American Society* (New York: Alfred A. Knopf, Inc., 1961) , p. 204.

28 Talcott Parsons, *The Social System* (New York: Free Press of Glencoe, Inc., 1951) , pp. 121, 127.

29 Talcott Parsons, *Structure and Process in Modern Society* (New York: Free Press of Glencoe, Inc., 1960) , p. 181.

the attainment of (anyone's) goals, so the polity "mobilizes" and "allocates" social "resources" for the attainment of (collective) goals. Hence:

> Power and wealth have in common that they are both generalized categories of "means," i.e., of "capacities" to get desired things done . . .
> Power . . . has specific reference to the goals of the collectivity, and hence implies, for its generation, *integration* of the collectivity with reference to such goals . . .[30]

The concept of authority, in turn, is treated on a somewhat lower level of analysis, the institutional, and again in terms of an economic parallel:

> From this point of view, authority would be the complex of institutionalized rights to control the actions of members of the society with reference to their bearing on the attainment of collective goals.[31]

The concepts of *both* power and authority, then, embrace the consensual, collective side of control processes. But, we must ask, what of the divisive, coercive, and private aspect of control? This aspect Parsons dismisses rather summarily as a "secondary and derived aspect" of power:

> A brief word should be said about the concept of power used here. It seems to me that it is one of the two principal alternatives which are current in the literature of political theory, the other being what may be called the "zero-sum" concept as used, for example, by Max Weber and by H. D. Lasswell. This is the conception that power is the capacity of one unit in a system to gain its ends *over the opposition* of other units—hence if the power of two units is equal there is a stalemate between them. The concept I am using here does not make opposition a criterion as such, though since I am talking about capacity to attain goals, it *includes* the overcoming of opposition. I thus consider the zero-sum concept to be a special case of the more general concept employed here.[32]

Though his book is concerned with structure and process in modern societies, he does not consider "opposition" important enough to treat other than as an aside. In keeping with his consistent theoretical emphasis on the stable, equilibrating, harmonious aspects of society, he avoids systematic treatment of the conflicting, disequilibrating, disorganizing aspects of society that are not merely "deviant" and thus taken care of by his "mechanisms of control."[33] What Parsons' discussion implies is

---

30 *Ibid.*, pp. 181–82.

31 *Ibid.*, p. 185.

32 *Ibid.*, p. 182.

33 Such considerations lead us to question the rationale for Parsons' taking Mills so strongly to task for his "bias" and his "highly selective treatment" in focusing his research on this latter aspect, and not defining "power" in the way that Parsons does. See *ibid.*, pp. 220–21.

that those modern Western societies that seem quite stable must have solved the problem of coercive power and integration.[34] In fact, as we have seen, the assumption of integration is built into Parsons' new definition of power which, in turn, is supported by a framework of analysis that leaves little room for the operation of what we might call *legitimate opposition*. Furthermore, Parsons' linking of both "power" and "authority" to the "attainment of collective goals," suggests that, to the extent that goals in a society are *not* "collective," but private and competitive, then malintegration, dissensus, and conflict may tend to be generated; but for some reason, this highly suggestive lead is not pursued. It is not without relevance to ask why Parsons should have dropped from his conceptual repertoire just that "pattern variable" that distinguishes between private *vs.* collective interests ("self-orientation" *vs.* "collectivity-orientation").

As a final illustration of the problem of consent *vs.* coercion in the definition of power, we shall mention Robert Lynd's conception, especially because he defined power in the same terms Parsons came to use, but on the basis of quite different considerations. Essentially, whereas Parsons' view of power as a "capacity" or resource derives from a conception of what a social system *is*, Lynd's view derives from a consideration of what a society *could be*. Reacting to "the traditional identification of power with domination," and the consequent tendency of liberal democracy "to resolve the problem of power by quantitative limitation of its use," Lynd argues:

> A central problem here is whether it is conducive either to clear thinking about power or to its effective use to lump together as dominance both arbitrarily imposed power and the uses of organized power by democratic means to achieve democratic purposes. The identification of power with dominance obscures the fact that power in a genuine democracy may be a human resource which can be used for the enlargement of human freedom.[35]

What we wish to point out is that if we translate Lynd's conception of "organized power by democratic means" into "consensual authority," we have yet another good argument against the identification of power and authority.[36]

---

34 Parsons states as much in several places in the work we are citing.

35 Robert S. Lynd, "Power in American Society as Resource and Problem," in *Problems of Power in American Democracy*, ed. Arthur Kornhauser (Detroit: Wayne State University Press, 1959), pp. 4–5.

36 In considering the views of Parsons, on the one hand, and Mills and Lynd, on the other, the temptation may be strong to evaluate all of them in ideological terms, which usually means to dismiss summarily one or the other on less than scientific grounds. This temptation, however, is to be energetically resisted: the issues involved here can be seen as genuine and fundamental problems *for social science*.

GROUP GOALS, POWER, AND BUREAUCRACY

A suggested solution to the paradox of power and authority, then, is to conceptualize the two aspects of control as polar types defining the ends of a continuum. As a suggested working definition, we may define *power* as control or influence over the actions of others to promote one's goals without their consent, against their "will," or without their knowledge or understanding (for example, by control of the physical, psychological, or sociocultural environment within which others must act). The mechanisms involved may range from naked force,[37] through manipulation of symbols, information, and other environmental conditions, to the dispensing of conditional rewards. The emphasis here is on the lack of ascertainable "consent," considered as something socially and psychologically deeper than mere acquiescence or overt compliance. A closely related characteristic is the emphasis on private goal-orientation rather than on collectivity goal-orientation.

Authority is the direction or control of the behavior of others for the promotion of collective goals, based on some ascertainable form of their knowledgeable consent. Authority thus implies informed, voluntary compliance, which is a definite psychological state, and a coordination or identity of the goal-orientations of controllers and controlled. As defined, authority is not a special form of power, nor is power a subtype of authority. These are polar types, with the various institutional areas of actual societies represented somewhere along the adjoining continuum. Historically, most societies have been heavily skewed in favor of the power pole, and must of history—especially modern history—can be seen as a struggle toward the authority pole, that is, toward the institutionalization of a process of informed, consensual self-determination of the whole, which we call "democracy."

The concepts of "will" and "consent" occurring in our definitions point up the need for a more adequate social psychological understanding, exemplifying especially well the recent arguments that sociology must of necessity make greater use of intervening psychological variables if it is to progress. As we suggested earlier, emphasis on structural concepts like institutionalization, legitimacy, and so forth—with an occasional mention of socialization—can carry us only part of the way. A more concerted

---

[37] In its pure form, naked power—brute force—is a purely physical phenomenon, outside the realm of the social or psychological. No group can be *based on* such coercion as a principle more fundamental than its common culture. We believe it to be a common error of the traditional political scientist to view the state's monopoly of coercive instruments as the foundation of civil society—as MacIver argued so well.

effort to relate these concepts to the lower-level propositions stemming from observations of the concrete interactions of individuals and groups is long past due.

It is axiomatic that power and authority are intimately related to the pursuit of goals in a social environment where the available goals are limited.[38] We shall focus now on the nature of this relationship, especially as it pertains to the pursuit of private goals *vs.* the pursuit of public, or collective, goals.

On the basis of research with small groups, Cartwright and Zander attack the problem of defining a "group goal."[39] They conclude that a satisfactory definition must recognize that a group goal: a) is related to a set of member "tension-systems" that are mutually interdependent in their arousal and release; and b) exerts influence over group members so as to activate and steer their behavior. More specifically, such a definition implies: 1) that a *group* goal exists only when action by *any one member* reduces the motivational tension of *all* group members (this is the core of the meaning behind the notion of interdependence of members' needs or goals) ; and 2) that a group goal exists only if it acts in some way on all the members alike, in contrast to unique or personal member goals.

Following this approach, Morton Deutsch proposes that a *group goal* be defined as existing when several persons are so interrelated that the activity of one helps reduce the "need tensions" of others, thus implying the conversion of individual needs into emergent, member-defined group "needs."[40] The type of group situation in which the interdependence of members is based on the existence of a group goal, in this defined sense, is referred to as a *cooperative situation*—one in which the goals of individuals are so related that the goal of any one of them can be achieved only if all the individuals can also achieve their respective goals. This suggests to Deutsch the very definition of a group: 1) a sociological group exists to the extent that its actors are pursuing "promotively interdependent goals" (group goals as defined above) ; 2) a psychological group exists to the extent that its members perceive themselves as pursuing promo-

---

38 We believe the term "limited" to be more accurate and less biased than the term "inherently scarce" so often used. In the modern "affluent" society, for example, there is no scarcity of the wherewithal to satisfy basic needs. If there is a scarcity relative to either basic or acquired needs in such a society, it is an institutionalized scarcity, not an inherent one. This follows from fundamental sociological principles pointing to the non-randomness of ends in a social system. To argue that men will always "want" more than is available is not too meaningful an assertion in the present state of our knowledge. Durkheim saw this point in discussing *anomie.*

39 Dorwin Cartwright and Alvin Zander, eds., *Group Dynamics* (New York: Harper & Row, Publishers, 1953) , Chap. 22.

40 Morton Deutsch, "The Effects of Cooperation and Competition upon Group Processes," in *Group Dynamics,* ed. Cartwright and Zander, Chap. 23.

tively interdependent goals, 3) a psychological group has cohesiveness as a direct function of the strength of goals perceived to be promotively interdependent, and the degree of perceived interdependence. Thus, Deutsch's definition of a "social group" is identical to the above conceptualization of the "cooperative situation," and to us it represents an advance over the usually vague sociological usage of the terms "common" or "shared" norms or values, "mutual" or "reciprocal" expectations, "functional interdependence" of parts, and perhaps "integration."

As a second basic type of group interdependence, contrasting with the above, Deutsch offers the *competitive situation:* if one member of the group reaches his goal, the others will to some degree be unable to reach their goals. This implies the lack of a group goal in the above sense. The goals in such a situation are scarce by social prescription, and cannot be attained by all.

Small-group experiments performed with such conceptions in mind led Deutsch to many findings or derived hypotheses of relevance to our thesis. For example: 1) In a group situation in which group goals are present there will be a readiness to substitute one member's activities for another's, since each person's activities are evaluated not by who performs them but by their contribution to the goal. 2) The primacy of a group goal implies a readiness to accept influence attempts from other members, since they all see that they are promoting each others' ends. 3) In a situation where group goals are absent or minimal the group will tend to split into more or less independent subgroups with mutually exclusive goals.[41]

Turning to another study of a quite different kind of group, we may find to be of some relevance many of the conclusions drawn by Margaret Mead from her investigation of cooperative and competitive preliterate societies, such as:

> . . . it is also instructive to look at the presence of the will to power over persons. This does not occur among the cooperative societies . . . The absence of will to power over persons among the cooperative societies correlates with the presence in these societies of shared ends among all members of the group. Since all individuals work together toward these ends, no individual requires servile individuals to do his bidding . . .
>
> In all the societies in which the will to power is obviously developed, there is a low degree of security for the individual, and in none of the societies with a high degree of security is there a will to power over persons. It is striking that will to power does not necessarily occur where there is strong ego development, for it is absent in Eskimo, Maori, and Iroquois.[42]

---

[41] Deutsch's work thus independently complements and deepens the very similar theory of cooperation and competition put forth by Mack A. May and Leonard W. Doob, *Competition and Cooperation* (New York: Social Science Research Council, 1937).

[42] Margaret Mead, ed., *Cooperation and Competition among Primitive Peoples* (New York: McGraw-Hill Book Company, 1937), pp. 496–97.

Many serious students have spoken in very similar terms in analyzing contemporary society. For example, Robin M. Williams, Jr., in his early monograph on *The Reduction of Intergroup Tensions,* pointed out that in every society people act in orientation to values that, on the one hand, can be shared by everyone and "are not scarce in the sense that one individual's sharing will reduce others' enjoyment," and on the other, to values that are "scarce, divisible, and divisive." "The main classes of scarce, divisible values are: wealth, power, and prestige . . ."[43] The manner in which such an emphasis may be built into a society has been discussed in corresponding terms by Gardner Murphy:

> . . . power, which was earlier simply the thrust of the individual against obstacles, becomes a struggle for relative control of the situation in the competitive atmosphere of the home or school or playground, and success in achieving power enhances the self . . . The child who struggles for an object or a privilege which he has been denied is therefore struggling for three things: the object itself, the prestige which this will add to his self-image, and the power which may be used in relation to the authorities on subsequent occasions . . . These relationships are built into our society . . . The advanced societies, without exception, are rigged in such a way that the three motives are more or less intertwined, but in our own society they are intertwined in special intimacy.[44]

The essence of authority, as we have defined it, is empirically illustrated in the studies of bureaucracy done by Peter Blau and by Alvin Gouldner. Blau's study included a comparison of performance and other characteristics of two separate interview sections of a state employment agency, one highly competitive in nature and the other primarily cooperative. It was found that the more productive and satisfied group was the one with what Deutsch would call "promotively interdependent goals." The differences in the two interview sections were found to be based on differences in three sets of social factors structuring the system of action and interaction. The supervisor in the competitive section relied heavily on performance records in rating his employees, thus giving rise to anxiety about individual performance. In the cooperative section, rating was more lenient and did not rely primarily on production records. Also, this latter section had developed a professional orientation during its members' earlier training, giving rise to a common professional code that discouraged hasty placement of clients, a practice which "transformed competitive practices from illegitimate means for desirable ends into illegitimate means for worthless ends,"[45] that is, hoarding of job referral

---

[43] Robin M. Williams, Jr., *The Reduction of Intergroup Tensions* (New York: Social Science Research Council, 1947).

[44] Gardner Murphy, "Social Motivation," in *Handbook of Social Psychology*, 2, ed. Gardner Lindzey, (Reading, Mass.: Addison-Wesley Publishing Co., Inc., 1954), pp. 623–24.

[45] Peter M. Blau, "Cooperation and Competition in a Bureaucracy," *American Journal of Sociology*, 59 (1954), 532.

slips to attempt to maximize one's own placements. The competitive group lacked this common orientation and code. Finally, members of the competitive group were not on permanent employment status and the insecurity thus engendered led them to overstrive to impress superiors. Members of the cooperative group, in contrast, had security of tenure. In sum, the competitive situation led to high status anxiety, low group cohesiveness, and consequently, inefficient group production. The higher social cohesion of the cooperative group enhanced its operating efficiency by facilitating cooperation among the members and by reducing status anxiety. And it is this kind of group situation that leads to a conception of consensus-based authority that goes beneath the mere fact of conformity or acquiescence to get at the non-normative elements of action underlying the consensus and hence legitimacy of that authority. Thus, Blau comes to define *authority* in the following way:

> . . . authority involves exercise of social control which rests on the willing compliance of subordinates with certain directives of the superior. He need not coerce or persuade subordinates in order to influence them, because they have accepted as legitimate the principle that some of their actions should be governed by his decisions.[46]

Gouldner's research in an industrial bureaucracy[47] led him to distinguish between what he called "representative" bureaucracy, and "punishment-centered" bureaucracy, each representing, respectively, one of the two main facets of Max Weber's conception of bureaucracy: the expertise or technical proficiency of the bureaucrat in attaining goals, and the emphasis on strict obedience of subordinates to bureaucratic authority. In any particular bureaucracy, primacy may be given to one or the other of these two types. "Representative" bureaucracy, Gouldner found, was characterized by an integration of the goals of both the subordinates and the officials, so that the bureaucratic norms were supported by both, satisfaction was high, and tensions at a minimum. "Punishment-centered" bureaucracy, however, manifested the opposite traits, and thus failed to meet Weber's "ideal" criterion of maximum efficiency. Thus, in the safety program studied by Gouldner the "representative" pattern was exemplified by the fact that the safety engineer was expected to have knowledge of the facts and to use them to prevent accidents, and the safety program itself sought to *persuade* conformance to the rules, through meetings, posters, and so forth. On the other hand, the "punishment-centered" pattern is represented by the fact that the foremen assumed the right to impose and enforce the rule "because of *their formal position of authority*":

---

[46] Peter M. Blau, *Bureaucracy in Modern Society* (New York: Random House, Inc., 1956), p. 71.

[47] Alvin Gouldner, *Patterns of Industrial Bureaucracy* (New York: Free Press of Glencoe, Inc., 1954).

In the punishment-centered pattern, then, the rule is treated as an end in itself. By contrast, however, the safety program, the prototype of representative bureaucracy . . . was designed to bring about another end, accident curtailment. Obedience was sought and given the safety rules, on the grounds that they would effectively lead to desirable consequences *beyond themselves* . . .

It may be that 'consent,' springing from a consensus of ends and values, also provides a clue for further investigations of punishment-centered bureaucracy. More specifically, it seems possible that this pattern arises not merely along with, but partly *because of a dissensus* in ends; that is, obedience would tend to be stressed as an end in itself, and authority tend to be legitimated in terms of incumbency of office, when subordinates are ordered to do things *divergent from their own ends.* If the no-absentee-ism rule had *furthered workers' ends,* for example, it could have been justified on these grounds. At best, however, this rule is related to management's need to regularize production and to make it more predictable—ends which are *not salient for workers.* It is in part for this reason that supervisors had only an authoritarian legitimation for the absenteeism rule . . .[48]

In sum, Cartwright and Zander, Deutsch, Margaret Mead, Williams, Blau, Gouldner, and many others arrive at the conclusion that the control, or directive processes of a group or organization are intimately related to, and must be studied in close conjunction with, the goals and more proximate values of that group or organization, the procedures by which the goals have been arrived at, the spread of participation in their implementation, and the distribution of their benefits. Especially must the social scientist be wary of confining his discussion to the level of assumed "common" or "shared" values without specifying the groups involved or without translating the values into the goals of individuals and the interrelation of these goals within a group or organization. It is the nature of the relation between such goal-orientations and the control processes of a group or organization that points to the possibility of the two relatively distinct phenomena that we have defined as power and authority. Although they may appear similar on the surface or from a narrow perspective, the differences on the level of psychological and sociocultural processes may be profound from the broader view.

SUBTYPES OF POWER AND AUTHORITY

If we attempt to develop a typology of power and authority it must reflect the conceptual distinction we have made between the two. It should also reflect the stipulation that "institutionalized" structures are not thereby necessarily "legitimized" in any full sense, even for a majority of group members. We shall make use of Weber's three types of

---

[48] *Ibid.,* pp. 220–21, 223–24.

"authority" or "domination" as a basis for discussion, though his typology may not be entirely adequate. What we suggest is that against the three types of legitimized *authority* (Weber's *Herrschaft*) may be placed three corresponding types of *power* (Weber's *Macht*) : traditional, charismatic, and rational-legal.[49]

Thus, an analytical distinction between "traditional authority" and "traditional power" makes conceptually explicit Weber's own recognition, that whereas this type of legitimized *authority* involves the exercise of control over others by virtue of inherited status and according to custom, it also implies a certain degree of arbitrary *power* by virtue of that status. Those exercising traditional authority have a dual advantage, as Bendix pointed out:

> Their commands are legitimate in the sense that they are in accord with custom, but they also possess the prerogative of free personal decision, so that conformity with custom and personal arbitrariness are both characteristic of such rule.[50]

In general, the distinction between traditional authority and traditional power alerts us to the distinction between the traditionally legitimized *social position or status* of the controlling decision-makers, and the possibly *non-legitimized, non-customary content* of their controlling decisions. The distinction thus leads us to question the often-held view of tradition-bound "folk" cultures as all of a piece, persisting in rustic tranquality through a control system made up entirely of internalized sacred norms, beliefs, and symbols unthinkingly adhered to as ends in themselves. We recall that Oscar Lewis has taken Redfield's "folk-urban" classification to task on a similar point, arguing that this classification "tends to obscure one of the most significant findings of modern cultural anthropology, namely, the wide range in the ways of life and in the value systems among so-called primitive peoples . . ." His critique of Redfield's Tepoztlan study continues by arguing:

> Throughout his study we find an emphasis upon the cooperative and unifying factors in Tepoztecan society. Our findings, on the other hand, would emphasize the underlying individualism of Tepoztecan institutions and character, the lack of cooperation, the tensions between villages . . .[51]

Adherence to the concept of folk-culture, Lewis suggests, may help explain Redfield's:

---

[49] Max Weber, *The Theory of Social and Economic Organization* (New York: Oxford University Press, 1947) ; Hans Gerth and C. Wright Mills, eds., *From Max Weber: Essays in Sociology* (New York: Oxford University Press, 1946) .

[50] Reinhard Bendix, *Max Weber: An Intellectual Portrait* (New York: Doubleday & Company, Inc., 1962) , p. 295.

[51] Oscar Lewis, *Life in a Mexican Village* (Urbana, Ill.: University of Illinois Press, 1951) , p. 429.

. . . emphasis on the formal and ritualistic aspects of life rather than the everyday life of the people and their problems, on evidence of homogeneity rather than the heterogeneity and the range of custom, on the weight of tradition rather than the deviation and innovation, on unity and integration rather than tensions and conflict.[52]

And in a later study of a peasant community in India, Lewis and Barnouw more specifically pointed out the *power* relations underlying the heavy cake of tradition.[53] They point out that most studies of the Indian caste system have avoided its economic aspects, especially the interaction of the subgroups in the production and exchange of goods and services. But it is in just this area of social behavior that we find the source of some of the most important determinants of control maintaining the long-standing system of differentiated and stratified positions and roles, namely, a clear-cut system of power relations based on property ownership that transcends even highest-caste membership as a determinant of local hierarchies.

Lewis and Barnouw suggest that W. H. Wiser, in his discussion of the *Jajmani* system, gives us a rather benevolent picture of the "peace and contentment" it provides the community.[54] Likewise, Opler and Singh tell us:

Not only does everyone have some place within the Hindu system, but it is significant that every group, from the Brahman to the Chamar caste, has been somehow integrated into the social and ceremonial round of the community and has been given some opportunity to feel indispensable and proud.[55]

But Lewis and Barnouw find otherwise:

Our picture of Rampur, however, leads to a quite different assessment, for it seems evident that the relationship between *jajman* and *kamin* lends itself to the exploitation of the latter. Land ownership is the basis of power in Rampur. All the village land, including the house sites, is owned by the Jats; the other castes are thus living there more or less at the sufferance of the Jats. It was this crucial relationship to the land, with the attendant power of eviction, that made it possible for the Jats to exact *begar* service from the Camars in the past and still enables them to dominate the other caste groups . . .
While the landowners are generally of higher caste in Indian villages,

---

52 *Ibid.*, p. 432.

53 Oscar Lewis and Victor Barnouw, "Caste and the Jajmani System in a North Indian Village," *Scientific Monthly*, 83 (1956) , 66–81.

54 William H. Wiser, *The Hindu Jajmani System* (Lucknow: Lucknow Publishing House, 1936) , p. 187.

55 Morris E. Opler and Rudra D. Singh, "The Division of Labor in an Indian Village," in *A Reader in General Anthropology*, ed. Carleton S. Coon (New York: Holt, Rinehart & Winston, Inc., 1948) , p. 496.

it is their position as landowners, rather than caste membership *per se,* that gives them status and power. In Karimpur, where the Brahmans are the landowners, the traditional caste hierarchy obtains. But in Rampur the Jats own the land, and the Brahmans are subservient to them. Majumdar and his colleagues present a similar picture in their description of the village near Lucknow: "The respect which the Brahmins enjoy is merely conventional; in daily life, however, the Brahmins are treated on an equal footing with the other castes . . ."[56]

Even Wiser, in his otherwise one-sided study, suggests the reason why the power exercised may not be too obvious at first glance:

> The serving ones have learned that as long as their subservience is un-questioned, the hand which directs them rests lightly. But let there be any move toward independence or even indifference among them, and the paternal touch becomes a strangle-hold . . . in every detail of life have the leaders bound the villagers to themselves."[57]

If such findings are borne out in other cases, then it becomes clear that the long-standing Sumnerian emphasis on pure "tradition" as a con-trol mechanism automatically regulating behavior with a wave of the classical economist's "invisible hand," has provided the sociologist with a very inaccurate perspective. But in reinstating the role of power, we are not thereby ruling out the force of "tradition" as at least a semi-autono-mous factor with psychologically and sociologically relevant laws of its own. All this suggests that in analyzing the control of behavior in tradi-tional societies, we would do well to look for both the power relations and the authority relations. This requires a closer look at the structure of goal-orientations, the extent to which they are self-oriented or "promo-tively interdependent," and the relative roles of coercion (no matter how subtle or latent) and consent.

Turning briefly to the "charismatic" type of control, it might be similarly instructive to consider the two poles of a continuum. Charis-matic *power,* at one end, might point to the psychic coercion or hypnotic force of the high-*prestige* figure over groups of people, who are thereby led to do things that are, in a real sense, against their "wills" or better judgment. Charismatic *authority* becomes direction or leadership by earned *esteem* based on a more clear-sighted recognition and acceptance of the leader's ability and concern to promote the goals of the whole collectivity.[58] Historical as well as everyday experience suggests the opera-tion of both types of charismatic forces, perhaps usually in a complex

---

56 Lewis and Barnouw, "Caste and the Jajmani System in a North Indian Vil-lage," pp. 77–78.

57 Quoted in Lewis and Barnouw, *ibid.,* p. 77.

58 We prefer to use the terms "prestige" and "esteem" more nearly as defined by the dictionary. Thus *prestige,* in one of its denotations, means "illusion, de-lusion, or blinding dazzlement." Another definition renders it as *"power* to *command* admiration." It is thus implied to promote a psychological reaction forced upon persons by certain characteristics of others, especially such charac-

mixture in which one or the other dominates. Social-psychological studies, especially small-group research, have begun to delve into this general area more systematically.[59] It would carry us too far afield, however, to pursue this subtype further here.

Of greater significance to the analysis of modern society, we believe, is the explicit introduction of the concept of "formally institutionalized power" as a polar type over against that of "formally institutionalized authority." (We use this terminology in preference to Weber's possibly misleading "rational-legal.") In the first place, this distinction makes it explicit that power is still power whether institutionalized or otherwise manifested. That is, it is control of others through a normative, at least partly legalized, sociocultural structure based, in some ascertainable way, on some form of latent or manifest coercion acting on groups directly or through their environment, and which holds together a structure of private goal-orientations. Though a difficult conception for the consensus theorists to accept, it has been rather well documented throughout history that small groups have often controlled large communities or societies through control of the normative or institutional apparatus. Modern sociology can no longer accept the Sumnerian view of norms and the institutional apparatus as a blind, unconscious evolutionary growth remote from the purposes and goal-seeking of men and their groups, and which therefore embraces some mystical, "natural" legitimacy, right, or sovereignty. For the contemporary structural theorist this means that the mere existence of established organizational positions and roles (defining, for example, relations of dominance and subordination) is not adequate evidence of their legitimacy.

Power, we argue, does not become sanctioned, legitimized, consensual authority simply by being clothed in institutional forms. We must disagree with Bierstedt's view that: "When social action and interaction proceed wholly in conformity to the norms of the formal organization, power is dissolved without residue into authority . . ." if this is taken to mean that "latent force" is thereby transformed into majority consensus.

---

teristics as power and wealth in full symbolic display. Unless it is clothed in broader cultural symbols internalized in others, the reaction tends to be mainly negative and of an abject nature, expressed concretely in deference gestures, obsequiousness, or servile fawning. Thus, prestige involves evaluation, but it is primarily an evaluation of one's *extrinsic* worth. *Esteem*, on the other hand, denotes the estimation or evaluation of the real or *intrinsic* worth of a person. It implies a more conscious, self-involved appraisal, manifested in gestures of praise and voluntary, spontaneous gift-giving (e.g., "in token of our esteem," rather than "in recognition of your prestige"). One cannot "command" or "claim" esteem—it can only be voluntarily given. There is implied a closer relation of the esteemed person to the self, as compared with a prestigious person. And we feel self-esteem rather than "self-prestige." It is implied that the esteemed person is promoting our own goals and values.

59 For example, see *Studies in Social Power*, ed. Dorwin Cartwright (Ann Arbor, Mich.: Institute for Social Research, 1959).

The issue, obviously, is the origin and basis of support for these norms. We are all too ready to grant this point when looking at Soviet society or a typical Latin-American country, for example, and might well consider it seriously in relation to others closer to home.

In the second place, our perspective forces us to look more closely at those very difficult terms, "institutionalization" and "legitimation." We tend to think of these as referring to role-structures of activities and interrelationships based on norms or standards internalized in the constituent role-playing actors, and thus representing a general consensus, even if only implicit, as to what is right and proper. But we easily jump to the conclusion that any concrete social structure that persists for any length of time must *therefore* be institutionalized or legitimized into a system of consensual authority. However, there is a very wide gap between large-scale participative, voluntary, informed consent to the role demands, on the one hand, and overt opposition to them, on the other. We cannot rule out the very real possibility that for a large percentage of actors in any social system the norms are accepted and obeyed merely as given conditions of action, with little understanding of their origin or ideological justification, and with even less comprehension that they might be otherwise; and that another sizable percentage feels oppressed by the norms and follows them unwillingly because no other course of action seems realistically open. If we accept these possibilities, the implication is that a social structure may be "legitimized" or "institutionalized" only from the point of view of a small minority of the members of the system. As a general proposition, we are forced to allow that, inasmuch as power and authority are relational concepts, what may be a system of authority to some actors may be a system of power to others. Once again, these points are rather obvious in the case of many of the "underdeveloped" and "newly emerging" societies of Asia, Africa, and Latin America, with their frequent internal struggles for control; in the "advanced" nations it is an empirical question, one of degree, depending on the institutional area in question.

It is true that, generally speaking, institutions may be viewed as crescive, but this cannot be interpreted to mean that their direction has not been plotted, often quite purposively, by some individuals or subgroups rather than, or more than, others. Thus, Sherif and Sherif have stated:

> All group members take part in the standardization of social norms. However, the process cannot be understood without considering the power relations which arise with the developing group structure. It is axiomatic that certain individuals contribute greater weight to this process than others . . .[60]

---

[60] Muzafer Sherif and C. Sherif, "Effects of Power Relations in Molding Opinions and Behavior," *Southwestern Social Science Quarterly*, 33 (1953), 289.

Likewise, the everyday maintenance of institutions must be seen as a very uneven affair, and not elliptically assumed to be simply the automatic result of general "societal forces," "systemic necessities," or the "functioning" of certain structures. Some time ago, Robert K. Merton pointed to the dangers here:

> Unless the theory of social institutions includes systematic consideration of the specific groups which support given "institutions," it overlooks the important role of sheer power in society. To speak of the 'legitimation of power' is to use an elliptical (and consequently, often misleading) phrase. For power may be legitimized for *some* without being legitimized for all groups in a society.[61]

And further implications of our view are brought out by Wolpert, who argues, "It must not be thought that states which do not have a political police are merely, by that fact, legitimate. The concept of legitimacy as applied to a social order is greatly in need of redefinition."[62] He goes on to suggest that in the Western contractual societies the idea of legitimacy relates to *Gesellschaft* norms defined in largely legal terminology. Under such conditions legitimacy is often "swallowed up by legality," and one need little wonder that "the basis of solidarity has been eroded."

> The divisiveness which is endemic to the social structure of the present Western capitalist world is a function of the way legitimacy is defined . . . In a contractual society the lack of a base for authority produces the insulated, atomized individual who is driven to accumulate power and wealth to compensate for his precarious insecurity. The lack of any genuinely recognized authority, whose place is taken by ersatz substitutes, is the condition for normlessness.[63]

What is suggested in much of the above, then, is that "institutionalized power" may be "legalized," but "institutionalized authority" alone is "legitimized." And, clearly, "legalized" and "legitimized" are, social psychologically, worlds apart. This, of course, constitutes a central facet of the great discussion of the last half century or more centering around the transition of society to the "secular," "contractual," or "mass" type, and the problem of finding newer bases of consensus and hence legitimacy.

Finally, a distinction between institutionalized authority and institutionalized power throws into relief a basic weakness in Weber's concept of "rational-legal" authority, one which perhaps accounts in part for his

---

[61] Robert K. Merton, "Discussion," *American Sociological Review,* 13 (1948), 168.

[62] Jeremiah Wolpert, "Toward a Sociology of Authority," in *Studies in Leadership,* ed. Alvin Gouldner (New York: Harper & Row, Publishers, 1950), p. 694.

[63] *Ibid.,* pp. 781–95, *passim.*

pessimism concerning the stability of this type of organization. This weakness stems partly from Weber's failure to appreciate the fact that rationality is not an absolute and therefore cannot serve as an absolute, independent source of social authority and solidarity.[64] Rather is it *relative* to the particular ends, goals, or values toward which the rational, efficient, expertise is aimed. And, as we have argued, the question of stable consensual authority and support *vs.* unstable, divisive, power struggles hinges on a further question: Whose ends, goals, and values are being promoted and by what (necessarily nonrational) process were they chosen for promotion over other ends? This is essentially the view to which Gouldner's research points:

> . . . it was noted that expert or representative bureaucracy was not legitimated *solely* in terms of the possession of technical skills. Examination of the safety program suggests several other conditions that must be satisfied before those who possess technical expertise will be acknowledged as legitimate authorities. One of these seems to be a consensus on ends or values. From this standpoint, it is not an irrelevant detail to note that *both* management and workers valued and sought accident-curtailment. If "voluntary consent" is vital to this pattern of authority, it would seem that this, in turn, rests on the subordinate's belief that he is being told to do things congruent with *his own ends and values* . . .
>
> If this view is correct, then it would appear that representative bureaucracy, or Weber's administration by the expert, entails a proto-*democratic* process of legitimation . . . The expert's authority is validated only when used to further the workers' ends, and when workers have a say-so in the enactment and administration of the expert's program. This would hardly be worth making such a point of, were it not for the fact that the role of "consent" and of democratic processes is blurred by Weber's theory of authority . . .
>
> For Weber, authority was given consent *because* it was legitimate, rather than being legitimate *because* it evoked consent. For Weber, therefore, consent is always a datum whose sources had to be traced. In consequence, he never systematically analyzed the actual social processes which either generated or thwarted the emergence of consent.[65]

This is not to deny, of course, that many individuals and groups in modern society grant a kind of "consent" to authority-figures *simply because* they are symbolic of, and legally supported by, an existing government. The psychological reasons for this are fairly well understood in principle. The main point, however, stands.

The final justification for any conceptual scheme, of course, is its ability to organize meaningfully the complex data of empirical reality, and thus throw a bit more light on otherwise confused phenomena. We believe the conception of power and authority we have suggested works

---

[64] Cf. Georges Freedmann, *Industrial Society* (New York: Free Press of Glencoe, Inc., 1955), pp. 375–76; Jeremiah Wolpert, *Studies in Leadership*, p. 689.

[65] Gouldner, *Patterns of Industrial Bureaucracy*, pp. 221–23.

in this direction. The events characterizing the emergence of new nations, as well as many of the problems seething within and between established industrial societies, can be analyzed fruitfully from this perspective.

For example, we might look at pre-Castro Cuba and ask what groups and for whose goals and values the Batista regime operated as a legitimized order of institutionalized *authority,* and for whom it functioned as traditional, institutionalized, or even naked, *power.* Certainly it would be of little analytical value to call it simply a system of legitimized authority, and let it go at that.

With the appearance of Castro—the charismatic figure *par excellence* according to Matthews of the *New York Times*[66]—we might ask for what groups and on what basis did he come to embody charismatic power or charismatic authority, and how has this distribution of attitudes changed, if at all, since his assumption of the direction of Cuban affairs? And what is the relationship of the goals and values of the Cuban exiles to those of the rest of the Cuban people: are they mainly "promotively interdependent," or divisively exclusive, or an indistinguishable mixture? On the answers to such questions rests much of the exiles' claim to legitimacy. Many United States government officials support the legitimacy of the exiles, and view them as the rightful Cuban "authorities," apparently because the goals and values of the latter are more promotively interdependent or consonant with their own. For opposite reasons, the Castro regime is viewed as a mere power group maintaining its position by coercion. The Soviet Union, on the other hand, has a contrary interpretation because, among other things, the promotively interdependent goals lie in the other direction. By providing a conceptual distinction between power and authority that emphasize their relational and hence relative nature, our framework makes room for both interpretations and makes unnecessary an argument over the meaning of words, as in the question of which group is "really" the legitimate regime? On the other hand, if we seek an answer to the question of whether a regime, as seen from *within* a society, is based predominantly on power or authority, we have a set of relatively objective criteria with which to assess the empirical conditions, though the research required would by no means be easily undertaken.

A second example in the "Communist" countries is not simply whether the public has the full vote, but whether and to what extent there is a predominance of institutionalized power or of institutionalized authority. Although the control centers in these countries have demonstrated their capabilities and commitment to promote some of the important group goals and values—such as health, education, employment,

66 Herbert L. Matthews, *The Cuban Story* (New York: George Braziller, Inc., 1961).

and some arts and sciences—to unprecedented levels, the crucial question is, of course, whether this is at the expense of the promotion of other goals and values felt to be important by large numbers of the citizens.

Likewise, in modern Western societies a central question involves the degree to which (in spite of the political vote) some institutional areas and their related goal-orientations and values are dominated by authority relations or power relations, and therefore produce and maintain promotively interdependent group goals and values as against divisive and competitive subgroup goals and values. For example, if we are to understand the central national and international issues of today, we cannot afford, as social scientists, to avoid or minimize the long-standing problem of the ambiguous role of private corporate influences upon the important decision-making of political democracies. The obvious question here is whether the modern corporation is predominantly a manifestation of institutionalized authority or of institutionalized power. It is quite clear that, to a substantial extent, it well illustrates the case of institutional power, although we may not wish to describe the situation in terms as blunt as those of Adolphe A. Berle, who argues that in the United States a smaller group within the largest 500 corporations have "the ultimate decision-making power" over two-thirds of the non-farm economy. Many of these corporations have budgets and payrolls which, "with their customers, affect a greater number of people than most of the ninety-odd sovereign countries of the world . . . Some of these corporations are units which can be thought of only in somewhat the way we have heretofore thought of nations . . ." Berle recognizes that "whenever there is a question of power there is a question of legitimacy. As things stand now, these instrumentalities of tremendous power have the slenderest claim of legitimacy."[67] Although management theoretically got its legitimacy by representing the will of the stockholders who supposedly chose them, in fact it was a "kind of quasi-amateur legitimacy" and the stockholders "were completely unable" to so choose:

> When the directors wished to renominate themselves or add to their number or to fill a vacancy, they did it. This is still the method by which the directors in a great corporation are chosen. This is an automatic self-perpetuating oligarchy.[68]

In another place, Berle continues in this line of thought and goes to the heart of our condition of institutionalized power:

> The argument is promptly made, both by scholars and by businessmen, that this power we have been discussing, if it exists at all, is not absolute, and that it is severely limited. There is force in the contention, but on examination the contention has less force than its proponents fre-

---

[67] Adolphe A. Berle, Jr., *Economic Power and the Free Society* (Santa Barbara, Calif.: The Fund for the Republic, 1957) , pp. 14–16.
[68] *Ibid.*, pp. 8–9.

quently assert. Some of the checks and balances alleged to exist upon this power require reexamination in the light of facts. . . .

The power we have been considering, though limited, is in large measure absolute. Around its use the law authorizes a mantle of sanctity, the legal "presumption" that management action is taken for the best interests of the corporate institution. . . .

As yet the community has not created any acknowledged referent of responsibility, no group from which they take their power mandate or get instructions in dealing with serious streams of events they can and do affect. There is no recognized body of doctrine by which they themselves must test their choice as they act from day to day. . . . Yet it seems the aggregate of their day-to-day decisions do form life and community. They do play a notable part in the physical base on which life is lived. They build or shift or direct frameworks of human experience within which great masses of men live. Indirectly they affect an even greater peripheral group. They do enter into those community institutions, now including colleges and schools and philanthropies, which are the proudest product of American life.[69]

Let us return now to Peter Blau's recent work on *Exchange and Power in Social Life*. We suggest that, despite some ambiguity in his use of the terms, Blau has developed a systematic conception of power, authority, and legitimacy that extends the general distinction between power and authority argued above. He devotes separate chapters to power (Chapter 5) and to authority and legitimacy (Chapter 8). Power is defined there (as we believe it should be) as control based on negative sanctions, regardless of how "voluntary" the transaction may appear outwardly. Power is:

> the ability of persons or groups to impose their will on others despite resistance through deterrence either in the form of withholding regularly supplied rewards or in the form of punishment, inasmuch as the former as well as the latter constitute, in effect, a negative sanction.[70]

Building on his exchange-theoretic perspective, Blau goes on to develop a simple but fundamentally important set of analytical classifications that extend the implications of his conception of power systematically and deeply into the area of institutional structure and dynamics. Power is seen to arise in exchange transactions when a person supplies needed services to others under the following four conditions of imbalance or "power-dependence" relations: 1) the others cannot reciprocate and supply him with services he wants badly enough to equalize the exchange relation; 2) the others cannot obtain the needed services elsewhere; 3) they cannot, for any reason, coerce him to furnish the services;

---

[69] Adolphe A. Berle, Jr., *The 20th Century Capitalist Revolution* (New York: Harcourt, Brace & World, Inc., 1954), pp. 35, 63, 181–83.

[70] Peter M. Blau, *Exchange and Power in Social Life* (New York: John Wiley and Sons, Inc., 1964), p. 117.

and 4) they cannot or do not resign themselves to do without the services or change the values determining the need. These alternatives, when stated positively, define the conditions of social independence of the power of others, and from them can be derived: a) the strategies required to attain and sustain power; b) the major types of issues arising in power conflicts; and c) the implications of power for the analysis of the basic problems of social structure. For example, to use his resources to acquire power over others a person must prevent them from choosing any of the four alternatives. That is, he must remain indifferent to benefits they can offer, denying them access to the required resources; he must bar access to alternative suppliers, for example, by monopolizing needed rewards or services; he must prevent the use of coercion, perhaps by discouraging coalitions among subordinates or blocking access to political power, or by dominating the sources of law and order and politically controlling the processes of exchange; and he must perpetuate the social values—be they materialistic values, patriotic ideals, religious convictions—that encourage the need for his kind of services, while opposing counter-ideologies.

The four alternatives also suggest four basic problems of social structure: the possibilities of reciprocating benefits point to the study of exchange processes and resource distribution; the possibilities of alternative opportunities direct attention to the emerging exchange structure and its competitive features, along with the normative standards tending to develop; the possibility of the use of coercive power leads the observer to investigate coalition formation and the organization of power, along with the processes governing the political power struggle in the society; and finally, the possibility of doing without something originally "needed" calls attention to shifts in values, formation of new ideologies, and conflicts between ideologies.[71]

In sum, Blau's systematic recognition of the power phenomenon is a large step toward filling the gap in the equilibrium-consensus model of social structure and dynamics. This model, for example, typically affords little room for the outstanding facts of social stratification, or tends to treat them only in positive or euphemistic terms. Blau's analysis of structural differentiation, in contrast, permits a deeper penetration into such matters, and in particular, demonstrates the serious shortcomings of Parsons' definition of "power" as a "generalized capacity of a social system to get things done in the interest of collective goals." Rather, he points out:

> Sufficient power enables individuals to monopolize resources and to make others increasingly dependent on themselves. While the perpetuation of their power is contingent on their continuing to provide *some* benefits to others, if only by refraining from punishing them, it is evident that the

---

[71] *Ibid.*, pp. 118–25.

very power that makes others dependent for these "benefits" cannot be considered in any sense to constitute a deserved reward for supplying services or an incentive necessary to produce them. In short, once superior power has been attained by furnishing services, it can be sustained without furnishing these same services. This self-perpetuating element of power is still more evident in the class structure of entire societies than in the differentiation of status in small groups, and failure to take it into account is a serious shortcoming of functional conceptions of social stratification.[72]

In a later chapter, however, when he comes to deal with legitimation and authority, Blau tends to forget that he has *defined* power as a coercive control based on the use of negative sanctions, and speaks of it as becoming legitimized into authority under certain conditions, thus introducing into his analysis the same conceptual confusions we discussed earlier. He suggests that legitimized authority rests on willing compliance which, in turn, rests on institutionalized and internalized social norms accepted and enforced by the collectivity of subordinates. It is argued that power is thus "transformed into" legitimate authority. But the conceptual linkage between power and authority prevents him from clarifying the important question of whether this means that control, though now encased in institutional and socialized forms, is *still* based on the coercive force of potential or actual negative sanctions, or whether it means that the originally private interests of the powerful have been "transformed into" collective goals that promote the interests of all. Do "legitimation" and "institutionalization" imply an informed, voluntary consensus concerning a given class structure? Or should we not make room in our conceptual apparatus, as we have already suggested, for a distinction between institutionalized *power* (in the essentially coercive sense that Blau used when he defined power) and legitimized *authority* (characterized by promotively interdependent goal orientation and willing compliance)? Some passing remarks of Blau's suggest this:

> Although legitimate authority rests on the social norms and sanctions of the collectivity of subordinates, this does not mean that all groups in a society support institutionalized authority, or even that a majority do. The crucial factor is that important and powerful groups of subordinates enforce the commands of institutionalized authority, putting external pressures to comply on those groups who refuse to do so voluntarily . . . The authority of the government, then, rests on its acceptance as legitimate and its support by the dominant groups of subjects, that is, by the majority of those who participate in political life and are concerned with public matters, not necessarily a majority of the total population.[73]

But Blau fails to follow through with the framework of his earlier chapter on "power." There he suggests that it is just such dominant power

---

[72] *Ibid.*, p. 197.

[73] *Ibid.*, pp. 212–13. It is worth noting the terminological usage, here. Blau, like many others, has defined "authority" as "legitimate power," but then feels it necessary to speak of "legitimate authority," a redundancy. And when the con-

groups who not only benefit most by the institutional arrangements in their society, but who contribute most to their creation and maintenance by monopolizing resources, controlling exchange processes, dominating the means of coercion, and perpetuating the supporting values and ideologies.

However, in the last part of his book Blau more than makes up for these confusions by introducing the concepts of "counterinstitutional components" and "opposition ideals," and the principles of inherent "imbalance" and "dialectic forces" underlying social change. Norms of fairness and justice, themselves always undergoing redefinition, are applied to the use of power or authority in society, and may lead to opposition. This implies (although Blau does not develop the point in quite these terms) that, in addition to a concern for how power comes to be transformed into legitimized authority, attention must also be seriously addressed to the possibility that what was once consensual *authority* can become "de-legitimized" and hence transformed into coercive *power*. Such a conception would seem essential for the understanding of many events of past and contemporary societies. It may be analyzed in terms of familiar social-psychological processes of tension arousal, problem-solving, or goal-seeking and goal blockage, leading to redefinitions of the situation of action—to new expectations, norms, roles, aspirations, and values. The dynamic models of the social interaction process that we discussed earlier suggest a number of relevant concepts: dissonance and a "strain toward symmetry"; selective processes tending to shape a more "congruent interpersonal matrix," "role-strain" and the resulting processes of negotiation and exchange; and the various strategies of conflict.

Blau develops the important principle that the cultural values serving to legitimize institutions also contain the seeds of destruction or reorganization of these institutions. "Opposition ideals" may form around accepted values which are unrealized and apparently unrealizable under given institutional arrangements. These opposition ideals, which are "culturally legitimated" for some groups, come into conflict with existing institutions and the authorities or the recognized power groups supporting them. The opposition ideals legitimate the leaders of opposition movements "and thus produce a countervailing force against entrenched powers and existing institutions in the society."[74]

Here we have, then, a firm recognition of one of the central prin-

---

notation of constraint or coercion is clearly desired, the term "power" is utilized, though it is sometimes used in other places where "authority" seems intended. Furthermore, we may object to the appropriateness of referring to a government as consensually legitimized when it is supported only by a minority consisting of dominant power (i.e., coercive) groups who constrain the majority. As we have suggested, the relativity of "power" and of "authority" needs to be brought out here.

[74] *Ibid.*, p. 271.

ciples we have been arguing: Institutionalization is not to be confused with legitimation in the sociological and social-psychological senses of these terms. It is an empirical question whether the institutional structure of a given society, or aspects of it, has a firm social and psychological foundation in an informed, cognitively and affectively undistorted, consensus on important norms, means, ends, and values.

Finally, Blau extends the implications of his views in a last chapter dealing with the "dialectical forces" of institutionalization and institutional reorganization as a fundamental principle of social change. The morphogenic nature of the social process, though referred to under an older terminology, is thus once again given a prominent place in sociological theory. Imbalance and structural elaboration, not equilibrium or homeostatic maintenance, are the characteristic, inherent features of sociocultural systems. The generation, self-perpetuation, or breakdown of such phenomena as those we label "legitimacy," "power," and "authority" are products of complex systemic processes that cannot be fully brought out in any piecemeal analysis. The self-perpetuating nature of established power, the self-maintenance of consensual authority, or the transformation of authority into power or *vice versa* are total-system processes of morphostasis or morphogenesis. They require study in terms of the sociocultural, social psychological, and psychological dynamics suggested in previous chapters. Our discussion in this chapter, of course, hardly constitutes such a study, but can only illustrate the fact that institutional or organizational analysis cannot be expected to go very far beyond its present state without a systemic treatment.

Conclusion

The general theme of this chapter has been the problem of "social control." In discussing various facets of this notion we have argued that a model of society as a complex adaptive system is required if the notion is to be sharpened in meaning. Social control, or social order, is not simply a function of men conforming to the demands of others, to divine precepts or natural law, or to fixed norms of an equilibrial or homeostatic system. Whatever control, order, or disorder there is at any time in society is a function of the interrelations and interactions of the components of an ongoing system process. Groupings of individuals seeking material and social goals in a physical and sociocultural environment generate meanings, interaction patterns, and ecological arrangements that are more or less temporary adjustments always open to redefinition and rearrangement. These social and cultural patterns involve, in varying degrees, an internal component of voluntary, informed self control and an external component of direct or indirect constraint. That is, legitimate authority and coercive power are both normally present in society, but one or the other may predominate at times.

A simple, cybernetic feedback model of explicit group goal-seeking does not fit most societies of the past and present because of a lack in those societies of informed, centralized direction and widespread, promotively interdependent goal behaviors of individuals and subgroups. In some cases in history, large scale, planned social development or change fitting this model has occurred, based on a strong centralized leadership and an efficient administrative apparatus; but the goals attained were not salient for large segments of the population, and problems of internal consensus and cohesion have usually arisen sooner or later to halt the process. Extensive, conscious attempts to direct a complex society in a viable, adaptive manner have only just begun in modern history, and much remains to be learned to avoid the mistakes of the past. An intimate understanding of the workings of the sociocultural level of complex adaptive system is essential.

Modern systems analysis suggests that a sociocultural system with high adaptive potential, or integration as we might call it, requires some optimum level of both stability and flexibility: a relative stability of the social-psychological foundations of interpersonal relations and of the cultural meanings and value hierarchies that hold group members together in the same universe of discourse and, at the same time, a flexibility of structural relations characterized by the lack of strong barriers to change, along with a certain propensity for reorganizing the current institutional structure should environmental challenges or emerging internal conditions suggest the need. A central feature of the complex adaptive system is its capacity to persist or develop by changing its own structure, sometimes in fundamental ways.

Underlying the criteria of stability and flexibility are the basic elements of the adaptive process: 1) a source for the continuous introduction of "variety" into the system, which may refine or revitalize the pool of commonly usable information and the set of common meanings and symbols that, by and large, represent adequate "mappings" of the physical and social milieu; but variety means deviance, and although some may be adaptive, some will be pathogenic; 2) maintenance of an optimum level of tension in the system, but also, a relatively high level of satisfaction of members' needs—both basic needs and those generated by the system itself; society is not a tension-reducing system—tension is produced by the normal impulses to action, the "role-strain" of everyday social relations, cognitive dissonance, incongruence of interpersonal matrices, and the like; 3) a full, two-way communication network extending throughout all parts of the system to provide adequate linkage of components and to make possible the various feedback loops essential to effective goal attainment; 4) a selective, or decision-making, system that is sensitive not only to changes in the external environment but also to those in its internal state (that is, it must be self conscious), and which is capable of "learning" or allowing for changes in its goals and values; and 5) effective mechanisms for preserving and propagating those meanings, symbol systems, and information sets that have, for the moment, passed the tests of truth, goodness, and beauty; and this newly structured variety becomes the basis of the sociocultural framework within which the next round of adaptive process occurs.

This kind of model is complex, and it is not as comforting as an equilibrium or functionalistic model. But the several recent theories of social interaction and institutional dynamics that we outlined in earlier chapters are intended to show that the challenge has already been accepted and a significant overhaul of sociological theory is well under way. And it is going in a direction, we reiterate, that is quite closely in line with modern systems analysis, which provides an integrating theoretical framework that may contribute to the advance—if we but choose to exploit it.

Selected Bibliography

Ackoff, Russell L., 1957–58, Towards a Behavioral Theory of Communication, *Management Science*, 4: 218–34.

———, Ed., 1961, *Progress in Operations Research*, I. New York: Wiley.

Allport, Gordon W., 1960, The Open System in Personality Theory, *Journal of Abnormal and Social Psychology*, 61: 301–11.

Angyal, Andras, 1939, The Structure of Wholes, *Philosophy of Science*, 6: 25–37.

Arbib, Michael A., 1964, *Brains, Machines, and Mathematics*. New York: McGraw-Hill.

———, 1966, A Partial Survey of Cybernetics in Eastern Europe and the Soviet Union, *Behavioral Science*, 11: 193–216.

Ashby, W. Ross, 1954, The Application of Cybernetics to Psychiatry, *Journal of Mental Science*, 100: 114–24.

———, 1956, *An Introduction to Cybernetics*. New York: Wiley.

———, 1960, *Design for a Brain*. New York: Wiley.

———, 1963, Induction, Prediction, and Decision-Making in Cybernetic Systems, in Henry Ely Kyburg, Jr., and Ernest Nagel, Eds., *Induction: Some Current Issues*. Middletown, Conn.: Wesleyan University Press, 55–73.

———, 1964, The Set Theory of Mechanism and Homeostasis, *General Systems*, 9: 83–97.

Attneave, Fred, 1959, *Applications of Information Theory to Psychology*. New York: Holt, Rinehart and Winston.

Baldwin, James M., 1900, *Mental Development in the Child and the Race*. New York: Macmillan.

———, 1906–1911, *Thought and Things, or Genetic Logic*, I–III. New York: Macmillan.

Bardis, P. D., 1965, Cybernetics: Definition, History, Etymology, *Social Science,* 226–28.

Bar-Hillel, Yehoshua, 1955, An Examination of Information Theory, *Philosophy of Science,* 22: 86–105.

———, 1964, *Language and Information.* Reading, Mass.: Addison-Wesley.

Barrett, F. D., and H. A. Shepard, 1953, A Bibliography of Cybernetics, *Proceedings of the American Academy of Arts and Sciences,* 80: 204–22.

Beauregard, O. C. de, 1961, Sur l'Equivalence Entre Information et Entropie, *Sciences,* 11: 51–58.

Beckner, Morton, 1959, *The Biological Way of Thought.* New York: Columbia University Press.

Beer, Stafford, 1959, *Cybernetics and Management.* London: English Universities Press.

Bentley, A. F., 1950, Kennetic Inquiry, *Science,* 112: 775–83.

Berkeley, E. C., 1949, *Giant Brains.* New York: Wiley.

Bertalanffy, L. von, 1950, The Theory of Open Systems in Physics and Biology, *Science,* 3: 23–29.

———, 1951, Problems of General System Theory, *Human Biology,* 23: 302–12.

———, 1952a, *Problems of Life: An Evaluation of Modern Biological Thought.* New York: Wiley.

———, 1952b, Theoretical Models in Biology and Psychology, in David Krech and George S. Klein, *Theoretical Models and Personality Theory.* Durham, N.C.: Duke University Press, 24–38.

———, 1962, General System Theory—A Critical Review, *General Systems: Yearbook of the Society for General Systems Research,* 7: 1–20.

Blake, D. V. and A. M. Uttley, Eds., 1959, *Proceedings of a Symposium on Mechanization of Thought Processes,* 2 Vols. London: Her Majesty's Stationery Office.

Blumer, Herbert, 1966, Sociological Implications of the Thought of George Herbert Mead, *American Journal of Sociology,* 71: 535–44.

Bock, Kenneth E., 1963, Evolution, Function, and Change, *American Sociological Review,* 28: 229–37.

Boulding, Kenneth, 1956a, General Systems Theory—The Skeleton of Science, *Management Science,* 2: 197–208.

———, 1956b, *The Image.* Ann Arbor: University of Michigan Press.

Brillouin, Leon, 1949, Life, Thermodynamics, and Cybernetics, *American Scientist,* 37: 554–68.

———, 1950, Thermodynamics and Information Theory, *American Scientist,* 38: 594–99.

———, 1956, *Science and Information Theory.* New York: Academic Press.

British Association, 1954, *Symposium on Cybernetics,* three papers:
    a. E. C. Cherry, Organisms and Mechanisms;
    b. W. E. Hick, The Impact of Information Theory on Psychology;
    c. Donald M. MacKay, On Comparing the Brain with Machines, *Advancement of Science,* 40.

Bukharin, Nikolai, 1925, *Historical Materialism: A System of Sociology.* New York: International Publishers.

Burgers, J. M., 1963, On the Emergence of Patterns of Order, *Bull. Amer. Math. Soc.,* 69: 1–25.

Cadwallader, Mervin, 1959, The Cybernetic Analysis of Change in Complex Social Organizations, *American Journal of Sociology,* 65: 154–57.

Campbell, Donald T., 1956, Adaptive Behavior from Random Response, *Behavioral Science,* 1: 105–10.

————, 1958a, Common Fate, Similarity, and Other Indices of the Status of Aggregates of Persons as Social Entities, *Behavioral Science,* 3: 14–25.

————, 1958b, Systematic Error on the Part of Human Links in Communication Systems, *Information and Control,* 1: 334–69.

————, 1959, Methodological Suggestions from a Comparative Psychology of Knowledge Processes, *Inquiry,* 2: 152–67.

————, 1960, Blind Variation and Selective Retention in Creative Thought as in Other Knowledge Processes, *Psychological Review,* 67: 380–400.

————, 1965, Variation and Selective Retention in Socio-Cultural Evolution, in Herbert R. Barringer, George I. Blanksten, and Raymond Mack, Eds., *Social Change in Developing Areas.* Cambridge, Mass.: Schenkman, pp. 19–49.

Cannon, Walter B., 1939, *The Wisdom of the Body.* New York: W. W. Norton.

Chapanis, Alphonse, 1961, Men, Machines, and Models, in Donald P. Eckman, Ed., *Systems Philosophy.* New York: Wiley, 113–31.

Cherry, Colin, 1961, *On Human Communication.* New York: Science Editions, Inc.

Chin, Robert, 1962, The Utility of System Models and Developmental Models for Practitioners, in Warren Bennis, et al., *The Planning of Change.* New York: Holt, Rinehart, and Winston, 201–14.

Churchman, C. W. and R. L. Ackoff, 1950, Purposive Behavior and Cybernetics, *Social Forces,* 29: 32–39.

Clark, Joseph T., 1962, Remarks on the Role of Quantity, Quality, and Relations in the History of Logic, Methodology, and Philosophy of Science, in Ernest Nagel, et al., *Logic, Methodology, and Philosophy of Science.* Stanford: Stanford University Press, 611–12.

Cohn, Stanton H. and Sylva M. Cohn, 1953, The Role of Cybernetics in Physiology, *The Scientific Monthly,* 79: 85–89.

Copi, I. M., C. C. Elgot, and J. B. Wright, 1958, Realization of Events by Logical Nets, *Journal for the Association of Computing Machinery,* 5: 181–96.

Crider, Donald B., 1956–1957, Cybernetics: A Review of What It Means and Some of Its Implications in Psychiatry, *Neuropsychiatry,* 4: 35–58.

Culbertson, J. T., 1951, *Consciousness and Behavior.* London: William C. Brown.

Cybernetica. Vol. I, 1958——.

Cybernetics, English translation of *Kibernetica,* published in Kiev starting January, 1965.

Deutsch, Karl W., 1951a, Mechanism, Organism, and Society, *Philosophy of Science,* 18: 230–52.

——, 1951b, Mechanism, Teleology, and Mind, *Philosophy and Phenomenological Research,* 12: 185–223.

——, 1952a, Communication Theory and Social Science, *American Journal of Orthopsychiatry,* 22: 469–83.

——, 1952b, On Communication Models in the Social Science, *Public Opinion Quarterly,* 16: 356–80.

——, 1955, Some Notes on Research on the Role of Models in Natural and Social Sciences, *Synthese,* 7: 506–33.

——, 1961, On Social Communication and the Metropolis, *Daedalus,* Vol. 90, *The Future Metropolis,* 99–110.

——, 1963, *The Nerves of Government.* New York: The Free Press.

Dewey, John and Arthur F. Bentley, 1949, *Knowing and the Known.* Boston: Beacon Press.

Dore, Ronald P., 1961, Function and Cause, *American Sociological Review,* 26: 843–53.

Easton, David, 1956, Limits of the Equilibrium Model in Social Research, *Behavioral Science,* 1: 96–104.

——, 1965, *A Systems Analysis of Political Life.* New York: Wiley.

Eckman, Donald P., Ed., 1961, *Systems: Research and Design.* New York: Wiley.

Fairbanks, G., 1954, A Theory of the Speech Organism as a Servosystem, *Journal of Speech and Hearing Disorders,* 19: 133–39.

Feibleman, James and Julius Weis Friend, 1945, The Structure and Function of Organization, *The Philosophical Review,* 54: 19–44.

——, 1954, Theory of Integrative Levels, *British Journal for the Philosophy of Science,* 5: 59–66.

Fender, Derek H., 1964, Control Mechanisms of the Eye, *Scientific American,* 211: 24–34.

Fields, William S. and Walter Abbott, Eds., 1963, *Information Storage and Neural Control,* Tenth Annual Scientific Meeting of the Houston Neurological Society. Springfield, Ill.: Charles C. Thomas.

Foerster, H. von, Margaret Mead, and H. L. Teuber, 1949–1957, *Transactions of Conferences on Cybernetics,* 5 Vols. New York: Josiah Macy, Jr., Foundation.

———, Ed., 1953, *Cybernetics.* New York: Charles Macy and Co., Inc.

———, and George W. Zopf, Jr., Eds., 1962, *Principles of Self-Organization.* New York: Pergamon Press.

Frick, Frederick C., 1959, Information Theory, in Sigmund Koch, Ed., *Psychology: A Study of a Science,* Vol. 2. New York: McGraw-Hill, 629–36; 611–615.

Fürth, R., 1952, Physics of Social Equilibrium, *Advancement of Science,* London: 8: 429–34.

Gabor, D., 1951, *Lectures on Communication Theory.* Cambridge, Mass.: M.I.T.

———, 1954, Communication Theory and Cybernetics, Milan Symposium paper, in *Trans. I. R. E. Prof. Group on Non-Linear Circuits.*

Garner, W. R., 1962, *Uncertainty and Structure as Psychological Concepts.* New York: Wiley.

General Systems: Yearbook of the Society for General Systems Research, edited by Ludwig von Bertalanffy and Anatol Rapoport. Vol. 1, 1956 ——.

George, F. H. and J. H. Handlon, 1955, Towards a General Theory of Behavior, *Nethodos,* 7: 24–44.

———, 1957, A Language for Perceptual Analysis, *Psychological Review,* 64: 14–25.

———, 1960, *Automation, Cybernation, and Society.* London: Leonard Hill, Inc.

———, 1965, *Cybernetics and Biology.* London and Edinburgh: Oliver & Boyd.

Gerard, Ralph W., C. Kluckhohn, and A. Rapoport, 1956, Biological and Cultural Evolution, *Behavioral Science,* 1: 24–33.

Gerard, Ralph W., 1957, Units and Concepts of Biology, *Science,* 125: 429–33.

———, 1960, Becoming: the Residue of Change, in S. Tax, Ed., *Evolution after Darwin.* Vol. II., *The Evolution of Man.* Chicago: University of Chicago Press, 255–67.

Goldman, Stanford, 1953, *Information Theory.* Englewood Cliffs, N.J.: Prentice-Hall.

Goode, William J., 1960, A Theory of Role Strain, *American Sociological Review,* 25: 483–96.

Grinker, Roy R., Ed., 1956, *Toward a Unified Theory of Human Behavior.* New York: Basic Books.

Guilbaud, G. T., 1959, *What Is Cybernetics?* New York: Grove.

Haberstroh, Chadwick J., 1960, Control as an Organizational Process, *Management Science,* 6: 165–71.

Hall, A. D. and R. E. Fagen, 1956, Definition of Systems, revised introductory chapter of *Systems Engineering*. New York: Bell Telephone Laboratories. Reprinted from *General Systems* 1: 18–28.

Hardin, Garrett, 1963, The Cybernetics of Competition: A Biologist's View of Society, *Perspectives in Biology and Medicine,* 7: 61–84.

Hartley, R. V. L., 1928, Transmission of Information, *Bell Systems Tech. J.,* 7: 535–63.

Hebb, D. O., 1949, *The Organization of Behaviour.* New York: Wiley.

Held, Richard and Alan Hein, 1963a, Movement-Produced Stimulation in the Development of Visually Guided Behavior, *Journal of Comparative and Physiological Psychology,* 56: 872–76.

——— and S. J. Freedman, 1963b, Plasticity in Human Sensorimotor Control, *Science,* 142: 455–62.

Henderson, L. J., 1935, *Pareto's General Sociology.* Cambridge, Mass.: Harvard University Press.

———, 1958, *The Fitness of the Environment: An Inquiry into the Biological Significance of the Properties of Matter.* Boston: Beacon.

Henry, Jules, 1955, Homeostasis, Society, and Evolution: A Critique, *The Scientific Monthly,* 81: 300–309.

———, 1959, Culture, Personality, and Evolution, *American Anthropologist,* 61: 221–26.

Herbert, P. G., 1957, Situation Dynamics and the Theory of Behavior Systems, *Behavioral Science,* 2: 13–29.

Jackson, Willis, Ed., 1953, *Communication Theory.* New York: Academic Press.

Jeffress, L. A., Ed., 1951, *Cerebral Mechanisms and Behaviour.* The Hixon Symposium. New York: Wiley.

Johnson, F. Craig and George R. Klare, 1961, General Models of Communication Research, *Journal of Communication,* 11: 13–26.

———, 1962, Feedback: Principles and Analogies, *Journal of Communication,* 12: 150–59.

Kaplan, David, 1965, The Superorganic: Science or Metaphysics?, *American Anthropologist,* 67:958–76.

Katz, Karl U. and Margaret F. Smith, 1966, *Cybernetic Principles of Learning, and Educational Design.* New York: Holt, Rinehart and Winston.

Khailov, K. M., 1964, The Problem of Systemic Organization in Theoretical Biology, *General Systems,* 9: 151–57. Translated by A. Rapoport.

Kilpatrick, Franklin P., 1961, *Explorations in Transactional Psychology.* New York: NYU Press.

Krech, David, 1950, Dynamic Systems as Open Neurological Systems, *Psychological Review,* 57: 345–61.

Kremyanskiy, V. I., 1960, Certain Peculiarities of Organisms as a 'System' from the Point of View of Physics, Cybernetics, and Biology, *General Systems,* 5: 221–24. Translated by Anatol Rapoport.

Kuhn, Alfred, 1961, Toward a Uniform Language of Information and Knowledge, *Synthese,* 13: 127–53.

———, 1963, *The Study of Society: A Unified Approach.* Homewood, Ill.: Irwin-Dorsey.

Kybernetica, published by Cybernetics Commission of the Czechoslovak Academy of Sciences, starting January, 1965.

Lange, Oskar, 1965, *Wholes and Parts: A General Theory of System Behavior.* Oxford: Pergamon Press. Translated from Polish by Eugeniusz Lejsa.

Latil, Pierre de, 1956, *Thinking by Machine: A Study of Cybernetics.* London: Sedgwick and Jackson. Translated from French by Y. M. Golla.

Leavitt, Harold J. and Ronald A. H. Mueller, 1951, Some Effects of Feedback on Communication, *Human Relations,* 4: 401–10.

Lehrman, Daniel S., 1964, The Reproductive Behavior of Ring Doves, *Scientific American,* 211: 48–54.

Lerner, Daniel, Ed., 1963, *Parts and Wholes.* New York: The Free Press.

Lewin, Kurt, 1947, Feedback Problems of Social Diagnosis and Action, Part II–B of Frontiers in Group Dynamics, *Human Relations,* 1: 147–53.

London, Ivan D., 1946, Some Consequences for History and Psychology of Langmuir's Concept of Convergence and Divergence of Phenomena, *Psychological Review,* 53: 170–88.

Luce, R. Duncan, and H. Raiffa, 1957, *Games and Decisions.* New York: Wiley.

McClelland, Charles A., 1962, General Systems and the Social Sciences, *ETC,* 18: 449–68.

McCulloch, Warren S., 1965, *Embodiments of Mind.* Cambridge, Mass.: The M.I.T. Press.

———, 1949, The Brain as a Computing Machine, *Electronic Engineering.*

Mace, C. A., 1953, Homeostasis, Needs, and Values, *British Journal of Psychology,* 44: 200–10.

MacIver, Robert M., 1942, *Social Causation.* New York: Ginn.

MacKay, Donald M., 1951, Mindlike Behaviour in Artefacts, *British Journal of Philosophy and Science,* 2: 105–21.

———, 1954, Operational Aspects of Some Fundamental Concepts of Human Communication, *Synthese,* 9: 182–98.

———, 1956a, Towards an Information-Flow Model of Human Behavior, *British Journal of Psychology,* 47: 30–43.

———, 1956b, The Place of 'Meaning' in the Theory of Information, in Colin Cherry, Ed., *Information Theory: Third London Symposium.* New York: Academic Press, 215–24.

———, 1961, The Informational Analysis of Questions and Commands, in Colin Cherry, Ed., *Information Theory: Fourth London Symposium.* London: Butterworth's, pp. 469–76.

Maclay, Howard, 1962, A Descriptive Approach to Communication, in Norman F. Washburne, Ed., *Decisions, Values, and Groups,* Vol. II. New York: Pergamon, 201–26.

Macrae, Donald G., 1951, Cybernetics and Social Science, *British Journal of Sociology,* 2: 135–49.

March, James G. and H. A. Simon, 1958, *Organizations.* New York: Wiley.

Maruyama, Magoroh, 1963, The Second Cybernetics: Deviation Amplifying Mutual Causal Processes, *American Scientist,* 51: 164–79.

Mead, George Herbert, 1934, *Mind, Self, and Society.* Chicago: University of Chicago Press.

——, 1938, *The Philosophy of the Act,* Ed., C. W. Morris. Chicago: University of Chicago Press.

Meier, Richard L., 1956, Communication and Social Change, *Behavioral Science,* 1: 43–59.

Mesarović, Mihajlo D., Ed., 1964, *Views on General Systems Theory: Proceedings of the Second Systems Symposium at Case Institute of Technology.* New York: Wiley.

Miller, George A., 1953, What Is Information Measurement?, *American Psychologist,* 8: 3–12.

——, 1956, The Magical Number Seven, Plus or Minus Two: Some Limits on Our Capacity for Processing Information, *Psychological Review,* 63: 81–97.

——, Eugene Galanter, and Karl Pribram, 1960, *Plans and the Structure of Behavior.* New York: Holt, Rinehart, Winston.

Miller, James G., 1955, Toward a General Theory for the Behavioral Sciences, *American Psychologist,* 10: 513–31.

——, 1965, Living Systems: Basic Concepts; Structure and Process; Cross-Level Hypotheses, *Behavioral Science,* 10: 193–237; 337–79; 380–411.

Moore, Omar K. and Donald J. Lewis, 1953, Purpose and Learning Theory, *The Psychological Review,* 60: 149–56.

Moulyn, Adrian C., 1957, *Structure, Function, and Purpose.* New York: The Liberal Arts Press.

Mowrer, Orval H., 1954, Ego Psychology, Cybernetics, and Learning Theory, in Donald K. Adams, et al., *Learning Theory and Clinical Research.* New York: Wiley, pp. 81–90.

——, 1960, *Learning Theory and the Symbolic Processes.* New York: Wiley.

Murphy, Gardner, 1961, Toward a Field Theory of Communication, *Journal of Communication,* 11: 196–201.

Nadel, S. F., 1953, Social Control and Self-Regulation, *Social Forces,* 31: 265–73.

——, 1957, *The Theory of Social Structure.* New York: The Free Press.

Nett, Roger, 1953, Conformity—Deviation and the Social Control Concept, *Ethics,* 64: 38–45.

Neumann, John von and O. Morgenstern, 1947, *Theory of Games and Economic Behavior.* Princeton: Princeton University Press.

——, 1952, *Probabilistic Logics.* California Institute of Technology.

——, 1958, *The Computer and the Brain.* New Haven: Yale University Press.

Newell, Allen, J. C. Shaw and Herbert A. Simon, 1958, Elements of a Theory of Human Problem Solving, *Psychological Review,* 65: 151–66.

Nokes, Peter, 1961, Feedback as an Explanatory Device in the Study of Certain Interpersonal and Institutional Processes, *Human Relations,* 14: 381–87.

Notterman, Joseph M. and Richard Trumbull, 1959, Note on Self-Regulating Systems and Stress, *Behavioral Science,* 4: 324–27.

Osgood, Charles E., 1952, On the Nature and Measurement of Meaning, *Psychological Bulletin,* 49: 197–237.

——, and Thomas A. Sebeck, Eds., 1954, Psycholinguistics, a Survey of Theory and Research Problems, *International Journal of American Linguistics, Memoir 10.*

——, 1957, A Behavioristic Analysis of Perception and Language as Cognitive Phenomena, in Jerome S. Bruner, et al., *Contemporary Approaches to Cognition: The Colorado Symposium.* Cambridge: Harvard University Press, pp. 75–118.

Ostow, Mortimer, 1951, The Entropy Concept and Psychic Function, *American Scientist,* 39: 140–44.

Pask, Gordon, 1961, *An Approach to Cybernetics.* New York: Harper & Row.

Penrose, L. B., 1959, Self-Reproducing Machines, *Scientific American,* 200: 105–14.

Pierce, J. R., 1961, *Symbols, Signals, and Noise.* New York: Harper & Row.

Pitts, W. and W. S. McCulloch, 1947, How We Know Universals, The Perception of Auditory and Visual Forms, *Bulletin of Mathematical Biophysics,* 9: 127–47.

Powers, W. T., R. K. Clark, and R. I. McFarland, 1960, A General Feedback Theory of Human Behavior, *Perceptual and Motor Skills,* 11: 71–88.

Pringle, J. W. S., 1951, On the Parallel Between Learning and Evolution, *Behavior,* 3: 174–215.

Quastler, H., Ed., 1953, *Information Theory in Biology.* Urbana: University of Illinois Press.

——, 1955, *Information Theory in Psychology.* New York: The Free Press.

Rapoport, Anatol, 1953, What Is Information? *ETC,* 10: 247–60.

————, 1956, The Promise and Pitfalls of Information Theory, *Behavioral Science,* 1: 303–09.

————, 1959a, Critiques of Game Theory, *Behavioral Science,* 4: 49–66.

————, 1959b, Mathematics and Cybernetics, in Sylvano Arieti, Ed., *American Handbook of Psychiatry,* Vol. II. New York: Basic Books, 1743–59.

————, and William J. Horvath, 1959c, Thoughts on Organization Theory . . . , *General Systems,* 4: 87–91.

————, 1966, Some System Approaches to Political Theory, in David Easton, *Varieties of Political Theory.* Englewood Cliffs, N.J.: Prentice-Hall, pp. 129–41.

Rashevsky, N., 1955, Is the Concept of an Organism as a Machine a Useful One?, *Scientific Monthly,* 50: 32–35.

Raymond, Richard C., 1950, Communication, Entropy, and Life, *American Scientist,* 38: 273–78.

Redfield, Robert, Ed., 1942, *Levels of Integration in Biological and Social Systems.* Lancaster, Pa.: The Jacques Cattell Press.

Rescher, Nicholas, 1963, Discrete State Systems, Markoff Chains, and Problems in the Theory of Scientific Explanation and Prediction, *Philosophy of Science,* 30: 325–45.

Romain, Jacques, 1959, Information et Cybernétique, *Cybernetica,* 2: 23–50.

Rosenberg, Seymour, and Robert L. Hall, 1958, The Effects of Different Social Feedback Conditions upon Performance in Dyadic Teams, *Journal of Abnormal and Social Psychology,* 57: 271–77.

Rosenblueth, Arturo, Norbert Wiener, and Julian Bigelow, 1943, Purpose and Teleology, *Philosophy of Science,* 10: 18–24.

————, and Norbert Wiener, 1950, Purposeful and Non-Purposeful Behavior, *Philosophy of Science,* 17: 318–26.

Rothstein, Jerome, 1958, *Communication, Organization, and Science.* Indian Hills, Colorado: Falcon's Wing Press.

————, 1962, Discussion: Information and Organization as the Language of the Operational Viewpoint, *Philosophy of Science,* 29: 406–11.

Ruesch, Jurgen, 1952, The Therapeutic Process from the Point of View of Communication Theory, *American Journal of Orthopsychiatry,* 22: 690–701.

Sapir, E., 1939, *Language.* New York: Harcourt, Brace.

Saporta, Sol, Ed., 1961, *Psycholinguistics.* New York: Holt, Rinehart and Winston.

Scheff, Thomas J., 1966, *Being Mentally Ill.* Chicago: Aldine.

Schelling, Thomas C., 1960, *The Strategy of Conflict.* Cambridge: Harvard University Press.

Schramm, Wilbur, 1955, Information Theory and Mass Communication, *Journalism Quarterly,* 32: 131–46.

Schrödinger, Erwin, 1945, *What Is Life?* Cambridge: Cambridge University Press.

Schweitzer, A. L. M., 1963, Sociologie en Cybernetica, *Mens en Maatschappij*, 38: 351–67.

Scientific American, 1955, *Automatic Control.* New York: Simon and Schuster.

Scott, William Abbott, 1962, Cognitive Structure and Social Structure: Some Concepts and Relationships, in Norman Washburne, Ed., *Decisions, Values, and Groups*, Vol. II. New York: Pergamon, 86–118.

Seward, John P., 1963, The Structure of Functional Autonomy, *American Psychologist*, 18: 703–10.

Seyle, H., 1956, *The Stress of Life.* New York: McGraw-Hill.

Shannon, Claude E. and Warren Weaver, 1949, *The Mathematical Theory of Communication.* Urbana: The University of Illinois Press.

————, and J. McCarth, Eds., 1956, *Automata Studies.* Princeton: Princeton University Press.

Shibutani, Tamotsu, in press, *Improvised News: A Sociological Study of Rumor.* Indianapolis, Ind.: Bobbs-Merrill.

Simon, H. A., 1962, The Architecture of Complexity, *Proc. Amer. Phil. Soc.*, 106: 467–82.

Slack, Charles W., 1955, Feedback Theory and the Reflex Arc Concept, *Psychological Review*, 62: 263–67.

Sluckin, W., 1960, *Minds and Machines.* Baltimore, Maryland: Penguin Books.

Sommerhoff, G., 1950, *Analytical Biology.* London: Oxford University Press.

Stanley-Jones, D. and K., 1960, *The Kybernetics of Natural Systems: A Study in Patterns of Control.* New York: Pergamon.

Strauss, Anselm, et al., 1963, The Hospital and Its Negotiated Order, in Eliot Freidson, Ed., *The Hospital in Modern Society.* New York: The Free Press, pp. 147–69.

Szilard, L., 1929, Über die Entropieverminderung in einem Thermodynamischen System bei Eingriffen Intelligenter Wesen. *Zeitschr. f. Phys.*, 53: 840–56. (Trans. by A. Rapoport and M. Knoller as: On the Increase of Entropy in a Thermodynamic System by the Intervention of Intelligent Beings, *Behavioral Science*, 1964, 9: 301–10.)

Taylor, Donald W., 1960, Toward an Information Processing Theory of Motivation, in Marshall R. Jones, Ed., *Nebraska Symposium on Motivation.* University of Nebraska Press, pp. 51–79.

Taylor, James G., 1962, *The Behavioral Basis of Perception.* New Haven: Yale University Press.

Taylor, Richard, 1950a, Comments on a Mechanistic Conception of Purposefulness, *Philosophy of Science*, 17: 310–17.

————, 1950b, Purposeful and Non-Purposeful Behavior: A Rejoinder, *Philosophy of Science*, 17: 327–32.

Tinbergen, N., 1953, *Social Behavior in Animals*. London: Methuen & Co., Ltd.

Toch, Hans H. and Albert H. Hastorf, 1955, Homeostasis in Psychology, *Psychiatry*, 18: 81–91.

Toda, M. and Y. Takada, 1958, Studies of Information Processing Behavior, *Psychologica*, 1: 265–74.

Tou, Julius T. and R. H. Wilcox, Eds., 1964, *Computer and Information Sciences: Collected Papers on Learning, Adaptation, and Control in Information Systems*. Washington, D.C.: Spartan Books.

Toulmin, Stephen and June Goodfield, 1962, *The Architecture of Matter*. New York: Harper and Row.

Tranöy, Knut Erik, 1959, *Wholes and Structures*. Copenhagen: Munksgaard.

Trincher, Karl Sigmundovich, 1965, *Biology and Information*. New York: Consultants Bureau. Authorized translation from the Russian by Edwin S. Spiegelthal.

Turbayne, C. M., 1962, *The Myth of Metaphor*. New Haven: Yale University Press.

Tustin, Arnold, 1952, Feedback, *Scientific American*, 187: 48–54.

Uttley, A. M., 1954, The Classification of Signals in the Nervous System, *Radar Research Establishment Memorandum, 1047*. England: Great Malvern.

Vickers, Geoffrey, 1959a, The Concept of Stress in Relation to the Disorganization of Human Behavior, in J. M. Tanner, Ed., *Stress and Psychiatric Disorder*. Oxford: Blackwell Scientific Publications, Ltd., pp. 3–10.

———, 1959b, Is Adaptability Enough?, *Behavioral Science*, 4: 219–34.

Vogelaar, G. A. M., 1962, *Communicatie, Kernproces van de Samenleving: Sociologie en Cybernetiek*. Haarlem: De Erven F. Bohn N. V.

Vogt, Evon Z., 1960, On the Concepts of Structure and Process in Cultural Anthropology, *American Anthropologist*, 62: 18–33.

Walter, W. Grey, 1953, *The Living Brain*. London: Gerald Duckworth & Co., Ltd.

Werner, Heinz and Bernard Kaplan, 1963, *Symbol Formation*. New York: Wiley.

Whitehead, Alfred North, 1929, *Process and Reality*. New York: Macmillan.

Whorf, B. L., 1956, *Language, Thought, and Reality*. Cambridge: Technology Press.

Wiener, Norbert, 1954, *The Human Use of Human Beings: Cybernetics and Society*. Garden City, N.Y.: Doubleday Anchor.

———, 1961, *Cybernetics*, 2nd ed. Cambridge: The MIT Press, and New York: Wiley.

———, and J. P. Schadé, Eds., 1963, *Nerve, Brain, and Memory Models*. New York: Elsevier Publishing Company.

————, and J. P. Schadé, Eds., 1964, 1965, *Progress in Biocybernetics,* 2 Vols. New York: Elsevier Publishing Company.

————, and J. P. Schadé, Eds., 1965, *Cybernetics of the Nervous System.* New York: Elsevier Publishing Company.

Wilkins, Leslie T., 1964, *Social Deviance.* London: Tavistock.

Wisdom, J. O., 1951, The Hypothesis of Cybernetics, *The British Journal for the Philosophy of Science,* 2: 1–24.

Woodger, J. H., 1952, *Biology and Language.* Cambridge: Cambridge University Press.

Yovits, M. C., G. T. Jacobi, and G. D. Goldstein, Eds., 1962, *Self-Organizing Systems.* Washington: Spartan Books.

Zeman, J., 1962, Le Sense Philosophique du Terme 'L'information,' *La Documentation en France,* 3: 19–29.

name index

subject index